ROCK
HARD
APPS

ALSO BY KATHERINE COHEN

The Truth About Getting In

ROCK HARD APPS

HOW TO
WRITE A KILLER
COLLEGE
APPLICATION

KATHERINE COHEN, PH.D.

HYPERION

NEW YORK

Library of Congress Cataloging-in-Publication Data

Cohen, Katherine.
    Rock hard apps : how to write a killer college application / by Katherine Cohen.—1st ed.
        p.   cm.
    ISBN 0-7868-6862-7 (alk. paper)
    1. College applications—United States.   2. Universities and colleges—United States—Admission.   I. Title.

    LB2351.52.U6C64 2003
    378.1'664—dc21

                                            2003044994

FIRST EDITION

10 9 8 7 6 5 4 3 2 1

For my students—and their parents

CONTENTS

☞ INTRODUCTION

THE CONCEPT

My motivation for writing this book was simple. It arose out of a fundamental misunderstanding about the college application process, one which plagued many of the students whose families came to me for help as a private college counselor. Stressed-out parents were largely to blame, parents who called me out of the blue, armed with their children's stellar GPAs and SAT I scores, desperate to know whether I thought they would be accepted at one of the nation's most selective colleges. A new round of parents would call right after decision letters were mailed out in April, again armed with their children's near-perfect GPAs and SAT I scores, desperate to know why their children hadn't been accepted at the college of their dreams. The very nature of these questions revealed the problem: By and large, these were students whose academic and personal profiles made them highly desirable candidates for selective school admission, yet their parents and counselors erroneously believed that mere statistics were enough to get them into the nation's most selective schools. I wish it weren't the case, but no one is a shoo-in anywhere, no matter what the record.

Every time one of these families came to me for help—usually reeling from the blow of multiple rejection letters—it would pain me to think of all the hard work the students had put in during four difficult years of high school. The countless hours they spent studying for exams, writing papers, and keeping up with classroom assignments; all the tiring nights of standardized test preparation; the grueling tests themselves; the numerous and time-consuming extracurricular activities; the endless college visits and research—all of this culminating in a sloppy, rushed, and underdeveloped application, one that did almost nothing to highlight and promote the students' significant personal achievements, character traits, and

Did you know?

That selective colleges view public and private high schools differently? Depending on the school, a regular level course at a private school may be considered more rigorous than the same level course at a public high school. Also, many public high schools don't require community service, so if a student does a remarkable amount of community work at a public school, it might look better than a student who simply fulfills the fifty required community service hours at a private high school. Since public schools tend to be bigger, if you are the top-ranked student in a graduating class of a thousand, it might look better to an admissions reader than if you are the number one student at a private high school with a graduating class of only one hundred. Similarly, SAT I scores coming from public and private schools may be considered differently because test score averages are usually lower at public schools and there is often less test preparation available to public high school students. Finally, the type of school from which you apply can affect the way an admissions reader looks at your college counselor's letter of recommendation. Because of their heavy student load, counselors at public schools often don't get to know their students as well as counselors at private high schools, and college admissions readers will therefore not weigh their letters as heavily in the admissions process.

strong desire to attend the college in question. These students, and the adults advising them, had not understood that an applicant's entire chance for admission rests on the strength of the application itself, a ten- to fifteen-page document that ends up sitting in a pile of nearly identical documents on the desk of an overworked college admissions officer who has no more than twenty minutes *at most* to read it, judge it against impossibly high standards, and decide on the fate of the student's academic existence. In failing to spend the necessary time fleshing out their applications, perfectly good students were ending up in the reject pile at colleges where they should have been accepted, simply because they believed statistics alone would do the trick. In the film world, it's known as the cutting room floor, the melancholic meeting place of all the well-intended shots that could have been part of the picture. I was shocked to meet so many great students who had ended up on the cutting room floor, students who now needed my help overcoming these self-created obstacles. How could they have hoped to make their applications stand out from the crowd when they had treated the application as a means to an end rather than as an end unto itself?

Ultimately, what these students had failed to understand was this: The selective college application is so much more than a few pieces of paper relaying the dry facts and statistics of your academic or personal experience. Far more, the application is a living, breathing document of your life's achievements, your successes and failures, your trials, tribulations, hopes, and dreams. The application is your proxy, your spokesperson, your ambassador, either your best friend or your worst enemy, depending on how well you treat it. It is your first and last chance to make a deep and lasting impression on a group of complete strangers sitting in a wood-paneled room in an ivy-covered building far from all the toil and trouble you have gone through in high school, far from the intimate details that make your life uniquely yours. It is, as Theodore O'Neill, dean of admissions at the University of Chicago, has said, a "conversation" between the applicant and the college. Wouldn't you rather have an eloquent, thoughtful, levelheaded, and razor-sharp speaker on your side, than some underprepared, hurried, and ultimately boring hack?

That's when the idea came to me to start a service for my clients called the Application Review. Although I prefer to counsel my clients over the course of many years, helping them to choose their courses in high school; strategize their work, community, and extracurricular experiences; offer them time-honored tips for improving their academic performance; guide them through the choppy waters of standardized test preparation;

From the Other Side of the Desk:

(1) **Performance in a rigorous curriculum** is the single most important aspect of the college application. Colleges want to see a challenging course load through the senior year and an incoming GPA commensurate with their average incoming GPA (3.7, unweighted at Emory). Emory bases many of its decisions on the **history of the high school** and on the student's performance in relation to that context. (Adam Max, Senior Assistant Dean of Admissions at Emory University)

(2) The University of Pennsylvania starts with **academic information** like the transcript and testing; then they look at extracurricular involvement for depth and commitment and the letters of recommendation for **anecdotes**. Finally, they look for **enthusiasm**, especially in the "Why Penn?" essay, because it shows that a student has done his research and is truly interested in attending their school. (Dan Evans, Regional Director of Admissions at the University of Pennsylvania)

You Know They Want You When:

When asked what a college will do to attract students they really want to accept their offers of admission, an anonymous admissions officer at Brown University has stated during an information session that Brown will first send a letter of congratulation from the admissions officer to the student. Letters from department heads will follow, urging the students to visit, to get to know the school in more depth, and familiarize themselves with departmental offerings. Finally, invitations are sent out to special students to attend a welcome event that honors their achievement.

Did you know?

That selective schools are extremely difficult to transfer into? Columbia University, for instance, has only a 4 percent transfer admit rate, nearly three times lower than their regular admissions rate. In 2002 Harvard took only 35 out of over 1000 applicants for transfer into sophomore year. All the more reason to research your college choices as thoroughly as you can before you make your final decision!

Insider Secrets!

• Students often don't realize a school's **institutional priorities**. For instance, Penn's legacy policy states that if an applicant's parent or grandparent is a Penn degree holder, and the student applies Early Decision, the Office of Admissions promises to give that candidate maximum consideration. (Dan Evans, University of Pennsylvania)

• Emory wants people who are interested in Emory. To this end, keep in close contact with the admissions office. **Show enthusiasm**. Let them know who you are and how you fit with Emory's offerings. A visit is not essential. There are other ways that you can show your interest—attend local receptions, high school visits, order a video, visit their booth at a college fair, contact local alumni, and so forth. It is important for families who cannot afford to

and help them research their college choices so they can arrive at an educated assessment of the best possible places to apply, I found that many students were coming to me much later in the game, many after they had applied. These students had been deferred from Early Decision, waitlisted, or even rejected outright and wanted to know why. They were desperate to increase their chance of regular admission, to get off the waitlist at their top choice schools, or even to reapply as transfer students. But the truth was, they had no objective way of analyzing their applications according to the standards they would be held to by the admissions readers and officers at the prestigious and selective colleges and universities to which they were applying. What they needed was a system for judging the relative strengths and weaknesses of their application *from the perspective of someone who knows.* In response to this, I began to offer my application expertise on a read-through basis, expertise I had gleaned from my experience as an admissions reader at Yale University and as a private, independent college counselor with a global clientele of competitive students. My goal was to be able to read through an entire application, pinpoint its weaknesses or "red flags," and come up with tailor-made strategies for improving its overall impact. As the students set out to rewrite their college applications, I urged them to remember that admissions readers at the nation's most selective schools were looking for reasons to put their applications in the reject pile. The goal of my strategies was to provide them with the tools necessary to *keep the reader reading*. After numerous back-and-forth sessions of editing and reworking all aspects of the application, my students would send off their work, far more confident about its potential impact and far more likely to receive the acceptance letters they so ardently desired—and deserved.

Thus I found myself, after many years of offering this service privately, in a great position to write a book with the needs and desires of the general public in mind. My goal was to create an official guide to the college application process, one that protected students from the shock and disappointment of unexpected rejection letters by making sure their applications were in the best possible shape *before* they were sent out. To do this, I wanted to use actual applications to some of the nation's most selective colleges as case studies, providing readers with the firsthand experience of reading and evaluating college applications from an admissions committee's point of view. Outside of Jacques Steinberg's recent book, *The Gatekeepers: Inside the Admissions Process of a Premier College*, which traces the fate of six applicants to Wesleyan University, there are virtually no books available to college applicants and their families that offer in-

schedule a campus visit not to feel at a disadvantage. (Adam Max, Emory University)

● Students may not realize that **every stone is turned over during the reading process**. Admissions readers dig into what you send them, so don't think that minor inconsistencies or weak areas will be overlooked. Conversely, it is worth including anything and everything you think might be of interest to your prospective school—they will look at it, even if just for a few minutes. (Lloyd Peterson, former Associate Director of Admissions at Yale, 1987–1995; Dean of Admissions at Vassar, 1995–2000; and now an independent college admissions counselor)

● You are not being measured against all other applicants but against the intellectual and cultural opportunities your community has provided. The question is not how many courses or extracurricular activities you have pursued but **whether you have taken full advantage of everything that your school and your community have to offer**. (Anonymous admissions officer during an information session at Harvard University)

● A typical NYU **application gets at most 35 minutes of review**. The first application reader spends 20 minutes, the second reader 10 minutes, and the third reader 2–5 minutes reading and evaluating an application. That means you must be able to communicate the salient aspects of your academic and personal profile clearly and completely. (Richard Avitabile, former Assistant Vice President for Enrollment at NYU, 1991–2002, and now an educational consultant at Steinbrecher and Partners.)

Off the Record

1. **Admissions readers are looking for a balance between preparation and potential**. Students with less preparation will be admitted if they show great potential for growth. Conversely, well-prepared students can hurt their chances if there are character issues that might continue to plague the student in college. (Lloyd Peterson, formerly of Yale and Vassar)

2. **If you can't find it, found it.** If your school doesn't offer a club or organization revolving around an activity you truly enjoy, **then invent it yourself!** Colleges love students displaying that kind of initiative and determination, plus you will earn a rewarding position of leadership that leaves a lasting legacy at your high school. (An anonymous admissions officer during an information session at Yale University)

depth explorations and elaborations of the college application evaluation process, start to finish, from the perspectives of the college applicants and the readers themselves. I wanted to write that book, highlighting and humanizing the application process, directly addressing each section of the college application, taking readers on a step-by-step analysis of salient strategies, offering expert advice from the points of view of the very same deans and directors of admission who would ultimately be judging their applications. I wanted to teach students the reasons behind the decisions, taking them into the mind of the application reader, offering a clear-cut system by which to judge the crucial parts of their own applications "from the other side of the desk." That's how *Rock Hard Apps* was originally conceived: as a practical guide to help college applicants assess and strengthen their college applications prior to sending them, based on the actual college application experiences of my clients.

The book you are about to read has a simple philosophy. Since so many of the problems I encounter in my practice stem from the frantic, obsessive, and ultimately self-defeating worry caused by the admittedly heavy competition for the nation's most desirable colleges, I want to put your mind at ease regarding the college application process. If you approach your application experience with a healthy attitude, a clear goal, a definite strategy, and the wisdom of an expert on your side, then you can write the strongest application possible—and actually have some fun in the process. I try to think of the college application as a body—a body of material, that is. Each segment of the college application equates to a group of muscles in the human body. Getting your application into the best possible shape, therefore, is roughly the equivalent of getting your body into the best possible shape at the gym. Those students who rely too heavily on their academic performance—to the detriment of their personal profile—are the equivalent of the jocks you see in the gym with massive shoulders and arms but flabby abs and skinny legs. They look ridiculous, don't they? The same can be said of college applications that boast extraordinary extracurricular activities but have mediocre grades or that contain a superstrong transcript but weakling test scores.

The best way to avoid this detrimental development is clear: *Train.* Just as your body requires a daily routine of cardiovascular exercise that works each crucial muscle group in careful rotation, you also need to put sustained and serious effort into all aspects of your academic and personal development in preparation for college admission. You must take seriously the daily

---

What's the biggest mistake applicants can make on their college applications?

● **Not following the instructions on the application.** (Brown University)

● **Not indicating clearly what it is you want to study.** For NYU and colleges with specific undergraduate schools, you must indicate which program of study you intend to pursue. (Richard Avitabile, formerly of NYU)

● **Rushing.** Not paying attention to the look of your application is the equivalent of not being thoughtful of your reader's experience. This includes not using spell check on your computer. One essay to the University of Pennsylvania continually referred to **The Wharton School of Bunnies**. (Dan Evans, University of Pennsylvania)

● **Reiterating** in your essay everything you talked about in **your brag sheet**. (Brown University)

● **Writing the same essay for ten colleges but forgetting to change the name.** (Adam Max at Emory University)

● **Burying genuinely outstanding accomplishments in a sea of more mundane activities.** (Marianne M. Kosiewicz, Associate Dean of Admission at the University of Virginia)

Your IvyWise Counselor Says:

"**If you think you can outsmart an admissions reader, think again.** Do not be tempted to plagiarize your essay or lie about your activities. Admissions readers have seen it all and have caught applicants cheating. The lesson here is to do only your own work."

Your IvyWise Counselor Says:

"**Put some gratitude into your attitude!** Be grateful for what you DO have: your health, your power of reasoning, your privilege to study and learn, your family, your friends, the food on your table and roof over your head. Try not to dwell on what you don't have. Try to have a good attitude even when you're annoyed. Life is not fair. Deal with it. Don't complain, and don't get paranoid. Maintain a good mood; let go of your negative feelings. Your day-to-day treatment of other people is what makes the difference. People notice a good attitude, a grateful attitude. People will be nice back. Counselors will write good recommendations, as will teachers. You will be elected to positions of authority. You will enjoy life. So help out and be thankful for all that you have. You can get the best grades in the world, but that doesn't matter if you are selfish, envious, and mean."

grind of going to class; participating in discussion; engaging in numerous extracurricular, work, and community service activities; preparing adequately for tests and exams; writing papers with plenty of time to spare; maintaining a healthy, positive attitude; and cultivating strong relationships with your peers, teachers, and high school's college counselor. Remember, like the human body, if all aspects of your college application are strong but one leg is weak, then you won't be able to stand up in front of an admissions committee and, excuse the pun, put your best foot forward. That is why I have chosen to highlight three students whose applications began as ninety-eight pound weaklings but who gradually trained themselves to become superb athletes and outstanding application performers. Through first-hand case studies of actual college applications to some of the nation's most prestigious schools, this book will provide you with the best possible training for the grueling endeavor ahead. It will also provide an objective analysis of all that is strong and weak in the body of your college application, and it will pinpoint strategies aimed at increasing your chances of getting the body of your application into the kind of shape you have always wanted. Only the perfect application, in the best possible shape, will be strong enough to stand up to the competition for a well-deserved admission to the college of your dreams.

THE BOOK

In an attempt to be as exhaustive as possible, I have organized *Rock Hard Apps* into an introduction and seven easy-to-understand chapters. The remainder of this introduction will familiarize you with my college application assessment process, called the IvyWise Index, an in-house system I have developed as a clear and rational way to rank each section of the selective college application. After that, in the first chapter, you will have occasion to meet the three students—David Horowitz, Ronald Siegal, and Stephanie Chase—whose profiles and applications form the basis of my analysis and interpretation. Through getting to know each student personally, you will come to understand the intricate highways and byways by which they traveled the complicated route to college admissions. Following that, *Rock Hard Apps* will lead you through the seven remaining chapters, each devoted to a crucial aspect of the selective college application:

(1) The student's personal profile

(2) The academic profile, including the student transcript and the high school profile

(3) The testing profile, including standardized tests and scores

(4) The brag sheet

(5) Personal support, including recommendation letters and interview

(6) The personal essays

(7) Extra-credit strategies, pinpointing things you can do to increase your chances of gaining admission to the college of your dreams

In each of these chapters, you will be presented with corresponding sections from the actual applications submitted by our three highlighted students. Following each application section comes my analysis of its relative strengths and weaknesses, as understood from the point of view of the IvyWise Index ranking system. In this way, you will get to know David, Ronald, and Stephanie as if you were their friend—as if you were going through the grueling college admissions process with them. As you follow my analysis and ranking of each section, you will come to understand what selective colleges are looking for in their applicants. You will also learn to spot the detrimental "red flags" in David, Ronald, and Stephanie's college applications, as well as become familiar with numerous ways to fix them. What I call "red flags" are lapses in the academic or personal profile of an applicant, such as C's or D's one semester without explanation or high test scores accompanying low transcript grades. These things—elements of your application whose impact you obviously want to diminish—are bound to make admissions readers at the nation's most selective schools raise their eyebrows. As you learn from the mistakes that David, Ronald, and Stephanie have made along the way, you will come to know—and anticipate—how admissions readers and officers at the nation's most selective schools will eventually be judging your own applications. Once those problems are fixed, each chapter will concentrate on ways to maximize the strongest elements in each application and how best to make those stronger elements stand out from the crowd and ensure that an admissions reader takes notice.

THE IVYWISE INDEX

In order to give you a rational, objective measure of the relative strengths and weaknesses of your college applications, I would like to spend a little time introducing you to the IvyWise Index college application ranking system. The IvyWise Index is based in large part on the actual application ranking systems of a number of the nation's most selective colleges and universities, taking into account the many intangible and subjective criteria that actual admissions readers use to judge their applicants. It is not identical to any one system; rather, it incorporates the rigorous standards to which selective schools hold their applicants in an effort to come up with a composite ranking system, which you can employ to evaluate your applications to any of the nation's top schools. The IvyWise Index draws primarily on my experiences as a reader in the Admissions Office at Yale University and as an independent college admissions counselor in New York. It also takes into account many insights provided by counselors, readers, officers, directors, and deans of admissions at some of the nation's most selective schools. In addition, it incorporates many of the rigorous standards that constitute the Academic Index, or AI, an application evaluation system used by the schools of the Ivy League to assess the strengths and weaknesses of their applicants. This gives the IvyWise Index greater applicability without losing any of its rigor. After all, only if you hold your college applications to the most rigorous standards of the nation's most selective schools do you stand a chance of gaining admission to the college of your dreams.

Above all, the index is designed for ease-of-use. Through my brief introduction in the following pages—and by applying it to David, Ronald, and Stephanie's actual applications— you should quickly learn how to use the IvyWise Index to judge your own applications, assigning a score to each relevant section and thereby coming to an expert understanding of your applications' relative strengths and weaknesses. The five application elements evaluated by the IvyWise Index ranking system are:

1. *Courses and Grades*: based on the rigor (e.g., honors, AP, IB), consistency, and exhaustiveness of the curriculum; as well as letter or number grades, grade trend, class rank, and AP exam scores.

2. *Standardized Test Scores*: determined by an average of the highest SAT I scores (for both the Math and the Verbal sections) and an average of the three highest SAT II subject area test scores—or the ACT composite score.

3. *The Brag Sheet*: judged according to the duration and level of involvement in extra-curricular activities and community service organizations, as well as any academic or community honors and awards received, significant employment and summer experiences, and general hobbies and interests.

4. *Personal Support*: based on the counselor evaluation, the two teacher recommendations, any outside letters of support, and the interview.

5. *The Essays*: including both the personal statement and any short-answer questions required by individual college applications.

IvyWise Index points are awarded on a scale from 1 to 9 for the categories listed above. As you can see from the point scales below, the individual aspects of the academic profile count twice as much as the individual aspects of the personal profile. This reflects the reality of the rigorous standards governing selective college admissions.

Academic Profile:

Courses:	9 possible points	×2	=	18 possible points
Grades:	9 possible points	×2	=	18 possible points
SAT I/ACT:	9 possible points	×2	=	18 possible points
SAT IIs:	9 possible points	×2	=	18 possible points*

Personal Profile:

The Brag Sheet:	=	9 possible points
Personal Support:	=	9 possible points
¼ Counselor Letter		
¾ Teacher Recommendations		
¼ Interview		
Essays:	=	9 possible points

TOTAL SCORE:	**=**	**99 possible points**

*If SAT II subject area tests are not required at the school in question, add 9 points each to Courses and Grades.

To determine the IvyWise Index ranking that corresponds to your standardized test scores, use the average of your highest Verbal and Math scores from the SAT I, your composite ACT score, and/or the average of your three highest SAT II subject test scores and apply them to the following chart:

SAT I	ACT	IVYWISE INDEX
780 or above	36	9 points
750 or above	34–35	8 points
720 or above	33	7 points
690 or above	31–32	6 points
660 or above	30	5 points
640 or above	29	4 points
620 or above	28	3 points
600 or above	27	2 points
590 or below	26	I point

The majority of admissions readers and officers that I have spoken to have stressed that nothing is as vital to a student's chances of gaining admission to a selective college as his or her overall academic standing. Keep in mind as you prepare to apply to college that Courses and Grades combined count twice as much as the SAT I score alone, so it would be counterproductive to waste an inordinate amount of time stressing and prepping for your standardized tests, to the possible detriment of your academic standing. Based on the transcript alone, most of the nation's highly selective colleges and universities will form preliminary acceptance and rejection piles.

Despite this, however, you should keep in mind that the majority of applicants to the nation's most selective colleges already have stellar scores in all academic areas. Since this is the case, the final, determining factors in college admissions often stem from the personal profile. Admissions officers at the most selective colleges often claim that 80 percent of their applicant pools are academically qualified to attend their institutions. When all course work, grades, and tests scores are equal, admissions committees will turn to the personal attributes of the candidate as expressed in the brag sheet, the essays, the letters of recommendation, and the interview. It is here, in the personal qualities demonstrated inside and outside the classroom, that less academically gifted students can stand out as great personal achievers and, conversely, more academically gifted students can appear less than stellar because of "red flags" or weaknesses in their personal achievement that they failed to realize would weigh so heavily against them.

EXTRA CREDIT

In addition to the application elements detailed above, each college applicant has the chance to earn extra credit points on the IvyWise Index based on the list of special criteria detailed below. The point-worth (and therefore impact) of each extra credit area depends on the quality and quantity of the demonstrated advantage. If you are a gifted athlete applying to a selective college, your IvyWise Index ranking will increase depending on whether you are a great tennis player on your high school's varsity team (2 points) or a nationally ranked junior star with major national tour victories (5 points). If you are an art student, your potential IvyWise Index advantage depends on the quality of your work as well as the interest of your target school in your particular artistic skill. For instance, the school you wish to attend may already have many gifted graphic artists in their freshman class and be looking for a gifted painter; or, alternatively, they may have many gifted artists in general and be looking for a gifted tennis player. If you are the child of parents who may be able to donate substantially to your future school, you are known as a "development case." The bump you receive on your IvyWise Index, and hence the increase in your chances of acceptance, depends on the size of your family's potential donation—anywhere from 1 to 5 points. Although this may seem unfair to students whose families would be unable to donate large sums of money to their children's alma maters, it is an unfortunate truth in our society that money talks. It certainly doesn't guarantee a student's chances of gaining admission to the school of his or her choice— and it certainly can't negate the negative effects of a spotty academic or personal record— but it can tip the scales in favor of a student on the cusp between acceptance and rejection. If two candidates vying for the last spot in a freshman class have similar academic and personal profiles, the potential giving power of one of the families could theoretically make the crucial difference. Again, this may seem unfair, but schools rely on alumni donations for everything from sports arenas and art centers to experimental educational programs, all the while freeing up more endowment money for scholarships and financial aid packages.

As many of you have probably heard, applying either Early Decision or Early Action to a school that offers such an admissions plan can dramatically increase your chances of admission, depending on your profile and the policies of the school in question. Columbia University, for example, estimates that its regular admission selectivity rate for the class of 2006 was somewhere between 10 percent and 13 percent. That number jumped to 47 percent when it came to the early applicant admission rate. In terms of real benefit on the college application, Christopher Avery and his colleagues at Harvard's Kennedy School of Government have concluded in their book, *The Early Admissions Game*, that applying early is roughly the equivalent of an increase of 100 points on the SAT. Elitist as they may seem, both ED and EA programs are here to stay, at least for now, so it is clearly to your advantage to apply early to the college of your choice if such a program is available and you have decided under no uncertain terms that the school in question is your number one choice (for Early Decision), *and* you have researched the school extensively, your essays are polished by mid-October of your senior year, your grades through your junior year have been consistent, and you have completed all necessary testing with adequate scores.[1] Applying Early Decision or Early Action is therefore a great way to increase your overall IvyWise Index ranking.[2] Depending on your original SAT I or ACT score, applying early can increase your Index ranking by as many as 4 extra credit points.

For the remaining extra credit areas, including minority status, legacy status, and first generation college applicant status, the numerical advantage for the IvyWise Index is roughly the same—about 5 points. Please note, however, that if you are a minority or first generation college student, you also have some flexibility in terms of your SAT I scores. Because it has been shown that the SAT I is biased toward affluent white students (those who can afford

---

[1] Please note that for the incoming class 2004–2005, both Yale and Stanford have switched from an Early Decision program to an Early Action program. The possible effects of this switch on their selectivity rates remain unclear.
[2] If you are applying for financial aid, I do not advise applying Early Decision. You can apply Early Action, however, and still compare aid packages from all schools that offer you admission in April of your senior year.

the best test preparation and whose backgrounds are similar to the test makers in Princeton, N.J.), an African-American applicant from an inner-city, low-income family who scores a combined 1350 on the SAT I might be awarded the full 9 points by our Index. The reasons are many: With a student such as this, colleges have an opportunity to increase their minority profile, as well as offer an excellent educational opportunity to a first-time college applicant. To further these worthy goals, schools cut these students a break on their applications because English may not have been the first language at home or extra test and course preparation services may have been unavailable. Finally, since the SAT I exam tests the acquired cultural knowledge of a mainstream American adolescent, those students who don't fall into the mainstream are at a disadvantage going into the test—colleges[3] will cut these students some slack on their scores in an effort to reverse this historical trend.

Here, then, is a breakdown of the Extra Credit areas in which a college applicant can earn extra points on the IvyWise Index:

(a) *Communication and interest*: demonstration of a high level of interest in the target school, including numerous and engaged college visits, frequent and substantial contact with school representatives, as well as exhaustive research done into the offerings of the target school

(b) *Distinctive athletic ability / recruitment*

(c) *Minority status*

(d) *Legacy status*

(e) *First generation college applicant*

(f) *Development case*

(g) *Distinctive artistic ability*: usually including application supplements such as portfolios, concert tapes, performance videos, and such

(h) *Early application*, resulting in an increase of 100 SAT I or 4 ACT points

---

[3]Colleges that do not use affirmative action excluded.

SCORE INTERPRETATION

IN THE "A" RANGE:

A score approaching 90 or above is needed to gain admission to the nation's most selective colleges. This means the application displays a powerful combination of academic and personal attributes. Everything must be excellent.

IN THE "B" RANGE:

A score of 80–90 does not immediately disqualify a student from admission, but the application must evince a special talent, demonstrate a strong and sustained desire to attend the school, and prove that the applicant has engaged in lengthy and relevant research on the college, as well as offer great support for the applicant's outstanding personal qualities through the brag sheet, the personal statement, the letters of recommendation, and the interview. Applications scoring in this range are on the cusp between admission and rejection; and without supplemental or extra-credit strategies, they will most likely receive a rejection letter. The important thing to remember here is this: *Being a bright, well-rounded student is not enough.* Typically, great students score in this "B" range and will probably not be admitted to the most selective colleges on their lists.

IN THE "C" RANGE:

A score below 80 gives the applicant very little chance of being accepted to a selective college unless "special" circumstances make his or her candidacy extraordinarily attractive (e.g., unusually large development case or "star" athlete). Even in this case, most colleges will have students applying under similarly "special" circumstances whose personal and academic profiles are much stronger.

THE SCHOOLS

Daunted? You shouldn't be. As you read through *Rock Hard Apps*, try to remember that the IvyWise Index college application ranking system gauges your chances of gaining admission to the nation's most selective colleges, those with selectivity rates lower than 40 percent. As such, the IvyWise Index may not apply as accurately to many of the other fine educational institutions in the country. In other words, you may be able to get into a number of excellent colleges with lower IvyWise Index rankings. However, no matter where you are thinking of applying, it is always good advice to hold your application to the highest possible admissions standards. Competition for what used to be considered "safety schools" has swelled in the last number of years, making it imperative that you go about your college applications with the same rigor and attention to detail as you would if you were applying to one of the nation's most selective schools. There is no reason to be caught off guard by a rejection letter in the spring when there is so much you can do to make your application the strongest it can possibly be. The following is a list of forty of the nation's most selective schools, categorized by type and listed alphabetically. The IvyWise Index applies most accurately to these schools, but if the schools to which you are applying do not appear on this list, you must still go the extra mile if you want to get in!

THE IVY LEAGUE

BROWN UNIVERSITY	HARVARD UNIVERSITY
COLUMBIA UNIVERSITY	UNIVERSITY OF PENNSYLVANIA
CORNELL UNIVERSITY	PRINCETON UNIVERSITY
DARTMOUTH COLLEGE	YALE UNIVERSITY

PRIVATE COLLEGES AND UNIVERSITIES

AMHERST	DUKE UNIVERSITY
BOSTON COLLEGE	EMORY UNIVERSITY
BOWDOIN	GEORGETOWN UNIVERSITY
CALIFORNIA INSTITUTE OF TECHNOLOGY	HAVERFORD COLLEGE
CARLETON COLLEGE	JOHNS HOPKINS UNIVERSITY
CARNEGIE MELLON UNIVERSITY	MASSACHUSETTS INSTITUTE OF
UNIVERSITY OF CHICAGO	TECHNOLOGY
DAVIDSON COLLEGE	MIDDLEBURY COLLEGE

NEW YORK UNIVERSITY

NORTHWESTERN UNIVERSITY

UNIVERSITY OF NOTRE DAME

POMONA COLLEGE

RICE UNIVERSITY

STANFORD UNIVERSITY

SWARTHMORE COLLEGE

TUFTS UNIVERSITY

WASHINGTON UNIVERSITY / ST. LOUIS

WELLESLEY COLLEGE

WESLEYAN UNIVERSITY

WILLIAMS COLLEGE

PUBLIC UNIVERSITIES

UNIVERSITY OF CALIFORNIA—BERKELEY

UNIVERSITY OF CALIFORNIA—
LOS ANGELES

UNIVERSITY OF MICHIGAN—ANN ARBOR

UNIVERSITY OF NORTH CAROLINA—
CHAPEL HILL

UNIVERSITY OF VIRGINIA—
CHARLOTTESVILLE

Chapter One

 PERSONAL PROFILES

Profiles of Three Students

There are three students whose selective college applications will form the backbone of my analysis and commentary in *Rock Hard Apps*. All three have generously offered their entire applications for our review. Please note that their names have been changed and some personal details altered in order to protect their anonymity.[1] Nonetheless, their applications appear much as they did when they were first sent to their prospective colleges, glaring mistakes and all. In choosing these three students to profile, I have tried to collect a broad cross-section of interests, high schools, academic performances, and family experiences. As with any human being, all three of these students have their personal strengths and weaknesses. In the end, all three ended up at excellent colleges—although not necessarily their top-choice schools and not necessarily the colleges they seemed destined for. As you read through the brief biographies below, try to identify attributes and experiences from the lives of the three profiled students that resemble aspects of your own history. Try to imagine how an author such as myself might talk about you and your experiences in the third person, as part of a coherent story meant for publication. This exercise will start to give you a sense of how an outside judge such as an admissions reader might assess the relative strengths and weaknesses of your personal and academic profiles. Imagining this outside perspective is essential if you want to become your own best college application judge— only when you can picture yourself and your applications in an objective manner will you be able to develop a clear understanding of the path that lies before you.

As you reflect on your own personal profile, you will want to ask yourself: What are the attributes of your character and personality that stand out, that allow you to excel, the ones that make you uniquely yourself? What are the significant experiences you have had that

---

[1] All high school names and hometowns have also been changed to ensure anonymity.

might help shed light on your personal development and the specificity of your character? As you notice some of the similarities and differences between yourself and the three students profiled below, can you start to imagine some of the things that will eventually help or hinder David, Ronald, and Stephanie's chances of getting into the colleges of their dreams? Conversely, what are some of the things you know you will have to work on before you start applying to college? If you start answering these questions consistently and methodically, you will come to be in fantastic shape when it comes time to write and submit your actual college applications. In other words, start your training now—with vigor, determination, and a realistic sense of your goals—and you will be well on your way to developing your very own *rock hard app*.

PERSONAL PROFILE: DAVID HOROWITZ

This shy, driven, Jewish Orthodox student from suburban Long Island appears in the pages of this book thanks to an all-too-common mistake he and his family made. He is the perfect example of an applicant who assumed that with straight A's mainly in honors and AP courses, and a high SAT I score, he would be a shoo-in at any college he wanted. Unfortunately, David learned the hard way not to take the college application process for granted: He was outright rejected from every school he applied to except for Rutgers University, Yeshiva University, and Johns Hopkins, where he was placed on the waitlist. Based on his stellar academic performance in the most rigorous curriculum at his yeshiva high school, as well as his considerable community involvement and extracurricular activities above and beyond his graduation requirements, David should have gotten in everywhere he applied. Why didn't he? Why did he have to suffer through rejection letter after rejection letter during what was supposed to be a relaxing spring semester of his senior year? The answer is simple: His applications were plagued with "red flags." Because of these oversights, David appeared far less desirable as a candidate than he actually was. Luckily, he was able to salvage a chance at attending the excellent Johns Hopkins University, now his number one choice, by employing my services for a full Application Review. Working with me, David was able to home in on the weaknesses in his application, develop strategies for improving each and every application section, and subsequently resubmit his vastly improved application to Johns Hopkins. Before launching into a detailed analysis of the ills that plagued David's initial application, as well as presenting the strategies we developed together, I would like to introduce you to Mr. David Horowitz.

David is the type of student who would rather chew his nails than file them. It's the nerves. And the time—chewing is so much faster than clipping, so much more . . . to the point. If only you could make them look as good by chewing. But who really cares about that in the long run—vanity gets you nowhere fast, right? At least that's what David believes. David has, as you may have guessed, a strong desire to get things done, to see things through to their most logical conclusion. Not that he's obsessive. Being logical and remaining focused free David up for other things, allowing him to move on to the next challenge.

This practical, goal-oriented enthusiasm for tackling problems stems from his religious upbringing. David has been raised in a Jewish Orthodox family, having what is a relatively common childhood for his tight-knit Long Island community but certainly quite uncommon for the average American high school student. It means that twenty-four hours of David's life every week are devoted to religion and prayer. It means David has to travel over an hour each way to attend the new yeshiva high school that opened a few townships away, spending numerous weeknights with friends who live closer to campus just so he can get to class on time in the morning and not be entirely exhausted. It means David's ability to participate in extracurricular activities has been hampered because he celebrates Shabbat, the Jewish day of prayer and rest, from Friday at sundown to Saturday at sundown. During that time, he is not allowed to work, use electronic equipment, go out with friends, talk on the phone, or read anything other than for pleasure. That means no homework—but also no video games. This is David's dedication to his faith.

As if that weren't enough, David's yeshiva high school requires him to follow a dual curriculum, devoting half his time to religious studies and the other half to more standard college preparatory courses. This is essentially the equivalent of going to two high schools at once, both a secular and a parochial school. In order to remain competitive with college applicants from other excellent high schools around the country, David has to fulfill the same general requirements as a normal high school student. Yet in order to satisfy the spiritual and intellectual requirements of his synagogue and faith, David must also study the Talmud and the Old and New Testaments, and become fluent in Hebrew. With a schedule heavy on academics, religious study, and spiritual reflection, as well as a commute that gets him home around 7:00 or 8:00 P.M. every night, David has obviously had little time for sports or any other activities that high school students long for as needed breaks from their busy days. This is okay with David, though—he isn't all that athletic to begin with, and he prefers to spend his free time listening to Israeli radio over the Internet. For relaxation, he plays the piano at home, often composing his own songs and entertaining his family after dinner. He also works hard during his summers, devoting 10 percent of his earnings to programs sponsored by his synagogue, as is the custom of his faith.

As a result of this extraordinary workload, and because of the demanding tenets of his type of Judaism, David has developed into a naturally driven young man. He is quiet and reflective, preferring a good book to a rowdy night with friends. The occasional dinner out is fine—if his parents let him, that is. They can be a bit strict. But that's because they are overachievers who have instilled in David a strong work ethic. They like to say that David is the type of kid they never have to tell to do his homework—a backhanded compliment that touts the subtlety of their parenting skills more than David's innate drive. Both are professionals: His mother, Ruth, is a lawyer while his father, Saul, is an ear, nose, and throat specialist. Deeply religious, they can be a bit controlling, especially when it comes to cars. A lot of David's friends drive to school, but he has to take the bus. Don't get me wrong: David doesn't resent any of the strictures placed on him by his family and his faith. That's the great thing about David—he actually thrives on the pressure and loves the hard work, and he is clearly dedicated to making his parents happy. It gives him a sense of accomplishment and a quiet confidence.

The only tension in the Horowitz household has come from Sarah, David's younger sister and a real firecracker of a young woman. As the middle child, she has always had to fight for attention, often acting out just to garner a response from her parents. Because David is such a dedicated high achiever and Ann, the baby in the family, is the sweet apple of her parents' eye, Sarah seems to have made it her goal in life to do whatever she can to disrupt the smooth running of the family. When she was younger, she once took all of David's action figures—David had a thing for Power Rangers—and threw them into the street. Like children who place pennies on railroad tracks and watch with delight as they are flattened by the heavy steel wheels of the locomotive, Sarah took a perverse kind of pleasure in watching David's molded plastic toys crack and crumble under the weight of their neighbor's SUV. Later, as it came time for Sarah to enter high school, she vehemently rejected Singer Yeshiva High School, where her big brother David had started just two years earlier. Threatening to run away from home if her parents forced her to go, Sarah ended up staying at the local public high school, where she fell in with a rough crowd of kids from the other side of the tracks.

Rejecting her faith, and her parents' way of life, Sarah's most recent ploy has been to sway young Ann to her side. To deal with Sarah tattooing herself against her parents' will, smoking cigarettes in the backyard, even sneaking out to boys' houses on weekends, David and his parents have tried to intervene with her, hoping to free Ann from her older sister's detrimental influence. As a result, a family feud has begun that threatens to wrench the Horowitz family apart at the seams. This has been especially taxing for David, who arrives home exhausted from a long day of school and a grueling commute only to find more trouble. Not long ago, Sarah and Ann had barricaded themselves in his room and were messing around with his computer files—not something David takes very lightly. This family trauma even played a role in David's college application plans. David has been reluctant to go too far from home for fear of losing Ann permanently to Sarah's rebellious way of life. Yet David also knows he has to make his college decisions based on his own needs and desires, not those of his family or his sense of moral obligation to others.

To his extreme credit, David has remained admirably even-keeled throughout the ordeal. In the end, David reasons, it's not really about him—it's about his sister's issues with their parents, something she will ultimately have to work out on her own. As you can probably guess from this story, David is a very humble person himself, not a braggart or a show-off like Sarah who needs so desperately to make an impression, regardless of whether it's positive or negative. David tries to concentrate on his schoolwork, focusing all his energy on the task at hand, trying his hardest to do a great job for the sake of doing a great job—not for any kudos, recognition, or hollow praise. David's extraordinary work ethic and genuine humility reflect his overall character. He is not an extravagant person and possesses a strong sense of frugality, which keeps his youthful passions in check. He has chosen reflection over confrontation and spirituality over materialism—except, perhaps, where computers are concerned. Nearly all the money he has earned went into buying new software and backing up his data so that Sarah's next terrorist act won't leave him bereft.

But most important of all his characteristics, David has a strong sense of justice. One of his heroes is Jack Ryan, Tom Clancy's globe-trotting do-gooder. The Napster situation annoys him—it's stealing, after all, right? At school and home, David possesses a natural sense of right and wrong, one that he is wary of imposing on others. He is a great listener and often plays the role of mediator between his parents and his younger siblings. This commitment to truth and justice has made David a very politically minded young man. If I had to guess at a future profession for David, I would say he has international diplomatic or legal experience in his future—a future in which he will be able to channel his considerable energy and his love of family and community into helping others help themselves.

PERSONAL PROFILE: RONALD SIEGAL

This artistic, fun-loving, and family-oriented student from a good public high school in the suburbs of Cleveland appears in the pages of *Rock Hard Apps* courtesy of the extraordinary time and effort he gave to his college applications. Ronald fearlessly took what could have been perceived as a modest academic profile and turned it into one of the strongest overall applications I have ever seen. And he had to—there was no other way he would stand a chance of being considered for early admission to a school like the University of Pennsylvania if he didn't put in a lot of extra effort. By employing certain IvyWise strategies developed in consultation with me, Ronald strove to achieve more than his academic performance might predict, and even though his college goals were nearly beyond his reach, he rarely ever wavered. As such, he is living proof that no matter what your background (within reason, of course!), you can do wonders to overcome weaknesses in your academic profile simply by writing a superlative college application. Ronald understood this from the beginning. We will learn later whether his hard work paid off, but either way, Ronald was a model client of mine from the get-go, remaining focused and dedicated throughout the process, never once taking for granted that he would have to go that extra mile to realize his post–secondary school dreams. As you read through the various sections of Ronald's application, consider it a point-by-point illustration of the numerous strategies you can employ to overcome obstacles in your profile and make yourself stand out in the mind of an admissions reader. In particular, analyze Ronald's use of extra-credit strategies, all of which aided his difficult attempt for early admission to U. Penn. Also remember that admissions readers at the nation's most selective colleges are looking for reasons to toss your application into the reject pile. It is therefore essential that you, like Ronald, do everything you can to keep your reader reading! Here, then, is Ronald Siegal.

Ronald Siegal is color-blind. This is no secret—he freely talks about it to his classmates and teachers, even in the personal statement that accompanied his college application. I mention it because this condition has shaped not only his vision of the world but also his outlook on life. Ronald, perhaps by necessity, is a creative young man. He is an explorer. Literally and figuratively, he sees the world in a different light. But this gift, if you will, comes with a certain responsibility: Ronald has to work to see the world the way other people do, to understand "accepted" notions of what is beautiful and right, to fit in. He also has to work to follow his true passion: art. As a color-blind student, choosing art wasn't easy. Just ask his art teacher. She has helped him develop a method for encoding his drawings and paintings so their colors are legible to the outside world in the formations and schemes he imagined. Ronald knows he has to make this kind of extra effort if he wants to be understood. Luckily, extra effort is what Ronald Siegal is all about. To a large extent, he has educated himself. Some of the more crucial aspects of his development have taken place outside the classroom. He attends the theater and visits museums whenever he can; he has interned at an art gallery; he takes advantage of all the cultural opportunities that both Cleveland and Chicago (the largest metropolis in the area) have to offer. And sometimes, Ronald likes to explore his own world, to delve into the abstractions of his unique color-blind vision, and to report back from a place that no one else can see.

This combination of creativity and old-fashioned hard work is what defines Ronald's personality. He is dedicated to his achievements, whether they be with pen, pencil, calculator, or Bunsen burner. He brings the same zeal and courage to everything he does, extracurricular activities and schoolwork alike. This confidence in his abilities, this comfort with himself, this optimism of spirit, may stem from his loving parents. They are the definition of supportive. Ronald's father, Kevin, is an insurance broker and a dedicated father—the kind of dad who comes to every student art show and sends digital pictures of his son's paintings to his friends and relatives over the Internet. He is the same father who sent away for college applications to every Ivy League school while Ronald was still in ninth grade, just to familiarize himself with the process, swearing it wasn't meant to put any undue pressure on his son! Ronald's mother, Linda, is a tour guide at the Cleveland Art Museum, specializing in High Modernism: the distortions of cubism, the effusions of expressionism, and the folly of the surreal—all interests she clearly passed on to her son. Surprisingly, Linda is the more down-to-earth of Ronald's parents, the one who calmly reminded her husband that Ronald still had two years to go before he would even think about college applications and that maybe all this fantasizing about the Ivy League was unhealthy for the emotional development of their son.

As parents, the Siegals qualify as staunchly middle class. They are solid, grounded parents who have taught their children a strong sense of community and an extraordinary work ethic. Kevin, Linda, Ronald, and his little sister Mimi are open, friendly, generous, and always surrounded by good friends. As a result, neither Ronald nor his sister is spoiled, self-centered, or materialistic. This does not mean they always see eye-to-eye, however. Despite sharing an upbringing and the joint genetic profile of their parents, Ronald and Mimi have developed into diametrically opposed individuals. Whereas Ronald seems to have inherited the surfeit of the creative genes from his family tree, Mimi is said to be the quintessential steel-nerved scientist through and through. More likely to be a forensics expert than a landscape painter, Mimi is currently in the throes of an obsession with skeletons and corpses. While Ronald has sketched a few bones in still-life class, Mimi apparently likes to play young Dr. Frankenstein, analyzing bones, studying autopsy books, and using her home chemistry set to concoct her own special blend of embalming fluid. Walking into Mimi's room is like stepping into a gothic novel—or an episode of *Six Feet Under*. And sometimes the whole thing is a little distasteful to Ronald, who tends to be squeamish.

I have to admit, however, that I never quite understood why it bothered Ronald so much that his little sister was so different from him—until I had an occasion to visit Ronald at his home. Shrouded in a permanent Halloween, Mimi's room is actually quite an artistic place. She has painstakingly rendered each of her macabre experiments in full-color lab drawings that display extraordinary precision and a fantastically unique perspective on the human body. Mimi showed me around her room not with the sober presentation skills of a rational scientist but more with the enthusiasm of a passionate curator guiding me through her favorite museum of horrors. It occurred to me as I toured the frightful place that Ronald must be experiencing a bit of jealousy. Their two versions of artistic production could not be more different and yet they were both clearly artists. I wondered if Mimi's obvious talent was a challenge to Ronald's confidence, a challenge to his art, or to his place as the "artist" in the family. Either way, I decided this was probably healthy for Ronald in the long run. He already displayed a canny confidence in his own work—half the battle for artists!—and a little competition might help him further innovate and evolve. Furthermore, he would have to get used to some competition if he was serious about pursuing a career in the art world, where you are only as good as your last show and upstarts constantly threaten to knock you off your pedestal of fame.

Ronald's personality could not be more different than the cliché of the lonely, angst-ridden artist. In fact, Ronald displays a genuine love of new experiences, a joy in the process of learning and discovering new things, which eclipses all self-doubt and worry. He puts a considerable amount of pressure on himself to succeed, especially in school, but he does so with a smile. In fact, he does most things with a smile. And because of his genuine love of learning, his unique vision of the world, and the great support system surrounding him, life is a naturally stimulating place for Ronald. He doesn't need to get into trouble, or drink or smoke or sneak out at night. This is even more impressive when you consider that bad behavior has been a constant temptation at his high school, where an unfavorable student-to-teacher ratio allows many fellow adolescents to slip through the cracks. The difference with Ronald is that he actually prefers to stay at home with his family, especially his mother, and plays constantly with his dog, Jess. He likes being surrounded by his artwork and his supplies. And, in the end, he loves his strange little sister dearly.

All in all, Ronald is an extremely loyal and dedicated person yet also a risk-taker, the type of young man who sets about the college application process with undaunted enthusiasm despite his modest grades, even applying Early Decision to the University of Pennsylvania because he had a "feeling" about the school. Even though it would make him cringe, I would also call Ronald a sweetheart. After all, he just went through a growth spurt and is evidently becoming quite a success with the young ladies. Of course, it still took him a month to get up the courage to ask his dream date to the prom . . . but all good things in all good time.

PERSONAL PROFILE: STEPHANIE CHASE

With two tattoos and a trio of nose-pierces, Stephanie Chase is not your typical boarding school girl. She is a free spirit, her hair more likely to be in cornrows than neatly combed, her clothes more likely to be off the cover of *Skaterad* magazine than off the rack at Lilly Pulitzer. Unfortunately, she appears in the pages of *Rock Hard Apps* not because of her eccentric looks and equally unique outlook on life—she appears here courtesy of her dismal family experience and a tragic event that sent her already troubled childhood into a tailspin, deeply hurting her chances of gaining admission to the college of her dreams. This tragic event, coming so early in Stephanie's young life, wreaked havoc on both her personal life and her academic life. One drinking bust, a serious grade dip, and some intense therapy later, Stephanie was left to pick up the pieces without much help from her distant, albeit wealthy, family. The net result of this disastrous series of events was an equally dismal performance on her college applications. Whereas Stephanie should have gotten into both Yale and Wesleyan—her top two choices, for very different reasons—she was eventually waitlisted at both, largely because they knew she had the potential to perform well at both schools but was clearly troubled emotionally in various ways. Although her family life could not be more different from David's, I selected Stephanie to be profiled in this book for reasons similar to his—she, like David, is an excellent student and individual who should have gotten in everywhere she applied but didn't, simply because of understandable yet wholly avoidable mistakes on her college applications. Here, then, is Stephanie Chase.

Stephanie Chase is a gifted writer. A poet in both words and action. Unfortunately, you wouldn't know this from her college applications. You wouldn't know this from meeting her, either. This is because Stephanie Chase is also a wounded young woman. Although Stephanie grew up in Brownville, Connecticut, a wealthy suburb, with parents who could afford anything and everything for their only daughter, Stephanie was left without guidance from an early age. Once she was old enough to take care of herself, her parents fired the nanny who had shouldered most of their parenting responsibilities and whom, understandably, Stephanie had grown to love. This was the first in a series of losses that left Stephanie an emotional wreck.

Stephanie's father, Dylan Chase, is a bigwig trial attorney in New York City whose firm has been involved in some of the most high-profile criminal cases in recent Manhattan history. Dylan works long hours. As a convenience, he decided a number of years ago to buy a pied-à-terre in the City—a natural complement to his London flat, his Gstaad ski chalet, his Bermuda bungalow, his Corfu villa, and of course his Brownville estate. This arrangement works well for Dylan, but not for poor Elizabeth, Stephanie's mother, who is left for weeks on end at the near-empty house in Brownville, wondering what exactly her husband is doing in Manhattan all the time, especially at night. So Elizabeth tries to keep herself occupied with her tennis league and her charity functions. She also spends a lot of time spending Dylan's money—throwing parties that he rarely attends and shopping on Madison Avenue, all the while fighting the urge to surprise her husband at his office, secretly hoping to confirm her suspicions by catching him in a noonday tryst. To while away her time, Elizabeth has also redecorated the house in Brownville three times in the past seven years, each time displacing Stephanie and all of her belongings to a different, more remote part of the house. That's just the type of mother she is—the type who would throw out her daughter's "clutter" without first consulting about its possible emotional worth. To relieve the nagging pain of her boredom and suspicion, Elizabeth has taken to drinking. It started with just a few gin and tonics at night, then quickly progressed to a level that even Stephanie couldn't imagine. Stephanie just knows to stay out of the way when Mom starts brooding or cursing her husband's name.

Where does Stephanie go to escape this life, this broken palace of aristocratic dreams? Two places. The first is an interior one—she flees into the life-giving illusions of her poetry and drama. Through her verse, Stephanie is able to escape the harsh reality of daily life in a universe entirely of her own creation. Through acting and playwriting, she is able, if only momentarily, to inhabit the soul of another person and to imagine complex, fantastical, and cathartic scenarios in which things always turn out better than they do in the real world. Through both forms of artistic expression, Stephanie is able to get in touch with herself and with the language she loves, not as the abstract series of guttural gripes that her parents toss at each other whenever they are together, but as the sweeter tones of a more private communication with the many poets and playwrights from the past and present whom she considers to be her true, more spiritual family. Here, in her writing, Stephanie's soul resembles her exterior—wild, unkempt, and free.

Stephanie's second place of exile is an exterior one. Although she lives only a few blocks away, Stephanie steps into another world whenever she visits her best friend, Charlotte Murphy. It's like night and day, the difference it makes in Stephanie's disposition. She and Charlotte got their tattoos together, after all—the happy and sad theatrical masks—and they will be forever linked because of this and so many other adolescent experiences too numerous to mention. Stephanie and Charlotte first bonded over their hatred of the makeup and brand names that so many of their classmates at Brownville Country Day began to covet as early as the fifth grade. Not ones to idle away the hours at the local mall with the rest of the lip-glossed grade-schoolers, Stephanie and Charlotte were more likely to attend an antiglobalization rally in their natty vintage clothes, taking government leaders to task for polluting our earth and our minds. Yet the two are different in a fundamental way: Whereas Stephanie evolved into her current freedom-fighter role as a form of rebellion against her parents, Charlotte embraced that position because of the love and freedom that her parents showered on her. Charlotte's mother, Barbara, is the polar opposite of Stephanie's own: a warm and loving family psychologist who cooks well and cares about the welfare of her family, both physical and spiritual. Charlotte's father, Richard, is a political science professor at Yale University whose left-wing musings have always fascinated Stephanie as well as armed her with knowledge in the fight against her parents' uninvolved pressure. It's no wonder she's over there all the time, eating Barbara's ethnic specialties, playing with the Murphy family dog, Buster (Stephanie can't have one of her own because of the furniture . . .). At the Murphys', Stephanie can be herself, feel at home, talk, and exchange opinions in a place that is loving and safe. Barbara Murphy, especially, is Stephanie's confidante—her savior.

Needless to say, Stephanie was devastated when Dylan began insisting that she go away to boarding school. You would think the prospect of escaping her parents for four years might interest her, but Stephanie couldn't stomach the idea of life away from Charlotte and Barbara Murphy. A few years prior to Dylan's unilateral pronouncement on Stephanie's future, Mrs. Murphy had been diagnosed with breast cancer. Even though Barbara was in remission, Stephanie wanted to be around this amazing, loving, and resilient role model as much as she could, just in case her status reversed. But Dylan was vehement—he had gone to Peter Egret Academy and so had his father. Without a brother to carry on the Chase family tradition, Stephanie would have to bear the brunt of Dylan's stubborn insistence. So, shortly after Labor Day, Stephanie was shipped off to a small town on the coast of Massachusetts, a few miles from the New Hampshire border—her new home for the next four years.

Already by the end of her first trimester, Stephanie was suffering from emotional problems adjusting to life on her own. More than anything, she missed Charlotte and Barbara, but she felt guilty about leaving her own mother behind in an empty house, too. Even though Elizabeth had supported the idea of sending Stephanie away, she was clearly an emotional disaster without her daughter to play tennis with and drag to her girls' lunches. For these reasons, Stephanie found it hard to commit to her new life at school and difficult to make friends at Egret, where her proto-punk look stood out like a bird of paradise in an English garden.

Stephanie survived two years at Egret by studying hard and taking plenty of trips "home" to the Murphys. Then it happened. As Stephanie hunkered down for her third year at Egret (traditionally called the "upper" year), Barbara suddenly died. It all happened so quickly that the whole thing was a blur. Up at school, feeling more alone than ever, unable to attend the funeral because of Saturday classes, Stephanie basically lost it. Angry at the world for taking Barbara, and at the school for not letting her go home, Stephanie did what so many adolescents have done before in her situation—she acted out. Just before Christmas vacation, Stephanie was busted for drinking in her room and, after a close vote of the executive committee, was placed on disciplinary probation. As part of her punishment, Stephanie was required to see Dr. Diamond, Egret's resident psychological counselor. During this period, Stephanie's grades suffered severely. In the most important year of high school, Stephanie was getting the worst grades of her life and had managed to alienate or confuse most of the people she had gotten to know at her new school.

In retrospect, all of this was understandable. The death of a mother figure is a traumatic event. But Stephanie made a few curious choices when it came to applying for college, mistakes that haunted her throughout the college admissions process. First, Stephanie decided not to tell her college counselor, Mr. Hayden, about the reasons behind the alcohol bust. Dr. Diamond, Stephanie's psychological counselor with whom she had started to meet voluntarily, even after her probation was over, urged her to confess the reasons both to Mr. Hayden and to the teachers writing Stephanie's letters of recommendation. When she refused, Dr. Diamond was bound by doctor/patient confidentially not to tell any of them himself. And although Stephanie's father, a major donor to Peter Egret, had made sure Stephanie's probationary "blemish" did not appear on her official record when it was sent to colleges, Mr. Hayden included the infamous "call me" at the end of his counselor recommendation letter. Counselors write this dreaded phrase when they want to inform an admissions committee of important circumstances that do not appear on the applicant's record. When the admissions officers at Stephanie's chosen colleges did indeed call, Mr. Hayden informed them of her probation for drinking and of the subsequent family cover-up. Since Stephanie had chosen not to explain the circumstances behind her drinking bust in any of her application materials, including her personal statements, admissions officers at her top-choice colleges were left with the impression that Stephanie had not only performed horribly during the first and second trimester of her junior year but that she had tried to cover up a bust—both significant, character-defining mistakes.

Stephanie's decision not to come clean about the reasons for her drinking, and to withhold any mention of the mitigating circumstance surrounding her grade dip, resulted in rejection letters from nearly all of her top-choice colleges. In the end, Stephanie was lucky to be waitlisted at both Yale and Wesleyan, her number one schools. Yale was Dylan's beloved alma mater, and they had most likely waitlisted Stephanie as a courtesy to him because he was a high-profile donor. With this type of courtesy waitlisting, Yale admissions was essentially giving Stephanie a chance to prove that she really wanted to attend their school and wasn't just applying because of her father, something her original application had not sufficiently indicated. On the other hand, Wesleyan, the school far more suited to Stephanie's needs and desires, waitlisted her primarily because she had expressed so much interest in their particular offerings that they wanted to give her one last shot at proving she was emotionally ready for four more years away from home. Much to Dylan's chagrin, Stephanie would have to do a lot more work—including some serious soul-searching and decision-making—before she would be allowed to enter the hallowed halls of either selective American college.

Chapter Two

 COURSES AND GRADES

Now that you have had a chance to get to know the three students whose college applications will form the basis of my commentary, we are ready to move on to their actual college applications. To begin with, we will examine the academic profile of each student. The academic profile is comprised of the student's courses and grades as reflected in the transcript as well as his or her standardized test scores. As I have stressed over and over to my clients in private practice, the single most important aspect of the academic profile is the student's overall academic standing. If you have poor or mediocre course selection—meaning you took easier courses just to get better grades, dropped courses mid-sequence because they were either boring or too hard, avoided courses you knew would be challenging altogether, or switched around from subject to subject throughout your high school career—you simply will not be accepted at one of the nation's most selective schools. Similarly, if you have mediocre or poor grades, it places undue stress on the rest of your college application—your test scores, your brag sheet, your letters of support, and your essays—a pressure they will not always be able to shoulder even if they are outstanding, since the academic profile of a selective college applicant counts twice as much as the personal profile. Unfortunately, courses and grades are also the two aspects of your academic profile you cannot significantly alter once they are completed. Since you will never have the opportunity to redo any courses you may have slacked off in during sophomore year, you absolutely must take it upon yourself to take the hardest courses you can and get the best grades possible *from the beginning of high school onward*. College is the culmination of your life's intellectual work, both in and outside the classroom. It is the stepping-stone to your future. So don't handicap yourself before you even get a chance to show the world how talented you really are. Treat the college admissions process like the ultimate challenge that it is—prepare for it as hard as you can in order to be performing at an optimum level when the actual college applications roll around.

Student Academic Profiles

As you read through the following academic profiles, imagine you are an admissions reader at a selective college or university. Think about the kind of student you would want to invite to your campus. Then try to spot the "red flags" in David's, Ronald's, and Stephanie's scholastic achievement, any aspects of their academic histories that might cause you to raise an eyebrow, or to question or doubt in any way their ability to perform in a rigorous academic environment. How do David, Ronald, and Stephanie compare to your ideal student? What advice would you give them for improving the various aspects of their academic profiles? Now think about your own academic profile. How do you compare to David, Ronald, and Stephanie on an academic level? How do you compare to your ideal college applicant? Are you taking the most challenging course load at your high school? Are you consistently achieving to the best of your ability? Can you already perceive some areas where an admissions reader might see a red flag in your academic profile? If so, what are you going to do about them? Whatever you do, don't fret: it's never too late to pinpoint those areas of your academic profile that need work and go about improving them to the best of your ability, right up until the time you apply to college in the fall of your senior year.

After each academic profile, I have provided the student's high school transcript as well as an abridged version of his or her high school's profile. By reviewing the transcripts, you can compare the students to one another based solely on their grades and on the rigor of their course selection. As you read through the high school profiles, you can begin to formulate an opinion as to whether or not each student has taken full advantage of the offerings at his or her high school. After the academic profile, student transcript, and high school profile for each student, I will begin my analysis of their applications, offering you a firsthand glimpse into the way I judge the selective college applications that cross my desk, from the point of view of both an admissions reader and an independent college counselor. Using the IvyWise

Index as my guide, I will rate each student's academic achievement and begin compiling a composite score for his or her entire application. Remember, each student's ranking on the IvyWise Index is roughly the equivalent of the rankings he or she would receive from an admissions office at one of the nation's most selective colleges. It is here, in my in-depth analysis of each section of these students' college applications, that you will be given a privileged view into the selective college admissions process *from the inside*.

After I have analyzed each student's academic profile and ranked it according to the criteria of the IvyWise Index, you will find the many suggestions for improvement that I offered David and Stephanie when they came to me for an Application Review. In the case of Ronald Siegal, there will be no such before-and-after analysis as he came to me early enough in the college admissions process to benefit from my expertise prior to turning in his final applications. In this way, Ronald Siegal's application, as it was sent to his top-choice college, the University of Pennsylvania, was the ideal IvyWise application. This does not mean he was the most gifted student I have ever seen—on the contrary, it means simply that he devoted extra time and effort to his college applications and was able to turn his modest academic achievement into a Hall of Fame perfor-

Did you know?

1. **A grade dip has to be explained in the counselor letter.** If you have suffered a momentary dip and there were extenuating circumstances, you must communicate with your high school college counselor and help him or her understand why.

2. **It's a huge red flag to drop a course.** Colleges like to see consistency and perseverance; dropping a course shows you couldn't handle the pressure or that you were too concerned about your grades to continue with a course in which you weren't performing well.

Do's and Don'ts of Getting Great Grades:

➲ **DO go above and beyond your assignments and show enthusiasm for a subject even if you're not interested in it.** If you are studying a foreign language, watch a film in that language every week. You can start and stop the film scene by scene, repeating lines out loud while blocking out the subtitles.

➲ **DON'T read works of literature in translation** when you are meant to read them in the original: You will learn nothing about the intricacies of the original language nor about the ways in which the great writers and thinkers of that culture express themselves in their mother tongue.

➲ **DO go to your teachers early on in the paper-writing process.** Discuss your topics with them. Show them your progress. Get them to recommend secondary sources for research. You can even ask them to sign off on your work at various stages along the way. If the teacher evaluates, makes suggestions, edits, and approves of your thesis, outline, rough draft, and first draft, the teacher is bound to give you a high grade on your final paper. This will not only educate you firsthand in the fine art of paper-writing but also forge a better relationship with a teacher outside of regular classroom hours.

➲ DON'T study just to get a good grade or cram at the last second!

From the Other Side of the Desk:

(1) Most applicants to Harvard need to have at least a solid B+ average, although some will have lower if they evince an upward grade trend or took an extremely difficult course load. Extraordinary achievement in another field such as sports, art, music, or a particular activity outside the classroom can help a reader overlook weaker grades. (Anonymous admissions officer at Harvard during an information session)

(2) Harder courses are more desirable on a student's transcript than better grades. A C in an IB or AP course must be looked at in context. If that's the best you could do, then fine: Tufts looks at the caliber of the course in relation to the offerings at your high school and judges your academic performance in relation to your fellow students, not in relation to the entire applicant pool. (Leon McLean,

mance, simply by following the tips and strategies contained in this book.

ACADEMIC PROFILE: DAVID HOROWITZ

As you may have guessed, David is an outstanding student. Although his nature is to be shy, he manages to speak up in class—just enough to participate but never enough to overtake discussion. According to his teachers, David always has something intelligent and insightful to contribute. He is the kind of student who genuinely wants to arrive at an answer, even if others beat him to it—which is rare if he really puts his mind to it. In the classroom, David likes to question, to think, to analyze, to communicate, and to arrive at a consensus. He studies for the sake of learning, not to get good grades. His outstanding record is simply a natural result of his extraordinary work ethic and his love of learning. Challenging himself to achieve, David took as many AP courses as he was able to given his dual curriculum, including the dreaded physics. He is what I would call a "true scholar."

Ironically, the problems with David's academic profile stem precisely from his strong desire to achieve. After a single year at his regional Long Island public high school, during which

David was unchallenged and understimulated, he boldly decided to switch schools for tenth grade. A new yeshiva had opened a few townships away, and although it would cost considerably more for his parents, everyone agreed it would be a far more suitable place for David's superior intellect. He began at Singer Yeshiva High School, however, with a distinct disadvantage in relation to the other students in his class, who had already spent a year getting to know their environment, making friends, and working out the kinks of going to a new school. It took David a while to adjust to the double course load, the long commute, and the more competitive academic atmosphere. Eventually he did, but with some emotional scars to show for it. If only David were more comfortable talking about his difficulties and insecurities, they might not have hurt him so much. But David is a trouper, if anything.

In fact, David jumped into his studies with such gusto that focus became a problem. For a while at the beginning of high school, David's interests ranged far and wide and his college counselor was worried that he was biting off more than he could chew. Luckily, by his senior year medicine and law—both of which he was well-prepared to pursue, given his strong background in science and the humanities—began to emerge as distinct career possibilities. Not that David had to decide on a major right away. Colleges don't

former Admissions Coordinator at Tufts University)

(3) Ninety percent of Brown applicants are qualified academically, but even those below the norm are encouraged to apply. Brown looks for **potential**. In the long run, better grades are less important than harder courses, which test students' ability to grow beyond their current knowledge as well as their willingness to challenge themselves. (An anonymous admissions officer at Brown)

(4) Straight A's in your high school's toughest classes would obviously give you the best shot at admission to your number one college. The "Courses and Grades" section of the application is a self-selection process: If you've taken only three out of a possible twenty-one AP's offered at your high school, you will have an extremely difficult time advancing through a selection committee. Of course, if you had to switch high schools midcareer because of family needs or other extenuating circumstances, or if your high school offers no accelerated courses, the school will take that into consideration and you would not be at a disadvantage. It is best if this information comes from the counselor in his or her letter. But as an applicant, you should always take the time to explain "your side of the story." (Dan Evans at the University of Pennsylvania)

(5) Emory has not published minimum grade point average or standardized test scores for admission. Competitive grade point averages in the past have fallen in the 3.5–4.0 range. A

lower grade point average can be offset by special talent, legacy status, or being a first generation college student. Emory is always on the lookout for an upward grade trend, with eleventh-grade marks counting the most. **At most highly selective schools like Emory, a GPA taken out of context means very little.** Admission committees evaluate strength of academic program, strength of secondary school, and many other subjective factors when viewing a prospective student's transcript. They know about the schools in their region from personal experience and will call the counselor if they have any unanswered questions. Whereas they may overlook a C, Emory considers F's and D's on a student's transcript **"warning signs."** (Scott Schamberger, Admissions Counselor at Emory University)

(6) Even students who have performed in the B-range (for one semester) have been admitted to both Yale and Vassar, but always under extenuating circumstances. The question we ask is: **Can we bring out the best and brightest in this person?** A dream student might be a genius kid from a one-room schoolhouse on the Montana prairie; the worst might be a student with a roller-coaster transcript from a prestigious school. In terms of the transcript, harder courses are more desirable than high grades. This is a faculty-driven decision: Professors want to know that the students they are getting are well prepared. (Lloyd Peterson, formerly of Yale and Vassar)

(7) **Tougher courses prepare students better for college but not to the detriment of one's**

necessarily seek students with a concrete agenda or a crystal clear idea of their career path. Undecided applicants are the norm, in fact. On the other hand, an undecided applicant who imagines studying seventeen different things at once in college—and none of them related—risks appearing wishy-washy, unrealistic, and/or confused in the eyes of a college admissions officer. If you remain focused on your studies, do the best you possibly can in school, and demonstrate skill in a number of academic areas, colleges will have absolutely no reason to doubt your ability to perform in any number of subjects at a collegiate level.

This brings us to David's college search. In the beginning, David really wanted to attend either Yale or Columbia—for reasons that had little to do with David's particular interests and more to do with the schools' names and prestige. He was a legacy at the University of Pennsylvania, so he applied there as well. As safety schools, David applied to Johns Hopkins and, more or less against his will, Yeshiva University and Rutgers University, where his parents wanted him to go so he could remain closer to home to help out with the "Sarah" problem. David was reluctant to leave his little sister Ann in Sarah's clutches, but college was supposed to be fun, right? And fun for David meant being as far away from the observing eyes of his parents as possible. Unfortunately, David was in the first graduating class of the brand-new Singer Yeshiva High School, and as a result, some of the kinks had yet to be worked out. Moreover, it was Singer Yeshiva's college-counseling services that were the most underdeveloped at the time. With David's outstanding course selection and his near-perfect grades, he should have been accepted to all of the colleges he applied to. But with little clue how to maximize his college application profile—and saddled with either absent or erroneous advice from his high school college counselor—David was rejected from Yale, Columbia, and, surprisingly, the University of Pennsylvania. By a stroke of luck, he was placed on the waitlist at Johns Hopkins University and accepted outright to both Yeshiva and Rutgers.

In addition to being in his high school's first graduating class, David was also the first of his siblings to go through the college admissions process. As such, David and his family were faced with many questions they did not know how to answer. They assumed that David was a shoo-in at the college of his choice simply because of his stellar grades, his great course selection, and his high SAT I scores. In May of his senior year, David and his family came to me for an Application Review. It became clear after my initial evaluation of his work that no one had taken the time to look over David's application as a whole. No one had considered it as a rhetorical docu-

grades. NYU prefers applicants with solid achievement—a 3.4 or 3.5 in the toughest curriculum over four years. Only if you are a star athlete or applying to a performance-based program can you get in with lower grades. Any F or bad semester must be explained by either the college counselor or the applicant. Certainly, it is much better if the grade dip occurs in the freshman year than in the junior year. (Richard Avitabile, formerly of NYU)

Beware!

Low grades but high test scores may force colleges to conclude you are an underachiever. The inverse—high grades and low scores—although not exactly desirable, is preferable. **Remember that, no matter what, grades count much more than test scores at the majority of the nation's top colleges!**

Your IvyWise Counselor Says:

"Students often tell me their high school teachers are unhelpful, unimaginative, or just plain bad. Even if this is truly the case, you still have to find a way to **learn on your own**. This takes discipline. It's not your fault if the teacher is poor, but you have to do something about it—complaining won't help. Always try to go above and beyond the assignments. Work with your teachers. Help them teach you. Get study aides on your own (especially in preparation for SAT IIs). **Don't put all the responsibility for your education in your teachers' hands.** This type of self-motivated work will be great preparation for college, where no one will be standing over your shoulder making sure you do your work."

Study Hard!

Fifty percent of your admissions decision could be based on grades and rigor of curriculum. (John Birney, Associate Director of Admissions at Johns Hopkins University)

Have an Academic Profile that POPPs!

If you want to maximize your potential during high school, try using what I call the **POPP strategy: Plan, Organize, Prioritize, and Pace.** Each week in your schedule should be planned out in advance. You should know all your assignments; know when they are due; and know when you are going to complete them. For this, you will have to learn how long assignments take to finish. Set aside a bit of time each day so you aren't caught with no time to spare. *Cramming is not learning.* Time is scarce, so prioritize. Papers and tests win out over ordinary assignments. If you're writing a paper, plan office hour visits and research/library time. The night before a paper is due you should only be proofreading. **If you need a nap, take one.** You can even learn how to power nap for twenty or thirty minutes. If you're sleep-deprived and cranky, you're not going to do well in your courses. Along the same lines, don't eat too many sweets because they zap your energy. Try eating energizing snacks like roast beef, vegetable crudités, or, my favorite, green apple with cottage cheese. Finally, try not to go out with your friends during the week. Set up friend nights on the weekends. Get enough sleep. **Complete your work first, then have fun.**

ment capable of either making or breaking his chances of being accepted at the college of his dreams. Now that dream was dashed—all because David, along with an inexperienced college counselor and parents who were entering the contemporary college admissions process for the first time, had failed to realize that the selective college application requires incredible attention to detail, as well as the finesse and marketing skills normally reserved for a job application. In fact, given the importance of the years we spend in college, the college application is perhaps the most important document of our early lives. It is thus all the more surprising that so many stellar students like David treat it with so little effort, and that so many parents and counselors underestimate its fundamental import.

As you look over David's transcript and high school profile below, you will see beyond a shadow of a doubt that David earned outstanding grades and scores throughout his high school career—all A's in the most rigorous curriculum he could take—as well as an 800 on his verbal SAT I, especially strong given the low mean SAT I scores at Singer Yeshiva. Despite this achievement, however, David's application was filled with a number of red flags. These weak or underdeveloped elements should have been rewritten or strengthened before he sent in his applications. In their current state, they took away from his overall chances of gaining admission to his top-choice schools. To begin with,

David's essays were inadequate and gave no clear sense of who he was as a person. Furthermore, he didn't sufficiently research the schools on his list in order to give the impression that he truly cared about attending them for their specific offerings. David also couldn't make up his mind on a first-choice school and didn't apply early anywhere, even though he was a perfect candidate for Early Decision at his top choice school, whichever that was. David's college list itself was strange—I still have no idea how he originally put it together and was shocked when I first saw the diversity of the schools to which he had applied. How could all of them be the "right fit"? Clearly David had been going on name recognition alone and hadn't taken the time to determine which schools were the best suited to his particular needs. As a final red flag, David used the electronic Common Application. Although this is a minor point, David should have taken the time to seek out the actual applications to each of his schools in order to demonstrate strong initiative. Who knows, something relatively small like this could have been exactly the bit of extra effort David's applications needed to set him apart from the many other qualified applicants vying for the same spot in the freshman class at Johns Hopkins. Because of these red flags, which will be discussed in more detail below, David and his parents decided to ask my help in getting him off the waitlist and into Johns Hopkins, now his number one choice.

THE TRANSCRIPT: DAVID HOROWITZ

To better understand and evaluate David's academic profile, examine his official transcript from Singer Yeshiva High School. As you read through his course selection and grades, keep in mind the criteria used to determine the IvyWise Index ranking for this application section. Does David take courses on a consistent basis with increasing difficulty in each of his chosen subjects? Does he follow each course through to an exhaustive enough level? Has he dropped any subjects prematurely? What are his obvious strengths and weaknesses? Are his grades consistently good or do they dip at any point in his academic career? Once you have familiarized yourself with David's transcript, examine the abridged version of the official Singer Yeshiva High School profile. In order to evaluate David's transcript and overall academic profile, consider any relevant information from Singer's school profile that might have a direct bearing on David's IvyWise Index ranking. Does David take full advantage of the academic offerings at his school? Does he take full advantage of the numerous extracurricular, sports, and community service opportunities provided by Singer? Finally, compare your own high school's profile to David's in order to determine the extent to which you yourself have been taking advantage of all that your academic community has to offer.

SINGER YESHIVA HIGH SCHOOL STUDENT TRANSCRIPT

Name:	David. J. Horowitz	**SSN:**	555-66-7777
Address:	123 North Walnut Ave.	**DOB:**	4/6/84
	Pearl Bay, NY 07789	**Gender:**	Male

GENERAL STUDIES

Department	Course Name	Grade	Credits
Electives			
2001–2002	Economics/Law	98.000*	1.00
English			
1999–2000	Honors English 10	99.000	1.00
2000–2001	Honors English 11	98.000	1.00
2001–2002	AP English 12	99.000*	1.00

Department	Course Name	Grade	Credits
Foreign Language			
1999–2000	French II—10	92.000	1.00
2000–2001	French III—11	93.000	1.00
History			
1999–2000	Jewish History 10	100.000	1.00
2000–2001	AP US History 11	95.000	1.00
2001–2002	European History	98.000*	1.00
Math			
1999–2000	Geometry 10	96.000	1.00
2000–2001	Algebra II—11	100.000	1.00
2001–2002	Pre-Calculus 12	100.000*	1.00
Physical Education			
1999–2000	Physical Education	A	.50
2000–2001	Independent Physical Education	P	.50
2001–2002	Physical Education Boys	A*	1.00
Science			
1999–2000	Honors Chemistry 10	93.000	1.00
2000–2001	AP Chemistry 11	100.000	1.00
2000–2001	Honors Physics 11/12	98.000	1.00
2001–2002	AP Biology 12	97.700*	1.00

JUDAIC STUDIES

Department	Course Name	Grade	Credits
Talmud			
1999–2000	Honors Talmud 10	96.000	2.00
2000–2001	Honors Talmud 11	95.000	2.00
2001–2002	Honors Talmud 12	92.000*	1.00
Bible			
1999–2000	Honors Bible 10	97.000	1.00
2000–2001	Honors Bible 11	97.000	1.00
2001–2002	Honors Bible 12	97.000*	1.00
Hebrew			
1999–2000	Honors Hebrew 10	98.000	1.00
2000–2001	Honors Hebrew 11	96.000	1.00
2001–2002	Honors Hebrew 12	95.000*	1.00
Judaics			
1999–2000	Sicha 10	A	.25
2000–2001	Sicha 11	P	.25
2001–2002	Sicha 12	P*	1.00

ACADEMIC SUMMARY

Year	GPA	Honor Roll
1999–2000	4.00	Yes
2000–2001	4.00	Yes
2001–2002	4.00*	*

Grade points are determined based on the conversion chart below:

100 − 90 = A = 4 grade points   69 − 60 = D = 1 grade point

89 − 80 = B = 3 grade points   59 − 0 = F = 0 grade points

79 − 70 = C = 2 grade points   Incomplete = 0 grade points

Singer Yeshiva High School does not rank students or weight grades. Both Judaic and General Studies courses are calculated into the grade point average (GPA). Course work completed at other schools is not calculated into the SYHS GPA. Course levels are designated in the transcript: Advanced Placement (AP), Honors (H), Accelerated (ACC), Level 1, 2, 3, 4, or A, B, C, D.

*Indicates courses still in progress—grades are not final

SINGER YESHIVA HIGH SCHOOL PROFILE

Singer Yeshiva High School (SYHS) is a four-year, private, coeducational, Jewish day school offering a comprehensive dual curriculum of Judaic and college preparatory courses. The school sits on forty pristine acres of suburban land in Rumsfield, New York, a suburban community of approximately 25,000 located in midwestern Long Island about twenty-five miles southeast of Manhattan. The majority of Singer Yeshiva High School parents are university graduates, many of whom have done advanced work in Judaic as well as general studies and are now employed in professional, managerial, or business occupations. The campus features extensive athletic facilities such as track, soccer and softball fields, basketball and tennis courts, and a floor hockey rink.

SYHS boasts forty-five professional full- and part-time faculty members averaging twenty-seven years of experience, many of whom hold master's or doctoral degrees with college teaching experience. The faculty includes two guidance counselors, a college guidance counselor, a learning coordinator/learning disabilities consultant, two school nurses, two librarians, and four physical education teachers. Its faculty to student ratio is 1:4. Its average class size is fifteen. It is important to note that Singer Yeshiva High School currently enrolls only 245 students and that the first Singer Yeshiva High School graduation took place in June 2002.

In order to graduate, students must take 17 credits of Judaic Studies, including Oral Law (four years), Bible (four years), Hebrew Literature and Language (four years), and Jewish Thought (one year). In addition, students must take 21.5 credits of General Studies: English Literature and Language (four years); Math (three years); Science (three years); History (four years); Spanish/French (two years); Physical Education (four years); Computer Applications (half year) plus three electives, selected from Math, Science, Humanities, Business, and Languages. Finally, Singer Yeshiva High School students are required to complete eighteen hours of community service per semester.

The mean SAT I scores for all juniors who had tested by June 2001 were 545 Verbal and 543 Math. The school's mean SAT II scores for all juniors who had tested by June 2001 were Biology: 631; Chemistry: 637; Math (IC): 602; Writing: 598; U.S. History: 615; Modern Hebrew: 570; Literature: 640; and World History: 715. At Singer, **Honors and Advanced Placement courses include** Honors Language and Literature in French and Spanish, Honors World Studies, AP U.S. History, AP Psychology, Honors Introduction to World Literature, Honors World Literature, Honors American Literature, AP English, Honors Algebra I, Honors Geometry, Honors Algebra II, Honors Pre-Calculus, Honors Calculus, AP Calculus, Honors Biology, Honors Chemistry, Honors Physics, AP Biology, AP Chemistry, AP Physics. Singer's **extracurricular activities include** Art, Band, Chess, Choir, College Bowl, Community Service, CPR, Dance, Debate, Drama, Israel Club, Jewish Literary Journal, Mock Trial, Model UN, Civics, Newspaper, Peer Counseling, Student Council, Technology, and Torah Bowl.

ACADEMIC PROFILE EVALUATION: DAVID HOROWITZ

Now that you have had a chance to familiarize yourself with David's academic profile, we are ready to start our analysis using the IvyWise Index as our guide. Keep in mind that the highest possible score for each section is 9 Index points.

David's Courses:	8 points

• Challenging course load

David's heavy course load and dual curriculum count very much in his favor. Colleges want to know if an applicant can handle significant, sustained work at a high academic level, and David's challenging curriculum, in addition to his superlative grades, proves this unequivocally.

• Rigorous courses

Four AP courses may not seem outstanding, but David's school only offers seven total. In addition to this, David's record of thirteen honors courses—including Hebrew, Bible, and Talmud—shows extreme dedication to academic pursuits, love of self-initiated challenges, and an extraordinarily high level of scholastic competency.

• Switched to a more challenging school

In some cases, students get expelled and have to switch schools in the middle of their high school careers. This clearly did not happen in David's case—he was the one to initiate a transfer because he was not sufficiently challenged at his old public high school. The choice was clearly a good one, as David thrived at Singer Yeshiva. This bold decision highlights David's initiative, his willingness to challenge himself, and his ability to adjust to new academic environments and teaching methodologies, as well as his perseverance, drive, and follow-through.

• Low level of math

Unfortunately, David did not take a high level of math and this ultimately detracts one point from his otherwise stellar transcript. The most selective colleges like to see at least a full year of Calculus.

• Dropped a course

In addition to not achieving a high level of math, another red flag appears on David's transcript: He dropped French going into his senior year. Two of David's lowest grades were in French, so it is reasonable to assume that he dropped French in order to improve his overall GPA. This is not a good reason, however, for it gives the impression that he was only in it for the grades, not for the love of learning. Normally this would merit a subtraction of a point from David's IvyWise Index ranking, but there are a few mitigating circumstances that come to his rescue. First of all, Singer Yeshiva requires only two years of Spanish or French, a requirement that David clearly met. Second of all, David has already mastered a foreign language: Hebrew. Although this is often viewed as a required skill in an Orthodox upbringing, it essentially makes French a second foreign language. As such, having three years (in grades 9, 10, 11) of a second foreign language is impressive, especially given the rigor of David's overall transcript. Third, David may have dropped French in order to make room for an elective his senior year in Economics/Law, a course that better reflects his overall academic interests. Finally, David doubled up on sciences in his junior year, making a difficult course load even more challenging in the process. Overall, David's course load is so impressive that I am inclined to forgive his dropping French his senior year.

David's Grades:	9 points

• Unweighted 4.0 GPA

An unweighted 4.0 GPA is as close to perfect as it gets. Unweighted means that none of David's honors or AP courses have artificially inflated his overall GPA. Certain schools offer 5.0 grade points for a perfect score in an honors or AP course. Singer Yeshiva does not. Given the many honors and AP courses David did take, it is all the more impressive that he was able to maintain a perfect A average. David's transcript is by far the strongest aspect of his application.

• High AP Scores

David's two AP exam scores of 5 and 4 in AP Chemistry and AP U.S. History, respectively, are great but not perfect. Ultimately, given David's astounding GPA, the 4 in Chemistry is not enough to bump him down a point.

ACADEMIC PROFILE IMPROVEMENT STRATEGIES: DAVID HOROWITZ

David Horowitz is essentially an outstanding student whose only flaw on his college application was his shyness. In fact, he's an academic superstar and schools were looking hard for reasons to reject him. Unfortunately, they found one in his tendency to keep personal information to himself and to hide behind his academic achievements. In order to change the Johns Hopkins admissions committee's mind about his application, David needed to come out of hiding and let them see who he really was underneath that hard, intellectual shell. Only this kind of personal exploration and self-expression would get off him the waiting list and into the freshman class. In the following chapters, I will address the changes we made to David's application along these lines, vastly improving the personal elements of his profile. As far as his "Courses and Grades" go, however, there was nothing for us to do. David's academic profile was the one area we had no need to improve.

ACADEMIC PROFILE: RONALD SIEGAL

Ronald Siegal is obviously a bright student who loves to learn. But in contrast to David Horowitz, Ronald probably won't end up pursuing a scholarly career. He simply isn't as academically gifted as either David or many of the other high-achieving students competing for his Early Decision spot at the University of Pennsylvania. Luckily, Ronald has other skills that helped him to achieve at a consistently high level in high school: He is extremely creative and open to learning new things, he enjoys a challenge, and his course load at Swanee High School was that of a definite overachiever. Yet despite working harder than others in his class, and despite maintaining an excellent attitude throughout, Ronald's grades never quite reached the level of achievement that would have immediately attracted one of the nation's top colleges. Somewhere in the top 20 percent of his graduating class, Ronald knew he had his work cut out for him if he wanted to get into U. Penn.

Despite the extra obstacles he faced because of his lower grades, Ronald's challenging curriculum counted very much in his favor. He had taken the most challenging course load he could without risking serious damage to his GPA. This does not mean that it was the most challenging course load a student has ever taken at Swanee High School. To begin with, Ronald took no college-level courses at a local community college, something many of the more supermotivated students at his large public high school did to bolster their academic profiles. In addition, Ronald didn't take all the Advanced Placement courses he could have. The most glaring inconsistency in his transcript, however, resulted from his unfortunate decision to sign up for AP Biology during his senior year when he should have enrolled in AP Studio Art. The two courses presented a scheduling conflict, so Ronald was forced to choose one over the other. Although I counseled him against it, Ronald mistakenly chose AP Biology. Since he was not truly interested in AP Biology and his strengths did not lie in the sciences, the class ended up being too difficult for him and he dropped it after three weeks. It was then too late for him to join the AP Studio Art class already under way, and Ronald was left in the unfortunate position of having neither course on his official transcript. More important, Ronald dropped his AP Biology class after he had submitted his Early Decision application to the University of Pennsylvania. Having dutifully completed his applications in the summer before his senior year, Ronald was eager to mail in his U. Penn application and get it out of the way. There seemed to be no harm in this at the time—but that was before Ronald decided to alter his senior year course load drastically. Ronald's transcript contained one fewer AP level course than it should have, and the discrepancy between Ronald's projected senior year courses as listed on his application (including AP Biology) and his midsemester school report (excluding AP Biology) would be visible to everyone in the admissions office at U. Penn. And finally, Ronald missed out on taking AP Studio Art, a course he most surely would have enjoyed and mastered, given his passion for art. Ronald made this mistake because he was too concerned with what he imagined colleges were looking for. He incorrectly assumed that AP Biology would look more "impressive" on his transcript than AP Studio Art. Although applicants can formulate reasonable assumptions as to what colleges are looking for in terms of *level* of achievement, there is no way to predict what a college is looking for in terms of *content*.

Despite this error, Ronald was able to rescue his application by employing a number of carefully formulated IvyWise strategies designed to overcome the potentially negative aspects of his academic profile. Swanee High School is a large public school that has traditionally fed a number of top liberal arts colleges in the Midwest. Perhaps out of habit or because they have forged strong relationships with these schools over time, the college guidance counselors at Swanee tend to recommend these few schools to the detriment of others. But instead of following blindly in the footsteps of his predecessors, Ronald chose to do intensive research into a number of schools around the country that interested him because he understood early on in the process that the right college fit was the most important thing for him. When his sights fell on the University of Pennsylvania, a school he had dreamed of attending since elementary school, Ronald's college counselor at Swanee wasn't motivated to help him—she was convinced, incorrectly, that Ronald would be happy wherever he went. One day while his mother was reading a magazine, Ronald spotted an article on IvyWise and begged her to call my office.

While putting together his college list, Ronald was reluctant to accept that there had to be such things as safety schools. This confidence stemmed not from an attitude of entitlement but from the knowledge that he was an extremely hard worker and wasn't going to settle for a college that didn't challenge him or that he didn't love from the get-go. But he also knew that a top-tier school like the University of Pennsylvania was going to be a real reach for him—there were many other gifted students in his class ranked higher than he who were applying to U. Penn, also Early Decision. But there was a difference. Whereas these other students, like David Horowitz, felt entitled to attend a school like the University of Pennsylvania because of their stellar academic performance, Ronald never once took the process for granted. This gave him an underdog mentality, a fire in his belly that provided him with an edge.

It is important to stress this aspect of Ronald's attitude about the college admissions process: Unlike David Horowitz, Ronald Siegal never once assumed he was going to get into one of the nation's best colleges.

When he decided to apply Early Decision to U. Penn, he understood it was a long shot, but he vowed he would do whatever it took to get in. Again, this was not arrogant. This was intelligent. As we have seen, with my guidance, Ronald also made sure that his other applications (eight in total) were completed and in the best possible shape *in the summer before his senior year*. This left Ronald plenty of time to concentrate on his studies and his test preparation for another shot at the SAT I. It also provided him with a backup plan in case things didn't work out with his first choice school.

THE TRANSCRIPT: RONALD SIEGAL

As with David Horowitz, I now invite you to spend some time studying Ronald Siegal's official high school transcript as well as an abridged version of the Swanee High School Profile. As with David, I will then evaluate Ronald's academic profile according to the criteria of the IvyWise Index. As you read through the next couple of pages, bear the same questions in mind that you did considering David's academic performance: Does Ronald take a consistently challenging course load, achieving ever higher grades in an ever more demanding curriculum? Does he take full advantage of the academic and extracurricular offerings at Swanee? How does Ronald compare to his fellow classmates? And again—how do you compare in terms of grades and course selection to Ronald Siegal?

SWANEE HIGH SCHOOL STUDENT TRANSCRIPT

Name:	Ronald P. Siegal	**Entered:**	September 1997
DOB:	5/7/83	**Graduation:**	June 2001

1997–1998

Course	Grade	Credits
English 212	A−	.50
English 212	A−	.50

Course	Grade	Credits
Earth Science 513	A−	1.00
Spanish 313	A−	1.00
Spanish 324	B+	1.00
Math 413	A	1.00
Physical Education 9	P	n/a
Physical Education 9	P	n/a
Studio Art	A	1.00
World History 612	B+	1.00

SUMMER 1998

Math 423	A	1.00

1998–1999

Biology 513	B+	1.00
English 222	A−	1.00
Spanish 334	B+	1.00
Group Skill	P	.25
Health	A−	.50
Math 433	A−	1.00
Photography 1	A−	.50
Physical Education 10	P	n/a
Physical Education 10	P	n/a
World History 622	A−	1.00

1999–2000

Chemistry 513	A	1.00
Drawing and Painting II	A	.50
English 234	B+	.50
English 234	A−	.50

Course	Grade	Credits
Spanish 344	A−	1.00
Group Skill	P	.25
Pre-Calculus 444	B+	1.00
Physical Education 11	P	n/a
Physical Education 11	P	n/a
U.S. History 635 AP	A	1.00

2000–2001: MIDTERM GRADES

AB Calculus 455 AP	C	1.00
American Dream	A	1.00
Art History	A	.50
English 244	A−	.50
Spanish Language 355 AP	A−	1.00
Physical Education 12	P	n/a
U.S. Government/Politics 645 AP	C	1.00

Grade Code:

A+	4.4
A	4.0
A−	3.7
B+	3.4
B	3.0
B−	2.7
C+	2.4
C	2.0
C−	1.7
D+	1.4
D	1.0
F	0.0
P	Pass
I	Incomplete
W	Withdrawn

Course Code:

Advanced Placement	5
High Honors/Honors	4
Enriched	3
Regular	2
Basic	1
Remedial	0
I.S.	Independent Study
A.C.	Accelerated

Course Key:

Hundreds digit:	Department
Tens Digit:	Year of Study
Ones Digit:	Level of Study

POINT AVERAGE

...th semester, includes all subjects in ...ing is given for honors or advanced ...aise a grade, the grade point average ...Students are not assigned a rank in

SW

In its ...ucation named Swanee High School "the ...e High School is a four-year college prepa ...ed in the town of Swanee, a suburban comn ...d County, Ohio. Most residents are midd ...technology company that dominates the a ...support for the public educational syster ...with enrollment and participation from ...ulturally diverse community, as the biotec ...n across the globe. Curricular offer- ings a ..., AB Calculus, English Literature, Spani ...t and Politics, to basic skill sections for students requiring special instructional approaches. Opportunities include extensive use of tutorials, independent study, and interdisciplinary courses, with a wide array of opportunities for in school/class governance, school and community service, publications, intramural sports, special interest groups, performing arts, interscholastic sports teams, and over thirty clubs that are student-initiated and -run. Swanee High School has a professional staff of 171 with a median teaching experience of sixteen years. The student to faculty ratio is 19 to 1. The Counseling Department, composed of a director and six school counselors, provides a comprehensive guidance program for each grade. All students are required to complete a minimum of 18.5 credits for graduation: English (4 credits), Arts (1 credit), Social Science (4 credits), Health ($1/2$ credit), Science (2 credits), Computers ($1/2$ credit), Mathematics (2 credits), Electives (3.5 credits), Foreign Language (1 credit), and Physical Education (4 years). Senior Options, an internship or independent project for five weeks, is required for graduation.

SWANEE STATISTICS

In 2000, the Swanee Mean Advanced Placement Score for all tests was 3.4. The SAT II Subject Test mean scores were as follows: Writing: 596; Math 1C: 627; Math 2C: 609; American History: 592; French: 589; Spanish: 602; Chemistry: 609; Biology: 601; Physics: 617; Literature: 576; and Chinese Listening: 653. The Swanee High school mean SAT I scores were 575 Verbal SAT I and 606 Math SAT I.

81 percent of the 539 members of the Class of 2000 continued their education. Of that group, 86 percent entered 111 different four-year national and international colleges and universities and 14 percent entered two different two-year colleges. Twelve students in the Class of 2000 (2 percent) were named National Merit Scholarship Semifinalists and thirty-four students in the Class of 2000 (6 percent) received National Merit Letters of Commendation.

ACADEMIC PROFILE EVALUATION: RONALD SIEGAL

The following is my in-depth analysis of Ronald Siegal's transcript and overall academic performance based on the rigorous standards of the IvyWise Index. Again, the maximum number of possible points for each section is 9.

Ronald's Courses:	7 points

• Dropped AP Biology!

Despite its overall level of difficulty, Ronald's course load would normally have ranked an 8 on the IvyWise Index because he took no community college courses and did not exhaust his school's curriculum. But his IvyWise Index ranking for this section dips to a 7 because he dropped AP Biology three weeks into his senior year—and U. Penn knew about it. It would have been far wiser to avoid this error by not taking AP Biology at all, or by continuing with it—using outside help, if necessary—and doing the absolute best he could both in the course and on the AP examination. As such, Ronald risked appearing lazy, unmotivated, and/ or unwilling to face the serious challenge of performing at a high scholastic level in a course he found difficult. Although admissions readers at U. Penn knew from the rest of Ronald's application that he was a hard-working student who never shied away from a serious academic challenge, this red flag, especially appearing in the crucial senior year, raises a question mark over the rest of his past achievement.

• Should have taken AP Studio Art!

Given Ronald's obvious talent and interest in art, any admissions officer reading his application would have noticed that AP Studio Art was missing from his transcript. They would have wondered at this conspicuous absence, especially since they would know it was offered at his school by reading the Swanee High School Profile. As I said, Ronald chose AP Biology over AP Studio Art—even after I urged him not to—because he felt it would "look better" on his transcript due to the difficulty and supposed "seriousness" of the course. In this, Ronald was mistaken. Colleges want students with demonstrated skill in whatever subjects they naturally gravitate toward. For Ronald, these subjects were clearly history and art. He may have felt more "free" and less "academic" when creating his art or when studying history, but this feeling was probably due to the fact that art and history were true passions for him. Colleges like nothing more than this kind of true passion for a subject: It tells them a lot about a student's interior life and gives them a pretty good idea of what the student will want to pursue in college. Unfortunately, Ronald missed a golden opportunity to spend an entire year in the studio, honing his craft with an excellent teacher and interacting with like-minded and equally creative art students.

• Not enough APs!

Since Swanee was a public high school where funding has always been an issue, the costs of implementing and teaching every AP course available nationwide were simply pro-hibitive. Ronald's total of four AP classes gives a college admissions office confidence that he challenged himself. However, he could have taken more. I am seeing more and more students take AP tests to further challenge themselves when there is no AP level course offered. Missing from Ronald's transcript were obvious choices, such as AP French Literature, AP English Language, and AP English Literature (in addition to the aforementioned AP Studio Art). Although Swanee didn't offer either AP English Language or AP French Literature, Ronald could have taken it upon himself to order the AP examinations in these subjects, take them on his own time, and send them to his prospective colleges. This is especially important for students applying from large public high schools like Swanee, regardless of their quality, where AP courses are often not offered because of budgetary difficulties. Few students are aware that you can order AP exams on your own, study independently, and turn in the results separate from organized courses or official test dates. It is a great way to show a prospective college that you care enough to pursue your studies to the highest possible level. It would have been a great way for Ronald to stay even with the undoubtedly difficult competition he faced from private high school applicants whose schools offer every AP course available. There is also little doubt, given his extraordinary work ethic and desire to succeed, that Ronald would have excelled at these exams.

Ronald's Grades:	6 points

• **Too many B's and a single low AP**

Of the many red flags contributing to Ronald's lower rank of 6 on the Grades section of the IvyWise Index, these were perhaps the most detrimental. With so many B's on his transcript—and some C's!—Ronald's academic profile ranked unfavorably in relation to other selective college applicants who were liable to have perfect 4.0 GPAs in addition to more impressive course loads. Although Ronald did try to challenge himself by taking increasingly difficult courses throughout high school, his grades suffered and his overall academic profile was affected. Ronald's decent score of 4 on his AP U.S. History exam redeemed him somewhat, even though he did not score at the highest level. Unfortunately, his single AP examination looked paltry in comparison to other Early Decision applicants who were likely to have taken as many as four AP exams by the time they applied. Had Ronald's letters of recommendation not attested to his dedication and perseverance in all areas of study, these lower grades would have resulted in an even lower IvyWise Index score. Within certain limits, colleges love to see a student who works hard, no matter what his or her natural abilities—and Ronald is certainly one of those students.

• Two C's in twelfth grade!

In addition to some rough spots on his transcript, Ronald appears to have either slacked off or bitten off more than he could chew in his senior year. By the time his midsemester report was sent to U. Penn, Ronald was receiving C's in both AP Calculus AB and AP U.S. Government/Economics. This is not acceptable, even if he did challenge himself by taking these difficult courses in the first place. If a borderline application like Ronald's were sitting in the "accepted" pile at a school like the University of Pennsylvania, and these midterm grades arrived at the admissions office, it could give the school occasion to question its initial decision. Admissions readers might be forced to conclude that Ronald had clearly been unable to remain focused after turning in his applications. More important, a school like U. Penn might have wondered whether a candidate like Ronald was still capable of doing sustained work at an advanced academic level. In the worst-case scenario, it could have sounded the death knell for Ronald's college dreams, essentially becoming grounds for the admissions office to withdraw its offer of admission. Either way, this much is clear: Lower grades later on in your high school career are something you want to avoid. An upward grade trend is the one major safety net that exists for a transcript containing a number of lower marks like Ronald's.

If a student such as Ronald can continue to do better and better during the course of his high school career, despite lower grades to begin with, colleges take stock of this student's potential for further growth in college. By getting his worst grades of his career in his most recent courses, Ronald risked alienating an admissions committee that had already fallen in love with his excellent personal qualities.

ACADEMIC PROFILE IMPROVEMENT STRATEGIES: RONALD SIEGAL

What I tried to help Ronald realize as we headed into the college application process together was that his strong personal qualities—especially his lifelong interest in art—were going to get him into college, not his grades and certainly not his test scores. We therefore concentrated on the personal aspects of his application in an effort to let his great character shine forth, all the while acknowledging the weaknesses in his academic profile and trying our best to work around them. As a primary strategy for achieving the latter, I suggested that Ronald address any confusing or mitigating aspects of his academic profile by talking directly to his college guidance counselor and the teachers writing his letters of recommendation. As it turned out, Ronald had been struck by an intestinal parasite during the spring semester of his junior year and the medication he was required to take directly affected his ability to study for both his final exams and his AP and standardized tests in May and June of that year. I found out about this sickness only after Ronald insisted on retaking the SAT I in October of his senior year. When I asked him why he thought he would perform better this time around, he told me about the illness. I told him that this is precisely the type of information that students must provide their college counselor and recommendation letter writers. By informing them of this mitigating circumstance behind his fluctuating academic record, Ronald would allow them to take it into consideration as they wrote their letters on his behalf. It was also a great excuse for Ronald to meet personally with his teachers another time, thus solidifying their image of him as a conscientious and dedicated college applicant. As a second strategy, I urged Ronald to include this information in a separate follow-up letter to the admissions committee at the University of Pennsylvania. Also contained in this letter would be an explanation as to why Ronald had dropped AP Biology after three weeks of his senior year, how he had been unable to enroll in AP Studio Art at such a late date, and how he now understood this to be a mistake. Preferably, Ronald would have avoided the entire scenario—or included these explanations in his original application—but the damage was done and we had to find the best way out. Please note, however, that extra letters such as this are recommended only if there were genuinely mitigating circumstances affecting one's high school performance, such as a scheduling conflict, an illness, or a family tragedy that directly hindered the candidate's academic performance. It is not meant as a way to pester an admissions committee with yet another list of your fabulous achievements. In this case, Ronald and I felt his illness was something the admissions officers needed to know in order to get a full picture of his academic and personal development, as well as to explain his mediocre academic performance during that period. In this way, Ronald was able to ensure his scores of 7 and 6 on the IvyWise Index for his Courses and Grades.

Here is the letter that Ronald wrote:

Ronald Siegal
Swanee High School
123-45-6789

Dear Admissions Committee,

In addition to the information provided in my application, I would like to make you aware that during the spring semester of my junior year, I suffered from an intestinal parasite during final exams, the AP examination, and SAT testing. The medication needed to treat the parasite caused headaches, nausea and dizziness.

I am also writing to inform you of a change in my academic profile since I first sent in my Early Decision application to the University of Pennsylvania. Originally, I was unable to enroll in AP Studio Art because it represented a scheduling conflict with AP Biology. Upon further reflection, however, it became clear to me that I had made a mistake. Although I am fascinated by biology, art is clearly my priority and a class such as AP Studio Art is much more in line with my interests and abilities. In addition, AP Biology was simply too difficult for a non-science student such as myself. Unfortunately, when I dropped AP Biology, I was too late to enroll in AP Studio Art as the class had been underway for three weeks. The teacher even declined my offer of making up the lost time with extra assignments. I therefore find myself in the unfortunate situation of having neither class on my transcript. I did, however, enroll in a studio-art elective for senior year.

I ask for your understanding in this situation and hope that you can see it as the result of a single oversight on the part of a momentarily confused student.

Thank you very much,
Ronald Siegal

ACADEMIC PROFILE: STEPHANIE CHASE

"From the moment she could talk, she was ordered to listen." This paraphrasing of an old Cat Stevens song pretty much sums up Stephanie's relationship to her father. From the moment she entered preschool, Stephanie was told she was going to Yale. Dylan had gone there and loved it. At least, that's what he told his own father, who had gone there before him. Back in the sixties, parents didn't really ask their kids if they were *enjoying* their college experience or if their college was in any way "the right fit." Certain things were taken for granted. Certain things were just done. Perhaps it's understandable, then, that a father who grew up under these circumstances would act the same way toward his own daughter, even if he had rebelled against his own father. But we are in a new millennium now. Stephanie is not a child of the sixties. Supposedly, we have made progress toward treating high school students like the young adults they are—which starts by allowing them to have a voice in the major decisions that deeply affect their future happiness. But Dylan Chase doesn't really live in the twenty-first century. Not yet, at least.

It all started toward the end of grade school. Brownville Country Day is a feeder school for Brownville High, the local public high school that enjoys a national reputation as one of the leading public high schools in the United States. Unfortunately, if you put the word "public" in anything—except perhaps Initial Public Offering—Dylan assumes it's second rate at best. Even though Stephanie wanted to stay in the public school system with her friends— especially Charlotte Murphy—Dylan insisted she go away to boarding school. And not just any boarding school. No, it had to be Peter Egret Academy, where Dylan and his father and his father's father had gone. Stephanie was hurt and confused by her father's unilateral decision: How would she cope with an ever more complex world, let alone her own, confusing life, without the guidance of Charlotte's mother, Barbara? But Dylan wouldn't budge. So Stephanie tried to look on the bright side, as was her way. Who knows, maybe a few years away from home would actually help her relationship with her parents. Doubtful, but it was worth a try.

So while Elizabeth stayed home and reupholstered the porch cushions, Dylan dragged Stephanie off to Egret. Needless to say, she had a hard time adjusting in the ninth grade (called the "prep" year at Egret), and her lower grades from this period reflect her anxiety and sense of displacement. In addition, Stephanie had always been more gifted in the humanities than in the hard sciences and this trend continued at Egret. Her math and science grades were mediocre at best, although Stephanie's English and History grades were some of the best that the school had ever seen from a prep. Egret has a reputation for being an extremely difficult school and most students spend their first year, if not their second, adjusting to the new standards. The school is so tough, in fact, that honors are awarded to anyone who maintains a B average over the course of a single term. Any student who routinely scores in the A-range in not one but *two* subjects is a true anomaly. All through Stephanie's second year, her grades continued to rise, even as her courses became more and more demanding. To cap it off, Stephanie received a National Gold Key for creative writing in the Poetry category, much to her sponsoring English teacher's delight. This is exactly what college admissions readers love to see—a national award accompanied by an upward grade trend in ever more difficult classes. Despite the rough start, Stephanie was on her way to becoming one of the best humanities students the school had ever seen, an easy candidate for early admission to the liberal arts college of her choice.

Then it happened. Barbara Murphy died from breast cancer, and Stephanie found herself living all alone all the way up in northern Massachusetts without a shoulder to cry on. Worst of all, Stephanie couldn't leave Egret to attend the funeral because of Saturday classes—all this in the middle of the first trimester of her junior year, arguably the most significant high school year in terms of courses and grades. Needless to say, Stephanie was hardly herself after this. She missed Charlotte desperately and wanted to be there for her and her father during this difficult time. Stephanie's parents, adopting the hard love approach, thought it best for Stephanie to stick it out at Egret, to "persevere" no matter what. Most likely they were dealing with their own conflicted feelings about the strength and depth of Stephanie's bond with Barbara. Maybe her death, and Stephanie's subsequent depression, reminded them unconsciously of how little they had done in terms of affectionate parenting. Whatever the reason, they insisted that Stephanie stay at Egret throughout the entire ordeal. In this they were wrong. I am not a child psychologist, but I have had significant experience with families going through difficult times. Had I been able to advise the Chases as a family, I would have suggested that Stephanie take a trimester off. It's clear that this type of personal tragedy can have devastating effects on one's school record, not to mention one's emotional health. Stephanie easily could have made up the coursework during the summer between her junior (known as the "upper") and senior years, not once missing a beat on the path toward college admissions.

Unfortunately, Stephanie stayed at Egret and tried to pretend that nothing was wrong. Deep down she was seething at her parents' decision and was still emotionally wrecked over the death of her true mother figure. Understandably, she became very depressed. Afraid that her parents might find out she wasn't living up to their stoic expectations, Stephanie opted not to go to Egret's on-campus psychological counselor, Dr. Diamond, until it was too late and she was forced to. As she withdrew further into herself, even her Haitian-American boyfriend Henri, who had been such help during her initial difficulties with accelerated French, broke up with her. A few weeks later, she broke down. Stephanie was busted, drunk and alone in her room after an all-night binge with some of the wilder girls on her floor. As she was taken through Egret's Kafkaesque disciplinary process, Stephanie let her grades slip drastically. Now she was facing the possibility of dismissal with only a few weeks to go before first trimester exams. In one of the closest votes in campus history, Stephanie was allowed to stay in school but was placed on disciplinary probation for the remainder of her upper year. Even though Dylan stepped in and threatened the school with withholding his massive annual donation if they didn't immediately erase this disciplinary blemish from her record, the emotional wounds of the entire episode would take a long time to heal.

After a miserable Christmas vacation during which Stephanie was forced to go skiing in Gstaad with her family—and not allowed to stay home in Brownville with Charlotte—

Stephanie began to pick up the pieces. During her winter term back at Egret, Stephanie rekindled things with Henri, to whom she finally explained the entire situation. She was also required to visit with Dr. Diamond as a condition of her probation. Unwilling at first to share anything with someone she took to be yet another representative of the administration and their heartless ways, she soon warmed up to Dr. Diamond, eventually lamenting that she hadn't gone to see him earlier, before the proverbial mud had hit the fan. Through long hours of counseling, Stephanie was able to survive the grueling New England winter and begin making some sense of what had just happened. Loss was one of the things they discussed. But the subject of Elizabeth and Dylan came up much more often. With Dr. Diamond's guidance, Stephanie began to construct the building blocks of an identity separate from her parents, one in which she could take pride, one that would equip her for an adult life in which she learned to follow her own heart, not the misguided will of her parents. With Dr. Diamond's and Henri's support—as well as a renewed bond with Charlotte back home—Stephanie's grades improved. She decided that as long as she was on probation, she might as well use her time to study and not jeopardize any more of her academic future. As a result of all the hard work she did during this period, Stephanie's grades returned to their normal high level and she was recognized as one of the strongest students in her English and History classes, eventually winning the coveted Saltonstall Award for third year U.S. History. She also did extremely well on her AP U.S. History, AP English Literature, and AP English Language exams, scoring a 5 on each.

During each spring trimester, Peter Egret Academy organizes college tours for its "uppers." Unbeknownst to her father, who had already dragged her to see Yale's campus on numerous occasions, Stephanie participated in a school trip to a number of small liberal arts colleges, including Wesleyan. This experience changed Stephanie's life forever. Here was a school that offered everything the larger, Ivy League schools did, yet it was smaller, more community oriented, and seemed to encourage and nurture the creative lives of its students. Things like the *Argus* student newspaper, the Wesleyan Writers Conference, the Alternative Music Social Collective, and the Second Stage Theater Group were perfect for Stephanie's blend of liberal arts acumen and creative ability. As she began to compile her college list, however, Stephanie's high school college counselor, Mr. Hayden, talked her out of applying

Early Decision to Wesleyan because he was worried that Stephanie's grade dip was too recent for Wesleyan to think it was a mere aberration, especially if they didn't get to see Stephanie's first trimester senior year grades. Secretly, Mr. Hayden also feared the wrath of Dylan Chase, who had called him several times to make sure he was pushing Stephanie toward Yale. If Stephanie applied regular admission, Mr. Hayden reasoned, then her target colleges would get a chance to see her initial senior year grades. Hopefully they would be high enough to convince the various admissions committees that the beginning of Stephanie's junior year was just a fluke—and he would avoid any confrontation with Mr. Chase. In the first instance, Mr. Hayden was right: With all the hard work Stephanie was putting into her studies, there was little doubt her senior year grades would be among her strongest, thus demonstrating a highly attractive upward grade trend. In the second instance, he was a coward who, like Dylan, acted out of self-interest and not with Stephanie's best interests in mind.

Then Dylan intervened yet again—this time directly with Stephanie. Over the summer between her upper and senior years, Dylan insisted that Stephanie apply Early Decision to Yale, since it was the only school "fit for a Chase." Dylan even went so far as to tell the Yale Alumni Relations Office that Stephanie was going to apply early, which Stephanie inadvertently corroborated in her hasty interview with a Yale alumnus. Unfortunately, Stephanie was not ready to apply early. She and her father got into a huge fight during which she told him about Wesleyan and about all that it offered for a student with her academic, extracurricular, and emotional needs. Dylan rudely countered that his law firm would never hire a Wesleyan graduate, so why would she want to go to a second-rate school like that? Despite all the research she had done into the specific offerings at Wesleyan—and all the passion with which she promoted her cause to her father—there was no convincing Dylan. Stephanie ended up applying to both Yale and Wesleyan regular admission along with Connecticut College, Vanderbilt (where her mother had gone), Pomona (where Charlotte wanted to go), and Brown, the Ivy League version of everything she loved about Wesleyan.

Unfortunately for this very intelligent and highly creative student, there were already a number of strikes against Stephanie's profile as she geared up to enter the highly competitive race for selective college admissions. As we know, she neglected to tell her college counselor about the reasons behind her junior year drinking bust. Had she come clean, Mr. Hayden might have written about the circumstances surrounding the bust in his counselor letter. He then would have urged Stephanie to write about Barbara's death on her application, preferably in her personal statement. In addition, Dylan's pressure to attend Yale made Stephanie work on all of her applications under extreme emotional duress. She felt like she was sneaking around behind his back, and like the entire college admissions process had been soured by his stubborn intrusiveness. Most likely out of unconscious rebellion, Stephanie did not spend an adequate amount of time editing or proofreading any of her applications. She also chose not to include a fantastic journal of poetry with her applications, a beautiful collection of her most intimate work that would have shed light on her emotional state—especially during the Barbara Murphy crisis—and accounted for a lot of her time spent outside the classroom. Stephanie also neglected to include her award-winning history paper and barely made mention of any of the great work she had done for *The Egret Bulletin*, the school newspaper, and *The Albatross*, Egret's literary journal. Most detrimental to Stephanie's chances of following in her father's footsteps was her refusal to do any substantial research into Yale, largely an ironic result of all the pressure Dylan exerted in precisely that direction. Had she applied early—which she should have done as a legacy—Yale most likely would have deferred her anyway, given Stephanie's clear lack of interest in their school. Not that Dylan is solely to blame: Even the best-intentioned parents often transfer their own desires onto their children, and nowhere does this drama play itself out with more intensity than in college and career choices.

As you can see from the outward details of her life, Stephanie is the perfect example of an applicant who should have been a shoo-in at schools like Yale and Wesleyan. But because of the red flags discussed in greater detail in the chapters to come, she ended up with nothing more than a courtesy waitlisting at Yale, a waitlisting at Wesleyan, outright rejections from Brown and Pomona, and offers of admission from Vanderbilt and Connecticut College. When the Chases first came to me for help, I could tell immediately where the problem lay: Dylan wanted me to get Stephanie off the waitlist at Yale while Stephanie desperately wanted to go to Wesleyan. They were working at cross-purposes, undermining each other. I told them in no uncertain terms that Stephanie stood a chance of being accepted off a waitlist only if she focused all of her energy on a single college—something she should have done from the get-go by applying early to her top-choice school. During our initial consultation, Dylan did everything he could to skirt the issue of Stephanie's drinking bust. Stephanie, however, blurted it out during a particularly emotional confrontation with her father. In retrospect, this was the best thing that could have happened because we used Stephanie's disciplinary problems at Egret—and the important reasons behind them—as a strategy for redoing her entire application. I pointed out that because Stephanie had been taught from an early age to stifle her emotions and keep her needs and desires to herself, her original essays revealed very little about her personal life. She would have to remedy this by writing a letter explaining the impact of Barbara's death and underscoring how it contributed to her decision to drink. Stephanie's parents had to understand that Stephanie held all the power over her future and that only by supporting her did they stand of chance of convincing an admissions committee that Stephanie's junior-year transgressions and her seeming lack of enthusiasm were not the product of a spoiled attitude but rather the forgivable mistakes of a passionate, soul-searching young woman who had suffered a major tragedy. Through this process, Dylan finally came to the realization that Wesleyan was better suited to his daughter's needs than Yale. He took his first, tentative steps into the twenty-first century—and toward accepting Stephanie as the independent young adult she had become long ago.

PETER EGRET ACADEMY STUDENT TRANSCRIPT

Student: Stephanie Chase   **Dorm:**   Wheelwright Hall
DOB: 10-29-84   **Adviser:**   Bob Hayden

FALL TERM 1998

Course	Grade	Points
Junior Studies 110: Rhetoric and Reason	A−	10.0
French 121: Accelerated Elementary French	B−	7.0
Health 110: Health and Human Development for Juniors	B−	7.0

Course	Grade	Points
Math 110: Algebra	C	5.0
History 101: People and Cultures of the Modern World	B	8.0
Physical Education 170: Instructional Tennis (Coed)	P	n/a
Term Grade Point Average: 7.4		

WINTER TERM 1998–1999

Course	Grade	Points
English 120: Junior English	A	11.0
French 122: Accelerated Elementary French	B−	7.0
Math 120: Intermediate Algebra	C+	6.0
Drama 101: Beginning Acting	A−	10.0
Health 120: Health and Human Development for Juniors	B−	7.0
Pec109: Drama-Sports (Coeducational)	P	n/a
Term Grade Point Average: 8.2—Honors		

SPRING TERM 1999

Course	Grade	Points
English 130: Junior English	A	11.0
French 210: Intermediate French	B	8.0
Math 130: Advanced Algebra	B−	7.0
Health 130: Health and Human Development for Juniors	B	8.0
Drama 102: Stagecraft	A	11.0
Physical Education 360: Girls Lacrosse (JV)	P	n/a
Term Grade Point Average: 9.0—High Honors		

FALL TERM 1999

Course	Grade	Points
English 211: Honors English for Lowers	A−	10.0
French 220: Intermediate French	B+	9.0
Math 210: Integrated Mathematics	B	8.0
History 213: Early Modern Europe, 1350–1660	A−	10.0
Chemistry 210: An Introduction to Physical Chemistry	B	8.0

Course	Grade	Points
Physical Education 171: Club Tennis (Coed)	P	n/a

Term Grade Point Average: 9.0—High Honors

WINTER TERM 1999–2000

Course	Grade	Points
English 221: Honors English for Lowers	A	11.0
French 230: Intermediate French	B+	9.0
Math 220: Integrated Mathematics	B	8.0
Drama 203: Intermediate Acting	A	11.0
History 214: Absolutism and Revolution, 1660–1800	A—	10.0
Chemistry 220: An Introduction to Physical Chemistry	B	8.0
Physical Education 109: Drama-Sports (Coed)	P	n/a

Term Grade Point Average: 9.5—High Honors

SPRING TERM 2000

Course	Grade	Points
English 230: Honors English for Lowers	A	11.0
French 310: Advanced French	A—	10.0
Math 230: Integrated Mathematics	B+	9.0
History 215: The European Century, 1800–1914	A	11.0
Chemistry 230: An Introduction to Physical Chemistry	B+	9.0
Physical Education 360: Girls Lacrosse (Varsity)	P	n/a

Term Grade Point Average: 10.0—Highest Honors

FALL TERM 2000

Course	Grade	Points
English 310: AP English	B—	7.0
History 331: AP United States History, 1763–1877	B—	7.0
French 320: Advanced French	C	5.0
Math 310: Advanced Integrated Mathematics	C	5.0
Physics 210: Introductory Physics: A Quantitative Approach	C	5.0
Physical Education 171: Club Tennis (Coed)	P	n/a

Term Grade Point Average: 5.8

WINTER TERM 2000–2001

Course	Grade	Points
English 320: AP English	A−	10.0
History 332: AP United States History, 1877–1945	A−	10.0
French 340: Readings in French	B+	9.0
Math 320: Advanced Integrated Mathematics	B+	9.0
Physics 220: Introductory Physics: A Quantitative Approach	B	8.0
Drama 301: Directing	A	11.0
Physical Education 109: Drama-Sports (Coed)	P	n/a

Term Grade Point Average: 9.5—High Honors

SPRING TERM 2001

Course	Grade	Points
English 330: AP English	A	11.0
History 333: AP United States History, 1945 to the Present	A	11.0
Math 330: Advanced Integrated Mathematics	B+	9.0
Physics 230: Introductory Physics: A Quantitative Approach	B+	9.0
French 443: French Drama	A−	10.0
Physical Education 360: Girls Lacrosse (Varsity)	P	n/a

Term Grade Point Average: 10.0—Highest Honors

FALL TERM 2001

Course	Grade	Points
English 411: Honors English for Seniors	A	11.0
Math 41d: Topics in Modern Discrete Mathematics	A−	10.0
History 425: World War and European Society, 1890–1945	A	11.0
Spanish 121: Accelerated Beginning Spanish	A	11.0
Anthropology 300: Cultural Anthropology	A−	10.0
Physical Education 171: Club Tennis (Coed)	P	n/a

Term Grade Point Average: 10.6—Highest Honors

WINTER TERM 2001–2002

Course	Grade	Points
English 421: Honors English for Seniors	A	11.0
Math 41m: Mathematical Modeling and Applications	A−	10.0
History 426: Europe Since 1945	A	11.0
Spanish 122: Accelerated Beginning Spanish	A	11.0
Drama 435: Advanced Acting: Senior Acting Ensemble	A	11.0
Physical Education 109: Drama-Sports (Coed)	P	n/a

Term Grade Point Average: 10.8—Highest Honors

SPRING TERM 2002

Course	Grade	Points
English 473: Poetry Portfolio	*	*
Math 41s: Descriptive Statistics and Probability	*	*
Senior Studies 431: A Little Course in Dreams	*	*
Religion 420: Introduction to Philosophy	*	*
Psychology 400: Introduction to Psychology	*	*
Physical Education 360: Girls Lacrosse (Varsity)	*	*

TESTING HISTORY

Test	Date	Score
SAT II: Writing	June 2000	800
AP: English Language	May 2000	5
SAT I	October 2000	800V/660M
AP: English Literature	May 2001	5
AP: U.S. History	May 2001	5
SAT II: U.S. History	June 2001	780
SAT II: Math I	June 2001	660
SAT II: French	June 2001	740
AP: Psychology	May 2002	*

*Indicates pending grades or scores

GENERAL NOTES

Peter Egret Academy does not weight grades, nor does it rank its students. It also does not fail students. Students earning a term grade point average of D+ or below at the midpoint of the term are placed on academic warning. Students receiving an overall term grade point average of D+ or below are placed on academic restrictions and assigned a tutor in the subject in question. Points are awarded for each grade earned in a term course according to the following scale:

A	=	11.0		C	=	5.0
A−	=	10.0		C−	=	4.0
B+	=	9.0		D+	=	3.0
B	=	8.0		D	=	2.0
B−	=	7.0		D−	=	1.0
C+	=	6.0		F	=	0.0

Students at Peter Egret Academy have the opportunity to earn honors, high honors, or highest honors for their academic achievement in a given term, according to the following scale:

Honors	=	Term Grade Point Average of 8.0 and above
High Honors	=	Term Grade Point Average of 9.0 and above
Highest Honors	=	Term Grade Point Average of 10.0 and above

PETER EGRET ACADEMY SCHOOL PROFILE

Peter Egret Academy is a private four-year college preparatory, boarding high school located in the bucolic hamlet of Lakewood, Massachusetts, population 26,700. Students from all fifty states and sixty-one different countries and principalities currently attend the academy. Of these, approximately 87 percent are boarders while the remaining 13 percent commute from local townships. Parents of Peter Egret Academy students are primarily employed in professional capacities, with doctors, lawyers, investment bankers, and university professors constituting the majority. Graduates of Peter Egret Academy have been presidential Cabinet members, presidents of major U.S. banks and corporations, world-renowned scholars, poets, painters, and athletes. With its commitment to diversity, creativity, and community service, and an endowment that rivals most colleges, Peter Egret Academy consistently ranks among the top three boarding high schools in America.

With a student body of 1,007 and 257 full-time teachers and administrators, Peter Egret boasts a faculty to student ratio of 1:4, one of the lowest in the country. Its faculty has an average of twenty-nine years' experience in secondary education, and a full 70 percent of classroom teachers have advanced degrees in their areas of expertise. Although there is no core curriculum at Peter Egret, students are required to take classes in four major subject area concentrations: science (consisting of biology, chemistry, computer science, physics, and astronomy); mathematics (ranging from algebra and economics to multivariable calculus and differential equations); arts and culture (including architecture, drama, dance, drawing, film, music, painting, psychology, religion, sculpture, and Senior Studies, an interdisciplinary seminar taught by senior faculty to top students in the graduating class); and language and history (including U.S. history, classical languages, Chinese language and history, English, European history, French language and literature, German language and literature, Japanese language and history, Russian language, literature, and history, as well as Spanish language and literature.)

Each of these classes is available to students on one of four levels: regular, accelerated, honors, and Advanced Placement. Peter Egret offers the complete array of thirty-three Advanced Placement courses in preparation for the Advanced Placement examinations. In addition to the four major subject area concentrations, Peter Egret allows students to pursue three different degrees: sciences, humanities, and classics. The sciences diploma carries with it extra math and science requirements and is excellent preparation for those students looking to pursue engineering or premedical undergraduate degrees. The classics diploma requires students to become proficient in Latin and Greek over the course of their studies and is excellent preparation, along with the humanities diploma, for a liberal arts education in college.

In addition to its extensive academic programs, Peter Egret Academy actively supports over forty varsity, junior varsity, and club level sports. With state-of-the-art facilities, including two indoor swimming pools, two indoor hockey rinks, twenty-four squash courts, thirty-six indoor and outdoor tennis courts, outdoor and indoor track and field facilities, an indoor batting cage, a football stadium, its own boathouse and river launch, extensive playing fields, and a thirty-six-mile cross country course, it's no wonder Peter Egret has produced over 125 interscholastic championship teams as well as a number of star college-level and professional athletes. All students are required to participate in some level of physical education each trimester, with club and general group activities attracting the majority of the student body.

In addition to these athletic programs, Peter Egret Academy offers students an astounding array of extracurricular activities and community service opportunities. These range from the Egret Social Services Organization, which does everything from planning campus parties to feeding the homeless in Boston, to numerous environmental groups, model UN, chess club, math club, and even a polar bear club, whose members trek out in their bathing suits each February to take a brisk dip in the Atlantic Ocean. Summer internship and study abroad opportunities abound, with chances for Egret Academy students to work on Wall Street and Capitol Hill or study in one of seventeen different foreign countries.

In 2001, the Peter Egret Academy mean SAT I scores were 740 Math and 710 Verbal. The mean Advanced Placement Test score was 4.4. The mean SAT II subject test scores were: Biology E/M: 725; Chemistry: 738; Chinese Listening: 703; French: 730; German: 719; Japanese Listening: 729; Latin: 780; English Literature: 731; Math 1C: 749; Math 2C: 731; Physics: 743; Spanish: 732; U.S. History: 722; World History: 721; and Writing: 731.

Ninety-nine percent of the 289 members of the Class of 2001 continued their education. Of that group, 98 percent entered sixty-seven different four-year selective colleges and universities and 2 percent entered two-year colleges or the military. Thirty-two students in the Class of 2001 were named National Merit Scholarship finalists, sixty-seven were semifinalists, and 132 received National Merit Letters of Commendation.

ACADEMIC PROFILE EVALUATION: STEPHANIE CHASE

Stephanie's Courses:	6 points

- **Inconsistent: opted out of AP French senior year**

Opting for personal reasons not to take AP level French—because the girl Henri had dated while he and Stephanie were broken up was in the class—was not really a smart move for Stephanie. Given her emerging talent in French, Stephanie was a perfect candidate for the AP course in her senior year and, based on her grades, she would have done well. At the very least, she should have taken an independent study in French to compensate. Of course, we all sympathize with her difficult situation, but deciding not to pursue a subject that has played a major role in your curriculum simply because your boyfriend's ex-girlfriend is in the class is a clear-cut case of misdirected anger: Stephanie ended up hurting only herself. Although she did fulfill her French requirement in terms of Peter Egret Academy, and she did end up adding a second foreign language—Spanish—Stephanie should have followed through on her significant commitment to French and thereby shown prospective colleges that she was capable of sustained rigor in all academic pursuits.

- **Not rigorous enough: no AB Calculus**

In addition, Stephanie chose to retire from competitive mathematics before taking Calculus, opting instead for the far less rigorous "Statistics and Probability" sequence—known on the Egret campus as "Spaz Math." This decision alone did not make or break her chances of gaining admission to either Yale or Wesleyan, but the majority of the nation's most selective schools like to see at least one year of Calculus on an applicant's transcript. In addition, it is clear from Stephanie's transcript that she decided to pursue an easier course in a subject she did not do well in. If you are tempted to do this, keep in mind that admissions officers are often forced to make quick and final decisions about your academic achievement based solely on the information contained in your transcript. If they see that you dropped math simply because you were not proficient, regardless of the relative worth of statistics and probability, the majority of college admissions readers will mark this down as a red flag. Whether you are predominantly humanities- or science-oriented, you don't want to measure up unfavorably against your competition, many of whom will pursue math to the Calculus level, even if Spaz Math is more fun!

- **Scattershot science**

Although Stephanie's passions clearly do not lie in the sciences, her single year of introductory chemistry and single year of introductory physics do not look very impressive when compared with the academic profiles of the best college applicants against whom she was competing. When combined with her lower math scores, and her utter lack of any science SAT IIs or APs, this is a student whose ability in these areas might be questioned by an admissions reader: Can Stephanie take on the significant challenge of college-level requirements in both areas?

- **Drama queen**

In her favor, Stephanie's exhaustive participation in drama helped her admissions committees understand where her true passions lay; however, significant achievement in an elective such as this does not make up for lower achievement in core courses like math and science. Her interest in the dramatic arts, while commendable, will weigh more heavily when it comes to the brag sheet section of her application.

- **Outstanding history and English**

Despite these red flags, Stephanie maintained an outstanding level of commitment to both English and history throughout her high school career. Her obvious interest and talent in these two fields make her a very promising candidate at a strong liberal arts college like Wesleyan. That she was able to maintain such a high level of commitment in these two areas despite her highly developed interests in drama, lacrosse, and French—still managing to take an English poetry elective her senior year!—is all the more commendable. Certainly, Stephanie's overall score for the "Course" section of the IvyWise Index would have been a lot lower had she not shown such extraordinary achievement in these two crucial core subjects.

- **Adjusting freshman year**

    Stephanie's first-year grades were normal at best. Although many students struggle when they first arrive at Egret, Stephanie's grades were lower than most when compared with her eventual achievement. On a more positive note, this difficult time allowed Stephanie to demonstrate a sustained upward grade trend over the course of her studies until she dipped during her junior year. Nonetheless, it is a rough introduction to her high school transcript.

- **Low science and math**

    In addition to a lower performance at the beginning of her high school career, Stephanie's grades in both math and science never reached the level that many college admissions officers have come to expect from their prime candidates. Again, no one is expecting Stephanie to be the next Nobel Laureate in Applied Mathematics—more like the next Poet Laureate—but colleges do like to know they are getting students who can perform well in each and every class they try to conquer.

- **High on humanities!**

    Despite this, Stephanie's outstanding grades in English and history help to make up for her lower marks in math and science. It is clear from her outstanding grades and awards in these areas that she is a truly creative thinker with a literary and/or scholarly life ahead. Colleges, especially small liberal arts colleges like Wesleyan, thrive on students such as Stephanie, who will be major contributors to the creative atmosphere on campus. In addition, her considerable achievement in drama helps to round out the picture of a student who excels at all aspects of the liberal arts.

- **Grade dip in junior year**

    Nothing, however, could overshadow Stephanie's dismal performance in the first trimester of her upper year. As we know, Stephanie suffered a personal setback during this crucial time. Unfortunately, no one at any of her target colleges knew why she suffered this horrible grade dip. Without answers, admissions readers were left to imagine that Stephanie had given up, or maybe that her upward grade trend came to a natural halt as she maxed out her intellectual abilities. Either way, her colleges had no idea why she slacked off that trimester. And even though she improved steadily over time after that, her poor performance in that first trimester left a deep impact on her overall academic profile.

- **Great AP scores!**

Stephanie scored 5's on all three of her AP examinations (English Language, English Literature, and U.S. History)—even earning a 5 in English Language after only the tenth grade! Above and beyond earning valuable credit toward college requirements, these excellent scores helped prove to colleges that Stephanie was able to synthesize and retain vast amounts of information in these subject areas, thus solidifying the impression that she was a truly gifted student of the humanities.

- **Outstanding writing ability**

Stephanie's lower year English teacher urged her to send in one of her papers to a scholastic competition and Stephanie ended up winning a National Gold Key for creative writing. In addition, Stephanie was awarded the coveted Saltonstall Award for excellence in historical writing. This later achievement is truly superlative when you consider that the beginning of her upper year was the most disastrous time in Stephanie's life. If only she had been more willing to talk about what happened at the time, the impressive history award would not have been clouded by the grade dip that haunted Stephanie throughout the college admissions process.

- **Upward grade trend!**

Finally, save for the one disastrous trimester at the beginning of her upper year, and a second trimester that same year in which she continued to rebound, Stephanie's grades were always climbing at Egret, eventually reaching a truly outstanding level. Not many students at Egret have maintained Stephanie's high level of performance in history and English *and* shown an upward grade trend. Had she not endured that one difficult trimester, Stephanie would have been in much better standing to apply for early acceptance to the college of her choice.

ACADEMIC PROFILE IMPROVEMENT STRATEGIES: STEPHANIE CHASE

Stephanie's main strategy for improving her chances at Wesleyan after she was waitlisted was to explain her academic profile and help the admissions committee to understand her grade dip during the first trimester of her junior year. She achieved this through a heartfelt letter that supplemented her resubmitted application to Wesleyan in which she discussed in intimate detail her godmother Barbara's death and the profound effect it had on her ability to concentrate on her studies. Since this letter served primarily to address her *emotional state* during the grade dip period and to supplement her less-than-perfect college essays, it is included in Chapter Six as part of the strategies Stephanie and I developed for improving her score in the "Personal Essay" category. As a result, the weak points in Stephanie's academic profile were explained retroactively. This does not erase the effects of her poor performance during that difficult period; it simply adds another dimension to her high school experience, something admissions readers would have wanted to know as they tried to understand Stephanie both as a student and as a human being.

Chapter Three

 STANDARDIZED TESTS

SAT I, SAT II, and ACT Tests

Despite the debate currently raging in admissions offices across the country about the overall fairness and relevance of the SAT I test, it is still required by most selective colleges and universities. There are a few high-profile schools, most notably the University of California school system, that have challenged the relevance of the SAT I. I happen to agree that the college testing system in this country is in need of a drastic overhaul in order to ensure that it is a fair assessment of each test-taker's knowledge and ability to perform at a competitive collegiate level. Numerous studies have shown that the SAT I, as it currently stands, is a biased examination that doesn't necessarily provide a clear depiction of a candidate's intelligence or potential performance in college. If you want to examine the various sides of the argument in further detail, I urge you to see the "Testing" section of my book *The Truth About Getting In.* For now, I will address the SAT I, SAT II, and ACT tests insofar as they are essential components of nearly all selective college applications.

As the system currently stands, students applying to the most selective colleges and universities in the country are required to take either the SAT I and up to three SAT II subject area examinations, or the ACT test. As you may have heard, the SAT I test was recently overhauled to account for changing pedagogical practices at our nation's high schools and to provide a more accurate picture of a student's preparedness for college. As of the March 2005 test date, the SAT I score will be transmitted via three numbers, all ranked on a scale from 200 to 800, with 800 being the highest. The SAT I Math section will be expanded to cover three years of high school math. Instead of just covering concepts from Geometry and Algebra I, the new SAT I Math section will contain concepts from Geometry, Algebra I, and Algebra II. The former SAT I Verbal section will be renamed Critical Reading. Instead of analogies, it will include short reading passages, in addition to the existing longer reading passages. Finally, a new section called the SAT Writing section will be added. It will contain multiple-choice grammar questions and an essay question. The responses to this essay will be judged by a panel of writing experts at the Educational Testing Service in Princeton, New Jersey, according to their grammatical accuracy, diction, rhetorical strength, and style. Unfortunately for you creative writers out there, the test will not take into account the beauty of your prose except insofar as it is a function of the essay's accuracy and strength. You should think of the new Writing section of the SAT I as a test of your ability to write a term paper on the spot. ETS will forward the Writing section to your target colleges, so if you are a great writer, this new section is clearly to your advantage. But beware: If there is too much discrepancy between the writing in your college application and the writing on your SAT I, college admissions officers may suspect you have received too much outside help on your essays. Although ETS claims this is not the reason for adding the new section, you should be aware of this secondary effect.

Personally, I believe there are more questions raised than answered by the unilateral and hasty introduction of a new SAT I Writing section. To begin with, does this new section make the Writing SAT II obsolete? If not, how are the two tests different? Furthermore, who are the so-called "experts" who will be judging the new tests, especially when most English teachers will be too busy with their own courses to devote time to the ETS? In the past, the Writing SAT II scores have arrived late because of a lack of adequately skilled judges. How can another writing exam be reviewed in time for students to send their scores to their prospective colleges, especially if over 1.5 million students will be taking and retaking the SAT I test next year? And finally, what are the uniform standards for judging something as subjective as a writing sample? Is it possible that all test-takers will be judged according to the same criteria? How do we interpret the new scores? What does a 2200 mean?

These problems aside, standardized tests are here to stay and the new SAT I will take effect in March 2005. As you prepare to take the SAT I, the SAT II, or the ACT, do not forget they are more than mere tests of your general knowledge in a given field: They are tests of your preparedness on the day of the exam. Therefore, even if you normally test well and feel you know your subject inside and out, it would be utterly foolish not to devote a significant amount of time to familiarizing yourself with the test format and rigorously reviewing your knowledge in each specific area prior to sitting down to take the test itself. Only with such thorough preparation will you be able to perform at an optimum level and earn both the maximum number of points on the IvyWise Index and the best chance at getting into the college of your dreams. Again, from the per-

cause every school in America has one. Combined scores below 1000 make it impossible for a student to get into most selective colleges, and all lower-scoring students who do manage to get in come from what admissions readers call the "hook" pool: kids with other strengths such as development potential, athletic ability, or first generation college applicant status. (Lloyd Peterson, formerly of Yale and Vassar)

(4) UVA does reject some 1600's every year as well as some valedictorians because not all have taken demanding course loads. They have also accepted students with modest test scores who had demonstrated outstanding talent or who had achieved in the face of overwhelming adversity. (Marianne M. Kosiewicz at the University of Virginia)

(5) The important thing to stress is that a lower SAT score can be offset by the rest of the application file. The lowest SAT I score ever admitted to NYU was probably around 1120, but this was for a student with super performance credits, strong leadership, and exceptional community service at a school where 1120 was relatively high. (Richard Avitabile, formerly of NYU)

At a Glance:

Test scores for the mid 50 percent of accepted students for the incoming class of 2006 (i.e., 25 percent of accepted students scored lower than the first number and 25 percent of accepted students scored higher than the second number):

(1) Brown University:
- SAT I composite = 1300–1500
- ACT = 28–32

(2) Yale University:
- SAT I composite = 1340–1540

(3) University of Pennsylvania:
- SAT I composite = 1350–1510
- ACT = 29–33

(4) Haverford College:
- SAT I composite = 1400–1450

(5) Georgetown University:
- SAT I composite = 1400–1495

(6) Emory University:
- SAT I composite = 1300–1430
- ACT = 29–33

(7) University of Virginia:
- SAT I composite = 1230–1410

(8) New York University:
- SAT I composite = 1350–1500

spective of a college admissions reader at a selective school, high test scores demonstrate a high level of general knowledge as well as solid work ethic, both qualities that indicate an applicant will be able to thrive in a college learning environment. Whether you agree with their format, duration, and subject matter, you will have to face these tests and they will count either for or against you. Just how heavily, you will come to understand as we survey and examine David, Ronald, and Stephanie's experience with their standardized tests.

TESTING PROFILE: DAVID HOROWITZ

David Horowitz opted to take the SAT I only once, scoring an 800 on the Verbal section and a 660 on the Math section. He was satisfied with his perfect 800 Verbal and didn't want to jeopardize it by scoring lower on a subsequent test. In this, he was mistaken. Although colleges will see both the Math and the Verbal scores for any test date you take the test, most admissions offices will only consider the two highest scores from each section. This means that David had at least a couple of opportunities left in which to try to improve his Math score. Instead, despite his perfect 800 Verbal, his overall SAT I IvyWise Index score is lower than his tremendous academic abilities would have warranted. Also, the large discrepancy between his Verbal and Math scores is a red flag because it prompts an admissions reader to question the well-roundedness of David's high school education. To avoid this, as well as to improve upon the 660 he received in Math, I would have urged David to take the SAT I test again in the fall semester of his senior year.

David's SAT I Scores:	7 points

• Perfect Verbal but mediocre Math!

David's SAT I scores of 800 Verbal and 660 Math give him an average of 730, which is a 7 according to the IvyWise Index ranking system. David's perfect 800 Verbal is so impressive that it might have bumped him up a point, but unfortunately the large discrepancy between his Verbal and his Math scores counts against him. A discrepancy is bad for a number of reasons: First, schools like to see a balance between an applicant's math and writing skills; second, they want to know you will be able to perform well in both areas in college; finally, you will be competing against students who have scored perfect 800s in both subjects, so you must really push yourself, if you are weak in either math or English, to perform to the best of your ability. Don't forget that the SAT I measures your test-taking ability, so practice as much as you can either in a test-prep course or by taking practice tests in books that contain real sample tests from prior years.

David's SAT II Scores:	9 points

• 790, 780, 770!

David scored very high on his top three SAT II subject areas tests: a 790 on the Writing test, a 780 on the U.S. History test, and a 770 on the Chemistry test. His average of 780 on his three SAT II's earned David 9 points on the IvyWise Index.

• An unimpressive 690!

However, despite these stellar scores, David also took the Hebrew SAT II at the end of his junior year, scoring a much lower 690—not very high for someone supposedly fluent in Hebrew.

Will the SAT I last?

(1) There is a big discussion going on right now among college counselors and admissions officers concerning the role of the SAT I. High schools and colleges are coming to realize the inherent limitations of the SAT I, but it is still required at most schools. Now that a new Writing section has been added and will go into effect in 2005, the test may gain in importance again. (Anonymous admissions reader at NYU)

The mistake he made was to report this low score even though he could have used Score Choice at the time he took the test. This counts as a red flag on David's application, but it is not enough to warrant a subtraction because most schools will only take the three highest SAT II scores. In the time since David and I worked together, the College Board has changed its policy on score reporting for the SAT II. Score Choice, allowing a student to decide after taking an SAT II test whether or not to report it, has been eliminated. This means that under the current system, David's Hebrew SAT II score would have been sent to his schools no matter what. Since this is now the case, it is all the more important to treat each SAT II testing situation with the requisite time and effort. Do not take an SAT II subject test unless you are well-prepared and absolutely sure that you will do well. Since you must take at least three SAT II tests for the majority of the nation's selective colleges and universities, you must treat each separate test with the same rigor and importance as you would the SAT I exam. You can, however, take each individual SAT II examination more than once if you want to try to improve your score. Like the SAT I, colleges will only look at the highest individual score in each subject area tested—although the psychological effect on your admissions reader of seeing a number of low scores replaced by higher ones remains undocumented. In other words, are the following two students judged equally: the student who takes the Math IC six times, scoring in the low 500's initially and finally scoring a 780; and the student who takes the Math IC once and scores a 780 right off the bat? Maybe the first student received excellent tutoring. Maybe the second just had a great day. If you were an admissions reader, how would you judge? In terms of your college applications, as with all things, moderation is the key. When Score Choice was still in effect, students could take the same SAT II test over and over, essentially using it as practice tests until they felt ready to report the score that counted. Such leeway is no longer possible—and even if colleges claim that taking the same test multiple times will not hurt you, why not try to ace each one the first time around?

TESTING PROFILE IMPROVEMENT STRATEGIES: DAVID HOROWITZ

By the time David came to me, it was too late for us to do anything about his testing profile. Again, if I had had the opportunity to work with David earlier in the process, I would have urged him not to send his Hebrew SAT II score and to take the SAT I at least one more time with the goal of improving his Math score.

TESTING PROFILE: RONALD SIEGAL

Understanding that he didn't have the world's strongest academic profile, Ronald became very concerned about his SAT I scores. The problem with Ronald was that he tended to get nervous in test-taking situations, a natural reaction to stress that was only compounded by the competitive atmosphere at Swanee, and by the strain of applying to some of the nation's most prestigious colleges. Bearing this in mind, I urged Ronald not to overdo it on his SAT I preparation. He took the test in the spring of his junior year and received a combined 1340. I was happy with this score and urged him to concentrate on his studies—only if Ronald were to score a good 100–150 points higher on a second test would it make any substantial difference to his overall application. Later I found out that Ronald was taking medication for an intestinal parasite at the time of his first test. Had I know this fact back then, I might have been more enthusiastic about his chances of improving his score and urged him to take a test-prep course. Believing he could still improve, Ronald retook the SAT I in October of his senior year. Unfortunately, his score went down 20 points. Maybe the parasite wasn't the problem. To make matters worse, these second, lower scores were sent to the University of Pennsylvania along with his initial scores. In retrospect, Ronald should have been happy with his original 1340 and used the time he spent preparing for the SAT I studying for class and continuing his numerous extracurricular activities. But hindsight is twenty-twenty. As with his overall academic profile, Ronald's testing profile was not the application element that was going to get him into college anyway, so we minimized our losses and moved on.

Ronald's SAT I Scores:	5 points

- **670/670**

Ronald's average score of 670—670 Verbal and 670 Math—earned him 5 points on the IvyWise Index. His second composite score of 1320 (he went down 20 points on the Verbal section) was also sent to the University of Pennsylvania, but they only considered his 1340.

Ronald's SAT II Scores:	6 points

- **670, 720, 710**

Ronald scored a 670 on the U.S. History SAT II test, a 720 on the Math 1C test, and a 710 on the Writing test, for an average of 700. This average, in turn, earned him 6 points on the IvyWise Index. Had Ronald scored higher or taken more than three SAT II tests— such as Spanish, Spanish with Listening, or English Literature—he may have been able to improve his overall IvyWise ranking for this category.

TESTING PROFILE IMPROVEMENT STRATEGIES: RONALD SIEGAL

When Ronald first came to me, I quickly realized we had our work cut out for us. Based solely on his transcript and his test scores, Ronald wasn't going to get into the University of Pennsylvania, especially not Early Decision. Ronald had never been a great test-taker and his grades, as you have seen, suffered somewhat under the weight of his extremely difficult course load. So instead of counseling Ronald to waste more time preparing for tests, I urged him to concentrate on the personal aspects of his application, since those were areas over which he had the most control and which, in the end, would prove the most attractive to the excellent school he wished to attend. With this in mind, we decided to focus on ways of making Ronald's application stand out from the crowd on a personal level, not only in relation to other applicants with similar grades but in relation to all Penn applicants, regardless of academic strength or extracurricular interests. We developed a number of strategies for increasing Ronald's IvyWise Index ranking in the personal profile sections of the application, strategies that stressed his achievement as an artist and as a member of his community. In so doing, we were able to strengthen Ronald's overall application in a number of areas, each of which will be treated in the following chapters. Unfortunately, his testing profile remained mediocre at best.

TESTING PROFILE: STEPHANIE CHASE

Stephanie Chase studied intensely for her standardized tests and took advantage of a number of excellent test preparation opportunities made available by Peter Egret Academy. Whenever I ask a prospective client what type of high school they attend, most assume that I want to hear "private" because rich private high schools are rumored to offer a better education than underfunded, overcrowded public high schools and hence to increase their students' chances of getting into a selective college. This is decidedly not the case. Although a well-funded private school would tend to have more money—and hence a greater number of curricular and extracurricular programs—college admissions officers try to look at everything in perspective. They want to know that you have taken advantage of all the offerings around you, whatever they may be. For a public high school student, this means going above and beyond the immediate offerings of the high school and pursuing courses at a community college along with volunteer, research, or employment opportunities in the community at large. For private high school students like Stephanie Chase, the challenge is almost greater. Schools like Peter Egret offer so many extracurricular opportunities that even a moderately engaged student can seem lazy or uninterested. On the other hand, Stephanie was offered certain test preparation opportunities that Ronald could only have dreamed of. In addition to these opportunities, Stephanie chose to take a Princeton Review course in the spring of her junior year. The highly competitive nature and reputation of the school was such that Princeton Review offered a number of review courses on the Egret campus itself, designed specifically for Egret students. As a result of this excellent preparation, Stephanie received a perfect 800 on the Verbal section of the exam. However, no amount of test preparation could overcome her lack of natural talent in Math, for which she received a respectable but much lower 680.

Stephanie's SAT I Scores:	7 points

- **800/680**

Stephanie's SAT I average was a 740, which ranks a high 7 points on the IvyWise Index. Stephanie should have been bumped up to an 8 for her perfect 800 Verbal, but the discrepancy between her two scores was a red flag.

Stephanie's SAT II Scores:	8 points

- **800/780/760/660.**

Stephanie scored a perfect 800 on the Writing SAT II test, a 780 on the U.S. History test, a 760 on the French test, and a 660 on the Math I test. Despite hiring a private tutor for help with her math exam, it was by far her lowest score. Luckily it did not count toward her applications, since Wesleyan required only the Writing SAT II, plus two tests of her choice, and Yale counted only her top three SAT II tests. This means Stephanie's II average for both schools was an outstanding 773, putting her on the cusp between and a 9 on the IvyWise Index. Because of her poor performance on the Math I test, which colleges were sure to see even if they didn't count it, Stephanie received 8 points for this section of the IvyWise Index.

TESTING PROFILE IMPROVEMENT STRATEGIES: STEPHANIE CHASE

Because Stephanie came to me so late in the process, there was nothing more for her to do on the testing front. Her scores were good enough that I felt confident we could concentrate on other, more pressing application needs.

Chapter Four

 THE BRAG SHEET

Importance of the Brag Sheet

I cannot stress to you enough the importance of the brag sheet for the selective college application. Everything you do, especially outside the classroom, tells an admissions committee who you are as a person. Your extracurricular activities, employment and summer experiences, community service, honors, awards, interests, and hobbies all paint a picture of you as a dynamic, living, breathing, human being. Colleges want to see a multidimensional personality emerge from this section of the college application; they want to know who they are inviting to their campuses for four years of intensive learning and equally intensive living; and they want to know what kind of lasting contribution you are going to make to collegiate life. Given the academic equality of so many applicants, admissions readers look to the likes and dislikes, passions and aversions of their candidates, as expressed in the brag sheet and the personal essay, in order to form a succinct view of the relative strengths and weaknesses of each applicant as a person. As the academic achievement of the average college applicant continues to rise, it is the personal attributes of the candidate's application that can make or break his or her chances of gaining admission to a selective college.

As such, it is essential that you develop a strategy for organizing and presenting the vast amount of information that your "activities and interests" convey about you. As with the personal essay, which we will analyze in more depth in Chapter 6, the brag sheet must tell a story about you. It must be a clear and user-friendly presentation of the many ways in which you spend your free time. Ideally, it will be rich in detail, exhaustive, and utterly, uniquely "you." In order to help you accomplish this necessary goal, I have spent many years developing a format for the organization and presentation of your personal data that will maximize its impact on an admissions committee. By analyzing the ways in which I helped David, Ronald, and Stephanie construct their elaborate brag sheets, you will learn both the format and the strategy behind it. You will notice that it resembles a résumé or curriculum vitae that you could submit to a potential employer during a job search. This is not a coincidence. If you do not treat the selective college application—and especially the brag sheet—with the same rigor as a major job application, you will not get into the top schools on your college list. If you follow the strategies contained in this chapter, however, you will be on your way to producing the best possible brag sheet you can and to realizing your college dreams.

BRAG SHEET: DAVID HOROWITZ

When David first went about applying to college, he was not aware that admissions officers at his chosen schools would be considering more than just his courses and grades. Of course, he knew about the essay, and he understood the importance of extracurricular activities and job experience, but David and his family erroneously believed that his excellent academic performance was enough to guarantee him admission to his top-choice colleges, regardless of how he treated the rest of the application. As you now know, this was decidedly not the case. One of the major applications elements that David left woefully underdeveloped was his brag sheet. He was under the impression that a rough list of his activities during high school—devoid of detail and completely underselling his accomplishments—was enough to convey to an admissions reader the passion he felt for his time spent outside the classroom. There is an obvious contradiction here: How could an admissions reader gain a sense of "passion" and "commitment" *from a brief list*? How was a college admissions reader supposed to see into David's private life, his hours spent composing in front of the piano, and his passion for Hebrew-language radio, when *David barely even mentioned these activities?!*

It might help to think about it like this: There is no part of the college application that works alone or as a simple list. The interview complements and, hopefully, enhances the more straightforward biographical aspects of the personal profile. The essay gives life to the application as a whole, placing your insight and experience into the context of personal anecdotes that reflect your voice, wit, and personality. Your grades and course selection are supplemented by teacher recommendations that serve to flesh out your numerical standing with intimate life details that shed light on your character. Even your standardized test scores help to paint a picture of how you take tests, of the subjects that interest you, and at which level you perform. The brag sheet, by extension, should be thought of as the personalizing complement to the activities grid that most applications, including the Common Application, require you to fill

kind of person an applicant truly is. **It's not only a question of leadership, but of commitment.** (Leon McLean, formerly of Tufts)

- The brag sheet answers the question **What do you make time for?** (An anonymous admissions reader at Columbia University)

- **Quality over quantity:** Penn is looking for commitment to a few activities over time, not a number. (Dan Evans at the University of Pennsylvania)

- **"What can you give back to Hopkins? How will you contribute?"** (John Birney, Johns Hopkins University)

- **Excessive length**—such as a packet of over a hundred pages for a complete application!—doesn't hurt a student, but admissions readers might not get a chance to read everything. If you are sending extra materials such as performance tapes or art portfolios, you can save time by sending them directly to the department most qualified to assess them. Alert the admissions office that you have done so and they will place a follow-up call to check on the quality of your submissions. (Adam Max at Emory University)

- I once received **a 14-page booklet** featuring the candidate's accomplishments, family, including photographs, illustrations, and awards. It was over the top, but it was well done and it worked! (Richard Avitabile, formerly of NYU) out. Let the admissions readers at your chosen schools know how long you've been involved in an activity, how many hours a week it takes, what your primary responsibilities have been, and what positions of leadership you have been elected to. Present this information in a format that reflects the serious commitment with which you have tackled the activities. Let them see you care by making the brag sheet a reflection of your skill at organizing, synthesizing, and presenting information. If, as has been said, the college application is a conversation between the applicant and the school, why would you speak in the equivalent of monosyllables when you could be communicating through eloquent turns of phrase?

Unfortunately, as smart as he was, David never considered these questions. Despite being a sensitive and careful student, he opted for the "Neanderthal" approach to organizing and presenting his activities: blunt labels that conveyed nothing of the specificity of the activities nor their duration, nor what they meant to him personally. It was truly shocking when I discovered the following "grid" on David's Common Application as it was originally sent to his top choice colleges, including Johns Hopkins University. It contributed largely to David's rejection letters and to the Johns Hopkins admissions committee's decision to place him on their waitlist. The activities look impressive, to be sure, but how could a reader really know from a mere list? In a sense, by placing him on the waitlist, the admissions office at Johns Hopkins was giving David one last chance to prove that he cared enough about his application to devote the same kind of energy and attention to it that he did to his high school studies and activities.

BRAG SHEET: DAVID HOROWITZ

ACADEMIC HONORS

Briefly describe any scholastic distinctions or honors you have won beginning with ninth grade:

Ninth Grade—Principal's Honor Roll

Tenth Grade—Honor Roll, Student of the Month (May)

Eleventh Grade—Honor Roll

Twelfth Grade—Honor Roll, Honors Society. Governor's Distinguished Scholar Award

EXTRACURRICULAR, PERSONAL, AND VOLUNTEER ACTIVITIES (INCLUDING SUMMERS)

Please list your principal extracurricular, community, and family activities and hobbies in the order of their interest to you. Include specific events and/or major accomplishments such as musical instrument played, varsity letters earned, etc. Check (√) in the right column those activities you hope to pursue in college. To allow us to focus on the highlights of your activities, please complete this section even if you plan to attach a résumé.

Activity	Grade level or post-secondary (PS)					Approximate time spent		Positions held, honors won, or letters earned	Do you plan to participate in college?
	9	10	11	12	PS	Hours per week	Weeks per year		
Piano	☑	☑	☑	☑	☐	3	52		☑
Model United Nations	☑	☐	☐	☑	☐	1	16	UNEP	☑
Hockey Team	☑	☐	☐	☐	☐	2	24	Defenseman	☐
College Bowl	☐	☑	☑	☑	☐	1	24		☑
Hospital Visitations	☑	☑	☑	☑	☐	3	2		☑
Yearbook Editor	☐	☐	☐	☑	☐	2	36	Hebrew Editor	☑
	☐	☐	☐	☐	☐				☐

WORK EXPERIENCE

List any job (including summer employment) you have held during the past three years.

Specific nature of work	Employer	Approximate dates of employment	Approximate number of hours spent per week
Billing Clerk	*The Daily View* (L.I. University Newspaper)	06/2001–08/2001	18
Assistant Publications Manager	L. I. University—Center for Urban Policy	06/2001–08/2001	20
Filing Clerk	Pearl Bay Medical	06/2000–08/2000	40

BRAG SHEET EVALUATION: DAVID HOROWITZ

It is immediately apparent that a computer-generated grid of this type does nothing to highlight David's particular interests, the reasons motivating these interests, nor the depth and duration of his involvement. This type of effort is simply not acceptable for a selective school like Johns Hopkins University or any of the other schools to which David applied. Luckily, David's major problems had little to do with the breadth of his activities nor with the depth of his involvement. David's weaknesses in this area had almost solely to do with his presentation skills and his unwillingness to share the more intimate details of his life. As such, his "activities" grid was an under-detailed disaster in which he neglected to include numerous important activities and accomplishments purely out of modesty.

David's Original Brag Sheet:	3 points

• **Barely filled in the simple chart!**

By simply and briefly filling in the chart provided by the Common Application, David gave the impression that his extracurricular interests did not rank high in his life and therefore did not warrant further explanation. Given the limitations of this format, David failed to go into enough detail about each activity, leaving the reader to guess at his level of involvement in each as well as his precise responsibilities within them. In addition, David did not include an attached brag sheet or résumé, which the Common Application specifically allows for, and which many other applicants were likely to do. This is not just a case of "keeping up with the Joneses," however. Colleges want to know as much as they can about an applicant's time spent outside the classroom, and a mere grid does nothing to enhance their understanding. In fact, it may do the opposite: give the impression that the candidate does not feel it is worth his or her time to share personal details with the college in question.

• Incomplete list

Overall, David listed far too few activities on his Common Application grid. Plus, there were a number of extracurricular interests that surfaced in his recommendation letters that he neglected to mention in this brief grid, let alone highlight. These included such impressive accomplishments as the Chess Team, Mock Trial, and learning Sign Language. David should have showcased and detailed activities such as these in order to grab his admissions reader's attention and help his brag sheet stand out from the crowd of other, equally qualified applications.

• Piano is number one

Specifically, piano seems to have been a major interest of David's, but none of his admissions readers could know the extent of his involvement with the instrument nor what genre of music he liked to play. If David spent as much time on piano playing as he said, then he absolutely should have revealed these details in order for an admissions committee to understand the importance of his playing.

• Lack of consistency with no explanation

As his activities grid stood, David displayed an unwelcome lack of consistency: He dropped hockey after ninth grade, participated in Mock Trial only in the twelfth grade, and was a participant in Model UN in the ninth and twelfth grades but not in between. Why this spotty record? What happened in between? Gaps in your extracurricular activities such as this must be explained in the brag sheet. If there are mitigating circumstances behind a spotty record, these must be elaborated or else an admissions reader must assume that you simply lost interest in certain activities along the way or, worse, that you are by nature scattershot in your interests.

• Shortchanged himself on time

David's volunteer hospital visits look impressive, but if they really lasted only three hours a week for two weeks per year, then they can hardly be considered worthy of mention. It seems David's modesty got the better of him here: When I questioned him about these visits, it turned out he spent considerably more time on them than he let on. Between commuting and preparing for his visits, David spent four to five times longer on this activity than the grid indicated. Also, David failed to explain why these activities were relegated to a two-week period during the year. When I learned that David visited elderly members of a Jewish nursing home during the High Holy Days through a program established by his local synagogue, I finally understood the nature of his involvement. An admissions reader needs to understand this, too! As such, David shortchanged himself by not counting prep time, commute time, and other time associated with this volunteer activity and by not

Do you catch applicants lying on their brag sheet?

(1) The Admissions Office at Brown University encountered an applicant who sent an audiotape of herself playing the piano masterfully. The problem was, neither her high school college counselor nor her faculty writers mentioned anything about her piano playing. Brown called the applicant's college counselor. He said he knew nothing about the piano playing either. Brown investigated and discovered that the student's mother was a concert pianist and had forged the tape in an effort to get her daughter into school. **Brown promptly withdrew its offer of admission.**

(2) Adam Max at Emory University has said that he and his colleagues catch students in lies all the time. Usually they have reported an incorrect SAT score, which is really quite blatant, since the Educational Testing Service (ETS) sends an official score report to colleges. In addition, Mr. Max has encountered students who lie about their grades or course selection—something equally obvious, since high schools always send an official transcript directly to the college, independent of the application, in a sealed envelope. More egre-

explaining why he didn't pursue this activity at other times of the year.

• One hour/week activities

Any activities that occupy only one hour per week of David's time should have been left off the chart completely. That, or David should have considered whether these activities really took only one hour, as with the example of his hospital visits above.

• Unknown responsibilities

Although David's work experience is solid and impressive, we learn nothing about his wages, his level of responsibility, or his intended use for the money he earned. No presentation of work experience is complete without this. Colleges don't want to know simply that you have worked; they want to know where, what you did, for how long, at what level, with which skills, and with what responsibility you have worked. Again, they are trying to get a picture of you as a candidate, as a student, as a human being, and as a productive member of our society.

• The bottom line is: *David did not brag!*

The single greatest mistake on David's activities grid was his unwillingness to impress his readers with the depth and duration of his interests and involvement. By nature a shy person, Da-

gious is a computer-doctored transcript or forged letter of recommendation. An admissions reader can discover the forgery by discrepancies in the application. **In these cases, the reader will always call the high school college counselor and get to the root of the lie.**

(3) Lloyd Peterson, formerly of Yale and Vassar, says lies are especially obvious in the case of a forged award at the state or national level. It is easy to call the counselor or the body presenting the award and verify the claim directly.

(4) Richard Avitabile, formerly of NYU, found so many activities listed on a particular brag sheet that he was forced to count up the hours—and there weren't enough hours in a week to get everything done!

Your IvyWise Counselor Says:
   "Your life is now. It doesn't start when you get to college, get a job, get married, and so forth. If you're sitting in a classroom doodling because you're bored, you're wasting time. **School is like a job.** You have to be there, so you might as well find out why you're learning and discover the joy in it. **It's not about grades.** Your education never ends. Everyone is still a student, so learn for the sake of learning. That's why your activities are so important. You're not doing them to put them on a résumé; you're doing them because you love to do them! **If you are forcing yourself to do things you don't like to do, you'll be miserable—and colleges don't want miserable kids!"**

vid felt it was inappropriate to brag. But if you fail to become your own strongest advocate—without sounding pompous or narcissistic, of course—then who is going to go to bat for you?

BRAG SHEET IMPROVEMENT STRATEGIES: DAVID HOROWITZ

As a corrective, I helped David overhaul his brag sheet according to the IvyWise format as delineated in my book *The Truth About Getting In*. I made sure David mentioned everything he did outside of school that might be of interest to his admissions reader at Johns Hopkins University, treating each activity with the detail it deserved. As you will undoubtedly see below, David's new brag sheet sheds much more light on his character than his previous one. It lets his admissions reader know the precise nature of his activities and his specific level of involvement with each, as well as their overall importance to him. I especially urged David to include his study of Sign Language and Modern Hebrew, as they both stress his natural linguistic ability. As you will also see, this extremely important section of his application went from being a vague list of generic, confusing, and under-described activities to being the cornerstone of his new, more powerful application.

IMPROVED BRAG SHEET: DAVID HOROWITZ

David J. Horowitz
555-66-7777
Singer Yeshiva High School

I. EXTRACURRICULAR ACTIVITIES	SCHOOL YEARS	HRS. PER WK./WKS. PER YR.	POSITIONS/HONORS
Classical Piano	9, 10, 11, 12	7/50	Play in recitals. Compose own music.

Activity	Grades	Hours	Description
School Band	11, 12	3/40	Founding Member. Keyboard player for monthly school programs.
Model United Nations	9, 12[1]	5/40	Founding Member at new school.
Israel Action Committee	11, 12	4/40	Distribution of flyers, fund-raising; planned programs to promote social causes, e.g., Israel Walk-a-Thon.
Mock Trial	12[2]	6/40	Member—starting witness.
College Bowl	10, 11, 12[3]	2/40	Practice sessions and day-long meets throughout the year.
Newspaper—*The Sentinel*	10, 11, 12	3/40	Reporter (10) and Columnist (11, 12).
Yearbook	12[4]	3/40	Hebrew Editor—solicited and edited works in Hebrew.
Pearl Bay High School Hockey Team	9	5/20	Defenseman.
Website and Computer Tutorial Design	11	2/6	Designed Singer Yeshiva High School Web page and Career Counseling Office tutorial.

[1]After ninth grade I switched schools; my new school was ineligible for competition until it had a senior class.

[2]I was unable to participate in other years due to scheduling conflicts.

[3]Ineligible for competition at my previous school (ninth grade).

[4]Available only to seniors.

II. HONORS AND AWARDS	SCHOOL YEARS	HONORS/TITLE
Governor's Scholar	12	State of New York Academic Excellence Scholarship.
Singer Yeshiva High School Honors Society	12[5]	Keynote Speaker at the school's first Honors Society Induction.
Singer Yeshiva High School Honor Roll	10, 11, 12	Requires a 3.5. cumulative GPA.
Singer Yeshiva High School Student of the Month Award	10	Awarded by teacher recommendation for classroom performance.
Pearl Bay High School Honor Roll and Principal's List	9	Requires a GPA of 90 or above.

III. COMMUNITY SERVICE	SCHOOL YEARS	HRS. PER WK./WKS. PER YR.	DESCRIPTION/ RESPONSIBILITIES
Program in Washington, DC, sponsored by the Washington Institute for Jewish Leadership.	11[6]	3 days, 30 hours of seminars	Seminars on activism, social justice, and public policy. Met with the homeless and various congressmen.
Jewish Federation of Greater Pearl Bay County	9, 10, 11 , 12	8/1	Volunteer on Super Sunday— telephone fund-raising to finance social and educational programs in the Pearl Bay County area.

[5]School ineligible for National Honor Society, which requires a graduated class.

[6]Only available to sophomores and juniors.

	SCHOOL YEARS	HRS. PER WK./WKS. PER YR.	RESPONSIBILITIES/ EARNINGS
Jewish Visitation Society for the Sick of Pearl Bay	9, 10, 11, 12	6/2	Basket preparation for Jewish Holidays. Drove and delivered baskets, and visited hospitals.[7]
Synagogue Prayer and Cantorial Services at Congregation Beth Alem	9, 10, 11, 12	3/52	Founding Member and Co-leader of the Teen Services group.

IV. EMPLOYMENT	SCHOOL YEARS	HRS. PER WK./WKS. PER YR.	RESPONSIBILITIES/ EARNINGS[8]
Babysitting	9, 10, 11, 12	3/20	$60 per month
The Daily View (the official student newspaper of Long Island University)	Summer 2001	18/8	Maintained financial records. Updated financial spreadsheets. Spoke with customers to solicit ads. Collected post-due balances. Installed and trained for new computer billing software. ($700)
Long Island University Center For Urban Policy Research	Summer 2001	30/8	Updated and maintained mailing list databases. Maintained book and position paper inventory. Retrieved books and position papers for faculty research. Responsible for filling book orders and file upkeep. ($850)

[7]Community service activity required for graduation from Singer Yeshiva High School.

[8]10 percent of my earnings I donate to synagogue charitable funds. The rest I have saved to buy a laptop for college.

Pearl Bay Medical	Summer 2000	40/8	Interacted face-to-face with patients. Prepared rooms for uninterrupted patient flow, including room setup for minor surgery. Took insurance information, scheduled appointments, fielded heavy call volume. ($700)
Summer Camp Counselor at local YM/YHWA	Summer 1999	40/8	Junior Counselor responsible for supervision of 25 children as well as daily swim instruction with certified instructor. ($600)

V. SUMMER EXPERIENCES	SUMMER	#WKS.	DESCRIPTION
Trip to Israel	2000	2 weeks each	Worldwide family reunion, with members attending from almost every continent.
Trip to London, England	1998	2 weeks	In-depth historical tour.

VI. HOBBIES AND INTERESTS	SCHOOLS YEARS	HRS. PER WK./WKS. PER YR.	DESCRIPTION
Reading novels and *National Geographic.*	9, 10, 11, 12	3/52	Mainly Tom Clancy and Ayn Rand. Favorite genres: mystery and fiction.
Softball and Tackle Football	9, 10, 11, 12	3/30	Usually on Sunday mornings.
Listening to Israeli Hebrew Radio over the Internet	9, 10, 11, 12	3/40	At night while using my computer.

| Automobile Enthusiast | 9, 10, 11, 12 | 3/40 | Informal club meetings to discuss new cars. Includes yearly trip to the NY International Auto Show. |

BRAG SHEET IMPROVEMENT RESULTS: DAVID HOROWITZ

David's New Brag Sheet:	7 points

David's new brag sheet, as it accompanied his resubmitted application to Johns Hopkins University, earned him 4 extra points for this section of the IvyWise Index. There are a few reasons why David's brag sheet did not rank higher. Although David's second brag sheet was much better in terms of detail, depth, and presentation, it was still not the greatest profile in terms of possible activities, jobs, and community service opportunities that a student could take advantage of. Primarily, David's lack of national awards, national competitions, and immediate community service beyond what his high school required of him kept him from getting a higher score for this section. Nearly every admissions reader and officer that I have spoken with recently understands that different high schools and different communities offer differing levels of possible activities and involvement. They want to see that their applicants have taken full advantage of the opportunities around them. In other words, although David's considerable community service activities may seem extraordinary when viewed in a vacuum, they are not as impressive when we learn from his brag sheet that he was required to participate in one of them as a condition for graduation. This same way of thinking can be applied to nearly all sectors of a student's life, both inside and outside the classroom: Colleges want to see that you will take full advantage of all that a college campus has to offer.

BRAG SHEET: RONALD SIEGAL

Unlike David Horowitz, Ronald Siegal had the advantage of foresight. Since Ronald came to me much earlier in the college admissions process, he and I were able to develop a number of strategies to ensure that his application made the most of his considerable interests and activities. Ronald followed my advice to stick to those activities that stemmed from his most passionately held interests, especially in the realms of art production and appreciation. In order to highlight his considerable achievement in these areas, I had Ronald construct a detailed brag sheet according to the IvyWise format. In this way, all of Ronald's time outside the classroom was accounted for in a well-organized and highly detailed document. By following the IvyWise format, Ronald ensured that the admissions officers reading his application would immediately understand his dedication to such activities as painting, peer counseling, the school newspaper, the March of Dimes, and the National Art Honor Society. They would also see his maturity and responsibility as demonstrated through his challenging and substantial employment, as well as his extensive summer experiences. Ronald's commitment to his community, his work ethic, his artistic talent, his attention to the needs of others, and his on-campus achievements all provided impressive support for the rest of his application and increased his overall chances of admission. The one thing I stressed over and over to Ronald about the brag sheet was this: The last thing he wanted to do was to sell himself short or raise more questions than he answered with vague accounts of underspecified activities arbitrarily organized. To avoid this, I urged Ronald to use the brag sheet as an opportunity to sell his unique qualities and experiences to his prospective colleges and to *never, ever be afraid to brag.*

Ronald Siegal
123-45-6789
Swanee High School

I. EXTRACURRICULAR ACTIVITIES	SCHOOL YEARS	HRS. PER WK./WKS. PER YR.	POSITIONS/HONORS
National Art Honor Society (responsible for beautifying the high school mainly by painting murals)	10, 11, 12[1]	6/40	President, Art Historian / Parliamentarian (12), Treasurer (11), Secretary (10).
Newman Art School (Cleveland, Ohio)	9, 10, 11, 12	4/40	Student: Studio Art, Elements of Drawing, and Painting.
Spanish Club	9, 10, 11, 12	4/40	Activities Coordinator/VP (11), Secretary (10), Member (9).
The Swan: School Newspaper	9, 10, 11, 12	7/35	Editor (11, 12), Business Manager (11, 12), Reporter (9, 10).
Peer Counseling	10, 11, 12[2]	3/40	Chosen to Counsel (11, 12), Member (10, 11, 12).
Patrons of Music and the Arts	11, 12	3/20	Student Liaison (11, 12).
National High School Honor Society	11, 12[3]	3/40	Member.

[1]Unavailable to ninth graders.

[2]Also unavailable to ninth graders.

[3]Unavailable to ninth and tenth graders.

Cleveland Teen Center	10, 11, 12	3/40	Assistant to Executive Treasurer (11, 12), Hiring Interviewer (10).
Group Skills	10, 11[4]	3/40	Treasurer.
Class Government	9, 10, 11, 12	2/20	Cabinet Member.
Student Activities Committee	9, 10, 11, 12	2/35	Club/Society Representative (10, 11, 12), Voting Member (9, 10, 11, 12).

II. HONORS AND AWARDS PRESENTED BY	SCHOOL YEARS	HONORS/TITLE
State of Ohio, Office of the Attorney General	11	Triple "C" Award in Recognition of Outstanding Character, Courage, and Commitment to the Swanee High School and Cleveland Communities.
Swanee High School	10, 11, 12	Major Volunteer Service Award— Shapiro Learning Center.
Swanee High School	11, 12	Major Volunteer Service Award— March of Dimes Foundation.
Swanee High School Student Government	11	Special Recognition for the Art Honors Society and the Beautification of Swanee High School.
Patrons of Music and the Arts	11	Only student art chosen to be displayed in *MADE: Music, Art & Dance Ensemble*.[5]

[4]Only available to tenth and eleventh graders.

[5]Slide numbers 1 and 2 in Art Portfolio.

Talisman	11, 12[6]		National High School Honor Society.
Summer Discovery at Michigan	11		John Davidson Leadership Award—only given to four Students out of 200 at Summer Discovery.
Swanee High School Art	9		Art Chosen for Display in The Free Space Gallery, a student art show.
Cleveland Community	9, 10		Best Overall for my age group (9, 10).

III. COMMUNITY SERVICE	SCHOOL YEARS	HRS. PER WK./WKS. PER YR.	POSITIONS/RESPONSIBILITIES
The Shapiro Learning Center—providing support for homeless children in Cleveland	10, 11, 12	3/40	Volunteer Art Instructor/Tutor.
March of Dimes Foundation	11, 12[7]	4/25	YOUNG HEARTS Youth Leadership Council in Cleveland: President (12), Member (11), Local Health Fair Representative (11, 12).
March of Dimes Walk America	11, 12	5/1	Central Cleveland Youth Coordinator (11, 12).

[6]Unavailable to ninth and tenth graders.

[7]Also unavailable to ninth and tenth graders.

		HRS. PER WK./WKS. PER	

MADE: *Music, Art & Dance Ensemble*, A Community Visual and Performing Arts Show	11	6/1	Volunteer.

IV. SUMMER EXPERIENCES	SUMMER	HRS. PER WK./WKS. PER SUMMER	POSITIONS/DESCRIPTIONS
Cleveland Art Museum	2000	40/6	Paid Summer Internship in Education Department ($200 per week).[8]
Bauer Fine Art Gallery (Cleveland, Ohio)	2000	5/8	Director's Assistant and Inventory Clerk.
The Art Workshop at Cleveland Community College	2000	10/8	Student—Projects in Painting and Advanced Drawing.
Newman Art School	2000	4/8	Student—Painting and Drawing.
ASA Spanish Language and Culture School—Madrid, Spain	1999	30/4	Community Volunteer and Student: Advanced Spanish Language and European Art History.
Summer Discovery at Michigan	1999	20/3	Student: Tennis and Photography.
Swanee High School Math Acceleration Program	1998	15/6	Student: Course II.
Newman Art School	1998	20/6	Student: Studio Art, Art History.

[8]Saved earnings to pay for art supplies.

V. EMPLOYMENT	SCHOOL YEARS	HRS. PER WK./WKS PER YR.	POSITIONS/EARNINGS
Bauer Fine Art Gallery	12	8/30 Clerk ($8/hour)	Director's Assistant and Inventory.
Private Spanish Tutor	11, 12	2/35	Earned Approximately $60/ Month (savings).
Baby-sitting	9, 10, 11, 12	4/50	Earned Approximately $80/ Month (savings).

VI. HOBBIES AND INTERESTS	SCHOOL YEARS	HRS. PER WK./WKS. PER YR.	DESCRIPTIONS
Drawing and Painting	9, 10, 11, 12	4/50	
Photography	10, 11, 12	2/20	Develop own black and white photos.
Cooking	9, 10, 11, 12	4/40	Traditional Spanish dishes.
Running	9, 10, 11, 12	2/40	2–3 miles/day outdoors.

BRAG SHEET EVALUATION: RONALD SIEGAL

Ronald Siegal's brag sheet was one area of his application where, despite his modest grades, he was able to shine. Through a detailed and well-organized account of his interests, activities, community service, honors, awards, and job experience, Ronald's character came alive in the minds of his admissions readers. His love of art and the museum life, his willingness to help less-advantaged members of his community, and his passion for Spanish language and culture were clear to all who read his brag sheet. Ronald's personal profile in this respect was truly excellent. Those of you who have read my book *The Truth About Getting In* will remember that I chose to highlight Ronald's brag sheet as an example of the perfect format. Now, by assessing it in the context of his entire application, you can see just how impressive it is. By following the IvyWise format, Ronald was able to stand out from the crowd and make a lasting impression at the University of Pennsylvania.

Ronald's Final Brag Sheet:	9 points

• **Strong commitment to activities**

Ronald's brag sheet demonstrates a clear and overwhelming commitment to artistic pursuits. Because he organized an account of his time outside the classroom in such a detailed manner, admissions readers at the University of Pennsylvania were able to learn *at a glance* about the murals he painted for his school, the classes he took at an art school outside of Swanee, his employment at both a gallery and a major museum, and, in general, his artistic interests in painting, drawing, and photography. The nation's top colleges like to see this type of passion and commitment in a student—it gives them a clear view of who the applicant is and of the kinds of things he or she is likely to pursue in college. In addition to art, Ronald's admissions readers were able to see that he was committed to a number of community service organizations, as well as to Spanish. Looking at the "School Years" column of his brag sheet, they also saw that Ronald remained committed to the majority of these activities throughout high school. Admissions committees love to see this type of consistency: They know they have a dedicated student on their hands, the type who will continue to make a significant contribution to extracurricular life in college and the surrounding community.

• **Great work ethic**

The numerous employment experiences contained in the "Summer Experiences" and "Employment" sections of Ronald's brag sheet demonstrated to his readers at the University of Pennsylvania that he had a high level of responsibility and maturity. They proved that

Ronald could collaborate well with others in an office-type situation, and they showed that he was not some spoiled rich kid willing to fritter away his summer lying in the sun with friends.

• Clear and concise presentation

By adopting the IvyWise brag sheet format, Ronald was able to present his numerous activities in a clear, concise, and highly detailed manner. Even if some material was repeated from the activities "grid" in the University of Pennsylvania application, it was important that he had all his pertinent extracurricular, community service, hobby, award, and employment information organized into a single, easy-to-read document. In Ronald's case, his exemplary brag sheet demonstrated to his admissions readers that he possessed great organizational skills and that he cared enough about his college application to take the extra time to make sure everything was presented in a reader-friendly way.

• Insight into character

Because of the wealth of detail contained in Ronald's brag sheet and because of his evident commitment to a small number of passionately held activities, the University of Pennsylvania was able to get to know Ronald intimately. Through this exemplary brag sheet, Ronald impressed his admissions reader with both the breadth of his activities and the depth of his interest.

BRAG SHEET: STEPHANIE CHASE

Stephanie Chase found herself in a position similar to David's, although under very different circumstances. Because of her general unhappiness at boarding school, the tragedy of her godmother's death, and her strained relationship with her own parents, Stephanie received very little guidance during the college application process. As a result, aspects of her application over which she exercised more or less direct control—such as the format of the brag sheet and the content and style of the personal statement—suffered, simply because she didn't have an adequate sounding board. Having grown up in the high-pressure world of the suburban moneyed classes, Stephanie certainly knew what a professional job application looked like. She also knew the extraordinary time and effort her fellow "Egretians" were putting into their college applications. In light of this, it is all the more astounding that Stephanie produced such a lackluster brag sheet. The vague list you will find below would have made her father cringe, had he taken the time to check it over, and Stephanie's own friends would certainly have advised her against it if she had shared her experience with them.

But Stephanie's problem was a dual one: On the one hand, she wasn't being pushed in the right direction by her parents and therefore never felt like she had emotional control over the college admissions process; on the other hand, she was still too devastated by Barbara's death to come out of her shell and ask for help, whether from friends at Egret or from her college counselor, Mr. Hayden. As a result, when it came time to compiling her brag sheet for her college applications, Stephanie was content to have a rushed phone conversation with her father's personal assistant, during which she enumerated her activities, work experience, community service, and overall accomplishments. Relying on Dylan's assistant—someone who had no interest in helping Stephanie get into college, other than to impress her boss with efficiency—to organize and type up this information, I suspect Stephanie never even proofread the document before adding it to her other application materials. As a result, Stephanie's "brag sheet" contained numerous typos, spelling mistakes, inconsistencies, lapses, and erroneous facts that must have contributed to the overall negative impression that this section of Stephanie's application had on her admissions readers. Plus, Dylan's assistant added an inappropriate hobbies list, thinking privileged activities would impress a college. As you look over the following document, you should easily be able to notice how little Stephanie seemed to care about making a positive, lasting impression on her readers. The red flags literally crowd out Stephanie's considerable achievements, making this one of her worst application sections.

BRAG SHEET: STEPHANIE CHASE

Drama: coursework, productions, directed own play.
    (All four years. 5 hours a week.)

Lacrosse: Award.
    (All for years. 4 hours a week.)

French Club.
    (Tenth grade and twelfth grade. 20 hours a week.)

Contributor to school newspaper: Cultural Editor.
    (All four years. 4 hours a week.)

Literary Journal: Poetry Editor.
    (All three years. 4 hours a week.)

National Gold Key for Creative Writing.

Saltonstall Award for Excellence.

Senior Acting Ensemble: the role of "Williams" in Miller's *The Crucibles*.

National Merit Scholarship Semifinalist

Abbey Road Program—Cannes, France: Summer 1999

Charity Fundraising: Summer 2000

University Research Assistant: Summer 2001

Hobbies: Tennis, Shopping, Yachting, Extensive Travel to our homes in Switzerland, London, Bermuda & Corfu.

BRAG SHEET EVALUATION: STEPHANIE CHASE

Comparing Stephanie's initial brag sheet for Yale and Wesleyan with Ronald's brag sheet for the University of Pennsylvania and David's resubmitted brag sheet for Johns Hopkins, you can see just how inadequate Stephanie's first attempt at organizing her interests and activities really was. In its current state, it contributed to the overall feeling that Stephanie had spent very little time on her college applications and that neither Yale nor Wesleyan had emerged as her clear-cut first-choice school. Had she really committed herself to the work involved in drafting her brag sheet, this section would have been an incredibly detailed and convincing advertisement for Stephanie as a candidate. Instead it was a bomb. Not *the* bomb, but a total dud. To add insult to injury, Stephanie also neglected to include a number of activities and events that she had initiated or participated in during high school and which a college admissions committee would have found extremely compelling. Why she slacked off is not clear, but it probably had something to do with her general emotional state at the time she wrote her applications. Not feeling clear about her college choices, her relationship with her father and mother still totally messed up, and the deep feelings of loss over the death of Barbara still swirling around inside her, Stephanie became utterly negligent.

Stephanie's Initial Brag Sheet:	1 point

• Inattention to detail

The major weaknesses in Stephanie's brag sheet lay in her inattention to detail. She had her father's assistant type up this list of activities and interests and neglected to proofread it prior to submission. It therefore contained numerous typos. For instance: The role is "Abigail Williams," not "Williams;" the play is *The Crucible*, not *The Crucibles*; the playwright's full name is Arthur Miller; the Saltonstall Award is for "Excellence in Historical Writing," not just "Excellence"; lacrosse lasted four years and not "for years"; the French Club occupied two instead of twenty hours per week; and, finally, lacrosse practice was more like three hours a day for five days a week instead of four hours a week! How could an admissions reader at either Yale or Wesleyan take Stephanie seriously if she didn't take her own activities seriously?

- **Too general and confusing.**

Although it was somewhat organized, Stephanie's first brag sheet offered very few details about her participation in each individual activity, and it completely failed to convey a sense of how much she cared about any of them. By simply listing such generic categories as "Drama," "Charity Fund-raising," "school newspaper," "Literary Journal," "Lacrosse," and "University Research Assistant," she gave no indication as to the nature of her interest nor the level of her involvement in any of these activities. Was she captain of the Girls' Lacrosse team or did she just sit on the bench? She seems to have won an award, but which one? Did she star in many school plays or man the lighting booth in a few? And which play did she direct? A reader may know what an Abbey Road Program is, but what exactly did Stephanie do in France? What else has she done abroad? What was her chosen charity and why? Did she raise $300 or $30,000? For whom did she conduct research and at which university? What was the subject of her research? And what the heck does "all three years" mean in the "literary journal" section? Knowing the general subject area of Stephanie's activities is worthless to a college—they want to know the details, all the specific pieces of information that make a candidate's interests and experiences utterly unique.

- **Passion or privilege?**

In addition to the typos, erroneous information, and vague nature of her first brag sheet, the quality of some of the activities contained therein was questionable. Although they are certainly telling in terms of her upbringing, activities such as yachting, extensive travel to exotic ports of call, references to family getaway houses, and the mere mention of shopping, all give the impression that Stephanie is a spoiled rich kid who doesn't have a clue about the real problems facing the world at large. She fails to indicate that the play she directed was a benefit to raise money and awareness for her chosen charity, the Breast Cancer Research Foundation. Had she mentioned this and written about Barbara's death in her essay, then an admissions reader would have seen the continuity between Stephanie's private and academic lives. They would have understood that she was able to use her passion for the dramatic arts to address some of the pressing needs from her own history. As it stood initially, however, her brag sheet gave the impression that she merely fulfilled the requisite number of volunteer work hours that her school required over one summer doing something mundane that she was not interested enough in to write about.

• Incomplete

Stephanie's original brag sheet was also too short, neglecting to include relevant experiences like her sustained involvement with ESSO, the Egret Social Services Organization. Stephanie also shortchanged herself on the time she spent outside the classroom reading and writing. Between tenth and eleventh grades, I later found out, Stephanie spent the summer with Charlotte and her sick mother. As Barbara was in and out of the hospital, Stephanie decided to volunteer in the cancer ward at Brownville County Hospital so she could spend more time with her. Stephanie even went so far as to produce and direct a theatrical production with some of the children from the ward. They did a sparkling rendition of *Alice in Wonderland*, which Stephanie herself adapted for the stage. At the same time, Stephanie started doing her own independent research on breast cancer and published a series of articles in the local newspaper. This was a truly miraculous summer for Stephanie, but we never knew any of this because she never wrote about it in her first brag sheet. Stephanie actually told me she felt like that summer had been a wash and that she had decided not to list any of these volunteer activities because they were not organized activities per se and because she hadn't made any money from the publication of her articles. Stephanie also felt that any non–school-related activities she initiated on her own—like her hospital play—were not the kinds of things colleges really cared about seeing on the brag sheet. As you know, this is decidedly not the case. Self-initiated activities show individuality, courage, and true passion. What they often lack in organization and the possibility for elected positions of leadership, they make up for in entrepreneurial spirit. With the example of lacrosse, Stephanie shortchanged herself by writing down far too few hours, ignoring all the time she spent training outside of practice, going to lacrosse camp over the summer, traveling to away games, and studying play books. I had suspected that she did this out of humility, but when I asked her why she hadn't included any of these aspects of her life, she told me because there wasn't very much room on the activities grid and she didn't want her attached sheet to be any longer. This is obviously not a valid reason. I also found out during subsequent conversations with Stephanie that she used to play tennis all the time during the summer and that her mother used to drag her to regional tournaments, where Stephanie would often win. She opted not to include these details because she felt that tennis wasn't a serious sport, that it was only something her mother told her to do because it was a social activity that you could play at the country club. The truth is this: The brag sheet is your opportunity to present all the pertinent information from your life outside the classroom, so let your admissions readers draw their own conclusions!

- ### Inconsistency for all the wrong reasons

Finally, Stephanie's first brag sheet revealed a number of inconsistencies that she should have explained or avoided altogether. Her flip-flopping in and out of the French club—which I later found out from her counselor letter was because of her boyfriend Henri!—not only deprived her of a deserved shot at being president of the club but also looked terrible on her brag sheet. Of course, many decisions are based in part on personal needs, but dropping the French Club entirely in eleventh grade after she and Henri broke up, only to join again during her senior year, demonstrates to a college admissions committee that Stephanie may still be too immature to handle positions of authority and that her priorities remain those of a self-centered rich girl. Since this was not the case, Stephanie should have gone out of her way to explain the circumstances surrounding this flip-flop in a letter to her readers. Extenuating circumstances such as the death of a relative or close friend, a move that necessitates a change of high schools, or a sickness that debilitates the student for a period of time are legitimate excuses for a lack of consistency in the brag sheet activities. Had Stephanie known this, she could have used the opportunity to explain what happened to her during the first trimester of her junior year and how this had affected her relationship with Henri and hence with the French Club.

BRAG SHEET IMPROVEMENT STRATEGIES: STEPHANIE CHASE

Had I been involved in Stephanie's college search from the beginning, I would have urged her to base the form and content of her brag sheet on the IvyWise model as it appears in *The Truth About Getting In*. As it was, we had to radically reconfigure her first brag sheet and include this new version with her resubmitted application to Wesleyan in the hopes that its strength and clarity would impress upon Stephanie's readers her commitment to her interests and activities. After a lengthy interview with me, Stephanie made a master list of all her activities, interests, honors, awards, jobs, summer experiences, and significant hobbies, and then set about organizing them into a format that would logically and coherently account for all of the time she spent outside of the classroom. In addition to improving the form and content of her brag sheet, I also urged Stephanie to turn in a number of "Exhibits" to show firsthand the quality of her many scholarly and artistic productions.

First of all, I urged Stephanie to submit a videotape of herself performing in the small stage play she wrote and directed in the winter of her upper year to benefit the Breast Cancer Research Foundation. It was clear to me from her commitment and achievement in drama class, her outstanding talent as a writer, director, and performer, and her obvious passion for the stage, that theater was something she would continue to pursue in college. Her admissions readers needed to know this. By watching a tape of her performance in a play that she herself had written, they would get a firsthand glimpse into the passionate, creative soul that I had come to know in the weeks we had been working together. You never know if someone in the admissions office will watch a video such as this, but it's better to include it than not, especially if it's such a star performance.

I also begged Stephanie to include a copy of the magnificent book of poetry she kept as a sort of journal throughout both grade and high school, including the poem that won her a National Gold Key for creative writing in her lower year. Not only did this book contain truly exquisite examples of Stephanie's poetry in many genres, it also provided invaluable insight into the more private Stephanie, especially during the crucial time of her mourning, depression, and subsequent disciplinary difficulty. I knew that this would help Stephanie's overall application not only because of its quality but also because of the openness and generosity that sharing such a document conveyed. On a more scholarly note, I suggested that Stephanie include both her award-winning History paper and the articles on breast cancer that she had published in the local newspaper at home. These pieces of writing helped to round out Stephanie's profile as a great expository writer in addition to being an exceptional creative writer. They would also help convince her admissions readers at Wesleyan that she was well-equipped to handle paper-writing at an advanced collegiate level.

Here, then, is Stephanie's new brag sheet. Please note that the tape and text of her stage play, the excerpts of her poetry journal, her history paper, and her published articles on breast cancer have not been included in *Rock Hard Apps* as they are the copyrighted material of the author and may be appearing in published form soon. Getting Stephanie to share them with Wesleyan was hard enough!

IMPROVED BRAG SHEET: STEPHANIE CHASE

Stephanie Chase
987-65-4321
Peter Egret Academy

I. EXTRACURRICULAR ACTIVITIES	SCHOOL YEARS	HRS. PER WK./WKS. PER YR.	POSITIONS/HONORS
Drama Club	9, 10, 11, 12	3/40	Chairperson (12); wrote and directed original play about breast cancer (11). Founding Member (9).
French Club	10, 12[1]	3/40	Member.

[1]Was unable to participate in eleventh grade due to personal conflict.

Girls Lacrosse	9, 10, 11, 12	15/15	Co-Captain (12); Varsity (12, 11, 10); Junior Varsity (9).
Senior Acting Ensemble	12[2]	3/40	Playing the part of "Abigail Williams" in Arthur Miller's *The Crucible.*
The Egret Bulletin, official newspaper of Peter Egret	9, 10, 11, 12	3/40	Contributor (12, 11, 10, 9), Cultural Editor (12, 11).
Class Government	9, 10, 11, 12	2/20	Member of Cultural Forum, responsible for booking on-campus performances and literary speakers.
The Albatross—Literary Magazine at Peter Egret	10, 11, 12	2/40	Poetry Editor (12); Contributor (12, 11, 10).

II. HONORS AND AWARDS PRESENTED BY:	SCHOOL YEARS	HONORS/TITLE
Peter Egret Academy	12	Finalist for Fourth Year English Award—results in June.
Saltonstall Committee at Peter Egret Academy	11	Saltonstall Award for Excellence in Historical Writing,[3] awarded to only one "upper"-year history student every year.
National Gold Key	11	National Award of Recognition for Outstanding Creative Writing, Poetry Competition.[4]

[2]Only available to seniors; try-outs required.

[3]Paper submitted with application as "Exhibit B."

[4]Poetry Journal submitted with application as "Exhibit C."

Peter Egret Academy Girls Lacrosse Team	11		Most Valuable Player Award.
National Merit Scholarship	12		Semi-finalist.
Windridge Lacrosse Camp	Summer 2000		Outstanding Camper Award.
Windridge Lacrosse Camp	Summer 1999		Most Improved Player Award.

III. COMMUNITY SERVICE	SCHOOL YEARS	HRS. PER WK./WKS. PER YR.	POSITIONS/RESPONSIBILITIES
ESSO: Egret Social Service Organization	10, 11, 12	2/40	Terminal hospital patient visitations.
Trigger	11	8/12	Produced, wrote, and directed original play about cancer to raise money for Breast Cancer Research Foundation—$4,300.[5]
Breast Cancer Research Foundation	Summer 2000	10/8	Raised $22,650 for the local chapter; organized "awareness" events for Brownville community.
Brownville County Hospital Oncology Research Center	Summer 2000	20/8	Volunteer in children's cancer ward; adapted, produced, and directed version of *Alice in Wonderland* with children from the cancer ward.
Abbey Road French Language and Culture Program in Cannes, France	Summer 1999	30/8	Community volunteer: Cleaned beaches and fed the homeless.

[5]Tape of *Trigger* performance submitted with application as "Exhibit D."

IV. SUMMER EXPERIENCES	SUMMER	HRS. PER WK./WKS. PER SUMMER	DESCRIPTIONS
English Department: Yale University	2001	40/8	Research Assistant for professor Jason Blume, writing book on literary theory.
Brownville Journal	2000	2/4	Published series of articles on children coping with parents suffering from cancer.[6]
Independent Cancer Research Brownville Public Library	2000	4/8	Researched causes and cures for breast cancer at local library.
Windridge Lacrosse Camp	1999–2000	40/2	Intensive lacrosse training.
Abbey Road French Language and Culture School in Cannes, France.	1999	30/8	Community volunteer and student: Advanced French Language.
Drama Camp at Brownville Community College	1998	40/6	Learned Principles of Dramatic Acting and Beginning Stagecraft; wrote and directed own short play about the fall of the Berlin Wall.

VI. HOBBIES AND INTERESTS	SCHOOL YEARS	HRS. PER WK./WKS. PER YR.	DESCRIPTIONS
Independent Reading	9, 10, 11, 12	7/50	Ashberry, Baudelaire, Rilke, Stoppard, Ionesco, Havel.

[6]Articles submitted with application as "Exhibit E."

Creative Writing	9, 10, 11, 12	5/50	Poetry, short stories, plays.
Tennis	9, 10, 11, 12	4/25	Advanced player.
Vintage Clothing	9, 10, 11, 12	2/50	Avid collector.

BRAG SHEET IMPROVEMENT RESULTS: STEPHANIE CHASE

Stephanie's Final Brag Sheet:	8 points

Although Stephanie's brag sheet shows overwhelming improvement, it still does not earn the top IvyWise score of 9 points. Stephanie's application was up against students from her own school with equally impressive community service and awards records who had also ranked at the top of national sports and music competitions and had worked their way through paid summer internships at major U.S. business institutions. Although Stephanie's deep interest and high level of achievement in drama, English, and history as well as her considerable volunteer experiences are quite impressive, they are not as outstanding when viewed within the context of the exceptional opportunities available at Peter Egret. In addition to dropping the French Club, Stephanie didn't have many school-spirited activities, and nearly all of her volunteer work was a direct result of Barbara's cancer. The question begs itself: If Barbara hadn't fallen ill, what would Stephanie have done? In the ninth grade she did no volunteer work to speak of. The very nature of this absence indicates that she may have lived a very sheltered—and perhaps even spoiled—life. No one would want her to spend less time with breast cancer fund-raising (or drama and creative writing, for that matter), but an admissions reader might be looking for a student such as Stephanie to set an example by getting involved in difficult social issues facing communities other than her own. Cleaning up beaches and feeding the homeless in France comes close but stands alone as an activity that had a direct impact on citizens of less wealth and privilege.

Chapter Five

 PERSONAL SUPPORT

The Importance of Personal Support

Although requirements differ from college to college, the Personal Support section of the application is usually composed of a required letter from your high school's college counselor, two teacher recommendations from instructors of your choice, and either an on-campus or alumni interview, although some schools do not require an interview at all. These four elements form an extremely important component of the selective college application, as they help an admissions committee understand who you are as a person both inside and outside the classroom. From the letters of recommendation, prospective colleges will learn about your character: how you interact with your peers and classmates, how well you prepare for your classes, the level of your engagement in the classroom, your reaction to setbacks, your contribution to on-campus life, and your dedication to your extracurricular activities. **The single most important piece of advice I give my students concerning the three letters of support is to start cultivating relationships with their counselors and teachers as early in their high school careers as possible.** The more time you give yourself, the better your odds of forging lasting bonds with those teachers you truly admire and respect. Nurture these relationships! By visiting your teachers often in office hours, taking an active role in your own education, and maintaining a positive attitude along the way, you will impress upon them your drive, determination, and love of learning, furnishing them with anecdotal evidence to support the positive claims they will make on your behalf in their letters of recommendation. By giving your letter writers plenty of time and reason to write glowing reports about your character and your performance, you can practically guarantee acing this section of the application, further convincing your readers that you would be an invaluable asset to their institution. It is important to remember not to request to see your letters of recommendation prior to their submission to your chosen schools. Your teachers will see this waiver clearly marked on the recommendation forms you provide them. Waiving your right to see their letters is essential to ensuring both honesty and trust in your teacher's assessments.

In terms of the interview, the main advice I give my students is to become a mini-expert in the college. Be prepared for each and every interview by doing extensive research into the curricular and extracurricular opportunities available at each college, arming yourself with a list of intelligent questions that you are prepared to ask the interviewer. In this way, you will ensure that the interview becomes a lively dialogue in which you learn as much about the personality of the college in question as the interviewer learns about you. As a result, the interviewer will be inclined to write a positive report about your meeting, another supporting document that will become a part of your college application dossier. In addition to the personal essay and the letters of recommendation, the interview is a unique opportunity for you to come alive in the mind of your admission reader. Outside of the information session and campus tour—which are clearly less about you and more about the school—this is a college's one real chance to see you up close and personal. So don't hide! Just be yourself!

As you read through David, Ronald, and Stephanie's personal support profiles and evaluations, you should compile a list of everything you will need to do in order to ensure the best possible reinforcement from this section of your own college applications. Please note that the letters appearing in this chapter were generously furnished to me after the fact by the many counselors and teachers who wrote them. Their names and some details have been changed to protect their anonymity.

PERSONAL SUPPORT PROFILE: DAVID HOROWITZ

A number of major red flags emerged from the Personal Support section of David's applications. These inadequacies revolved primarily around David's overall unwillingness to engage with his counselor and teachers outside of their normally sanctioned interaction. In general, David's admissions readers probably found cause for worry in the discrepancy between David's great academic productivity and his general shyness in the classroom. An admissions reader would also have assumed that David's tepid counselor letter was a result of his infrequent visits. Although this may not have been the case, most of the colleges David applied to saw nothing that refuted the interpretation of David's shyness as a lack of interest in the college itself. David also displayed inadequate preparation in his first interviews, which sent a negative message to the admissions committees. Here was a kid, they must have imagined, who was a genius on

low students. Try to maintain a good attitude. If you treat your teachers and peers with respect, people will notice and be much more willing to write nice things about you. **Everything you do in the classroom can and will be used either for or against you in your recommendation letters.**

• **DON'T forget to write a thank-you note** to your counselor, your teachers, and anyone who has written a letter of recommendation on your behalf.

What do you think about outside letters of support?

(1) Dan Evans at the University of Pennsylvania has encountered application files with close to fifty letters. Of course, most of them started sounding the same. Mr. Evans welcomes letters that provide new information about the applicant, regardless of the length of the letter or the prestige of the writer. Length for the sake of length, however, is bad. If you turn in twenty to thirty letters, the reader will not have enough time to do more than skim each one.

(2) John Birney at Johns Hopkins University has seen in excess of fifty letters of recommendation in a single application. Just to get an idea how outrageous that is, Hopkins prefers two or three.

(3) Marianne M. Kosiewicz at the University of Virginia has said that letters of support can augment an application but cannot compensate for weak credentials. Meaningful com-

ments in one letter are more influential than quantities of letters that merely reiterate the transcript.

(4) Richard Avitabile, formerly of NYU, warns that too many letters cause admissions readers to look deeper into the candidate's profile to discover what is being compensated for. The best outside letters are heartfelt—letters from a neighbor, for instance, who praises the applicant for baby-sitting their developmentally challenged son and mowing their lawn just to help out, without asking for any compensation. Now that's character!

paper but who didn't feel compelled to share anything personal—probably because he considered himself a shoo-in. Of course, we know that David acted this way only because of his natural shyness— but how can a college admissions committee tell the two attitudes apart? That is the problem with being quiet: No one knows how to interpret silence with any measure of surety. David was certainly qualified to attend many of the colleges he applied to, but he did very little on his original application to prove to his admissions reader that he deserved to be given the opportunity to go there.

With these general criticisms in mind, please read through the following pages, where you will find David's counselor letter and the two teacher recommendation letters that accompanied David's original application to Johns Hopkins University, now his top-choice school. Following each letter, you will find my evaluation of its relative strengths and weaknesses as judged from the perspective of the IvyWise Index. At the end of the section, I will share with you the advice I gave David as well as the results of the strategies we developed to radically increase his score in these areas.

COUNSELOR RECOMMENDATION

For: David Horowitz
From: Carol Himmelfarb
           College Guidance Counselor
           Singer Yeshiva High School

David arrived at Singer Yeshiva High School at the beginning of his sophomore year from a large public high school in his area. An academically gifted young man, David felt that his former school was not challenging enough. The majority of his grades there were in the 90's, and he received a perfect 100 in four out of eleven courses. The move, and the much longer commute (over an hour each way!), have had little effect on David's superb academic achievement. David has a perfect 4.0 GPA (we do not weight grades), and he is on the school's National Honor Society. He makes significant contributions to the group dynamics of Singer's classrooms, and his ability to maintain his academic excellence in a dual curriculum of Judaic and General Studies here is yet another mark of his distinction. His high SAT scores are just icing on the cake.

The achievement that stands out most in my mind is David's performance in his Honors Physics course with Mr. Bulga during his junior year. This is one of our high school's most challenging classes, even for those who are naturally gifted in math. David was at a disadvantage coming into it: His former high school offered no accelerated math program. As was expected, David struggled during the beginning of the year. But through rigorous application of his considerable abilities and his natural giftedness in math, David had achieved the highest grade in the course (96) by the end of the first semester.

As a person, David is quiet and unassuming. This does not mean he is lazy or unin-

---

Have you ever received a negative letter?

(1) Adam Max, at Emory University, says it is usually more a question of tone than of any overt statements condemning the applicant. Normally, writers will hint that the student has not been working to his or her potential and is therefore a risk in terms of long-term college-level performance. Letters like this might contain phrases such as "I can't write about Amanda without first saying..." or "Lynn is capable of stronger work..."

(2) Lloyd Peterson, formerly of Yale and Vassar, received negative letters nearly every day of the admissions season. Some of the telling phrases, words, and signs that convey negative feelings without coming out and saying them are:

● "It is my professional obligation to share with you..."

● "Robert didn't work up to the level of the class..."

● Any sentences that contain the words "arrogant," "intimidating," "underachiever," "classroom distraction," or "disciplinary case."

● Any indications of behavior that is anti-Semitic, homophobic, racist, or criminal by nature.

volved. On the contrary, David is quietly proactive and engaged, especially when it comes to a perceived injustice in the classroom. He is always willing to speak up and explain what is wrong and how best to fix it. I witnessed this personally when I sat in on his Honors Physics course one day and students were asked to use a malfunctioning computer program to respond to an in-class assignment. The majority of the students in the class were openly frustrated by the malfunction and responded angrily to the teacher, who was not prepared for such an uproar. As communication broke down, David jumped in, procuring the necessary help without offending anyone and even offering the programming solution that eventually brought the computers and the classroom back on-line. David was calm, quick, courteous, and effective throughout the entire affair.

Overall, David is one of the most thorough, dedicated, concentrated, and fastidious students I have ever met. There are times, however, when he is too focused on his academic performance to the detriment of the learning process itself. For example, one of his French teachers last year commented that while he receives excellent grades, has fantastic pronunciation, and is one of his star pupils, he could use a healthy dose of self-confidence—it seems this humble student believes he is going to fail every quiz and is honestly shocked when he receives one of his typically excellent grades. Although this clearly motivates him to study harder for each exam, it can get annoying for fellow students who may misinterpret his angst as melodramatic gloating.

With his dual curriculum and his grueling daily commute, it is a truly remarkable sign of David's dedication to all aspects of the community that he is still able to participate in numerous extracurricular activities in and around school. David was a member of the Hockey Team and Model UN in ninth grade at his former public high school. For the past three years, David has been an important member of our school's College Bowl. He has also taken piano for the past eight years and will be contributing his considerable musical talent this year to the School Band. During our "club hour," David was a member of our Chess Team for the past three years and even tackled Sign Language for a semester. Last year, David participated in a special trip to Washington, D.C., called "Panim El Panim," sponsored by the Washington Institute for Jewish Leadership Values and The

George Washington University. This only deepened David's interest in government, history, and law. This year he is also the Hebrew Editor of the school yearbook. This comes as no surprise, since David reads a Hebrew newspaper daily to stay informed about the Israeli political situation.

David has also been a volunteer computer technician in my counseling office, leading a group of several students who maintain our complicated website. He works well as a leader and his fellow students appear to respond to him favorably. David was especially efficient at setting up a college interest tutorial on the computer and scheduling counselees to take it. David is an excellent young man and I have no doubt that he is going to be very successful in his adult life. David would be an asset to any college, both in and outside the classroom. He has the makings of a true scholar, always striving to learn more and understand the way our world functions.

I recommend David Horowitz most enthusiastically.

Sincerely,
Carol Himmelfarb

COUNSELOR LETTER EVALUATION: DAVID HOROWITZ

David's Counselor Letter:	5 points

• No insight into personality

One-fourth of David's entire Personal Support score stems from this letter. Although it certainly recommends David's excellent academic abilities, it contains only a single telling anecdote about David's personality. And even that story—that David was able to rescue the class from a computer meltdown in a calm and conscientious manner—tells an admissions reader much less about David's personality than it does about his trust in his own technical abilities. That he worked as a computer technician in the College Counseling Office corroborates this—his greatest contribution was a tutorial that he programmed on the computer. All in all, we get the sense of a student who would rather interact with a computer than another human being, an unfortunate association for a student whose application already stressed the technical over the personal. We are left making the logical conclusion that David had no other interaction with his college counselor outside of these moments when he impressed her with his technical skill.

• Dropped activities

In addition, David's counselor letter inadvertently reveals that he dropped Hockey and Model UN when he came to Singer Yeshiva. Although David had no direct control over the content of his counselor's letter, it hints to an admissions reader that he failed to explain his personal record adequately to Ms. Himmelfarb prior to having her write her letter. Either David should have explained to her why he was unable to pursue these particular interests at his new school, or he should have asked Ms. Himmelfarb to leave indication of such inconsistency completely out. Although this may sound presumptuous, keep in mind that most college counselors have written hundreds of letters and are well aware of what works and what doesn't work. Given their often grueling student load, however, it is often up to the student to help point his or her counselor in the right direction. If your counselor balks when you attempt to do this, you must simply trust that he or she will write the best letter they feel comfortable writing.

• Laundry list of activities that should be in brag sheet

A large part of David's college counselor letter reads like a laundry list of activities. These bits of biographical data should have been covered in David's brag sheet—which they weren't—leaving room for the counselor to comment on David's more personal qualities. Lack of personal detail must have forced the admissions committee at Johns Hopkins (and the other schools where he was flat-out rejected) to assume that his counselor never really got a chance to get to know David. If she was going to highlight an activity, Ms. Himmelfarb should have done so in the context of an anecdote. Ultimately, it was David's responsibility to meet with her more and provide her with such anecdotes before she set about writing her letter.

• Inconsistency

There are many activities that emerge in David's counselor letter that David neglected to mention elsewhere. Colleges want an application that is consistent, one that stresses the same abilities and proclivities in each of its elements and thus produces a clear and elaborate picture of the applicant. Was David being modest by not mentioning Sign Language anywhere on his application? Or did he hate it enough never to refer to it again? Or was he simply lazy or distracted during the actual writing of his college applications? If questions such as these linger after reading his counselor letter, then the letter did not serve its purpose. Again, David should have been more forthcoming, both to Ms. Himmelfarb and on his application, about his passionate commitment to his numerous activities.

LETTER OF RECOMMENDATION FOR DAVID HOROWITZ

To whom it may concern,

Mr. David Horowitz is an exceptional young man. Well-organized, full of talent and as intelligent as they come, he is a model student and citizen. He is acutely focused while also very broadly read; he is intensely serious while also wonderfully easygoing. I count myself lucky to have worked with David on numerous occasions and in widely varying circumstances. I have witnessed him interacting with his peers, our faculty, and the administration. In each of these dealings, he is spirited, fair, courageous, and open-minded. He grapples with new concepts, challenging himself to learn and grow. He has a deep understanding of people and the world. He uses his many talents to serve his school, his classmates, and his community. Throughout all our shared experiences, I have been consistently impressed with David's maturity, intelligence, even-keeled personality, drive, and determination.

David greets new intellectual challenges head-on, with a refreshingly precise attention to detail and bold, undaunted creativity. In all things, he displays an admirable degree of stamina and focus. In order to fully comprehend the scope of David's achievement, you must understand that his school day, including his commute, begins at 7:00 A.M. and ends at 7:00 P.M., during which time he carries a daily academic load of nine courses and participates in numerous extracurricular activities. Despite the challenges facing him, David never fails to bring to his classroom presence and laboratory work a noteworthy balance of enthusiastic industriousness and solid workmanship. David was consistently an integral part of the most memorable discussions and interchanges in both my Judaic Studies and science classes. He is extremely cooperative in groups, listens well, and challenges others to achieve at his high level of accomplishment. David is responsible and self-disciplined in all that he does, an orderly and brilliant mind unencumbered by vanity or self-righteousness.

There is one area in particular in which David distinguishes himself, even from the other brilliant, energetic, and highly successful young scholars it has been my privilege to teach. David shows great sensitivity to the poetical and ethical lessons of the Biblical prophets and Talmudic sages. His considerable linguistic skills have given him access to those works in their original, powerful form, allowing David to shape his growing young mind around many of the conceptual, artistic, judicial, and ethical cornerstones of our civilization. Alongside his general education, David has developed a deep concern for the welfare of his fellow man and for the societal laws that govern us. This sensitivity to the needs of the individual governs his interactions with others, as well as the goals he sets for himself. It is a true mark of his efficiency and hard work that he is able to juggle both a dual curriculum and a wide range of outside interests including sports, music, computer technology, Sign Language, political theory, and student government. That he excels at all of these is indicative of his natural talent and his sustained determination. Complementing these superlative academic abilities is an innate professionalism, a truly refined character, a generous nature, and a delightfully grown-up sense of humor. He is respected and liked by all those who come into contact with him, making a lasting impression with his maturity, honesty, perseverance, and positive outlook on life.

All in all, Mr. Horowitz is truly a remarkable, multifaceted young individual whose insight and compassion will contribute significantly to any college community. I wholeheartedly endorse his commanding intellect with full belief that he will continue to educate and motivate himself to ever loftier pursuits, helping to shape our country's future with brilliance, modesty, and understanding.

Sincerely,

Rabbi Dr. Eugene Maccoby

Chairperson, Physics Department

Teacher, Judaic Studies

Singer Yeshiva High School

FIRST TEACHER RECOMMENDATION EVALUATION: DAVID HOROWITZ

David's First Teacher Recommendation:	7 points

• Telling, not showing

David's first teacher recommendation letter left me breathless. Not with admiration for its beauty, but with frustration at its exhausting descriptions. While obviously quite strong in support of David's character, the letter fails to cite any specific examples of David's abilities in action, eschewing anecdotes for adjectives. It all sounds quite impressive, until you realize that the entire letter is simply a list of descriptive phrases that, in the end, risk sounding insincere or contradictory. This is a classic example of what high school English teachers mean when they decry the evils of "telling" in favor of "showing." In short, David doesn't come to life for the reader. There is very little recourse for students in a scenario such as this. Not knowing the contents of his letter, David had to rely on Dr. Maccoby to do the best job he could. Unfortunately, an admission reader would most likely infer from Dr. Maccoby's letter that their relationship remained largely formal. Had David spoken more often with him in a personal manner, Dr. Maccoby may have learned a few telling details about his subject or even a few revealing anecdotes. More important, David might have received a higher score for this section of his application on the IvyWise Index. As it stands, however, despite its stylistic shortcomings, this recommendation letter is obviously very strong and certainly counts more in David's favor than against him.

LETTER OF SUPPORT FOR DAVID HOROWITZ

David is a pleasure to work with as a student and a delight to know as a person. He is a curious, keen observer. He thrives off complexity and is always involved in class discussion. He reasons well and demonstrates superior intellectual ability. He learns rapidly and easily, efficiently making use of what he has learned. His scores on the AP Chemistry test and the Chemistry SAT I demonstrate this. He must be challenged in order to do well. He has strong moral and social concerns and a fantastic sense of humor. He will be a great asset to any college.

Sincerely,

Jon Glickman

Chemistry Teacher

Singer Yeshiva High School

SECOND TEACHER RECOMMENDATION EVALUATION: DAVID HOROWITZ

David's Second Teacher Recommendation:	2 points

- **Way too short**

With its overall brevity and total lack of detail, this second letter detracted more from David's application than enhanced it. An admissions committee must have gotten the distinct feeling that this teacher didn't know David very well or that he was being brief in order to avoid saying anything negative. Although David had no control over the final contents of his letter, he clearly did not choose a teacher with whom he had worked closely and felt comfortable sharing. My suspicion is that David chose this writer because he teaches Chemistry, a subject that David was interested in highlighting to his prospective colleges. Based on its generic quality, however, an admissions reader would have been forced to conclude that David must have run out of teachers with whom he had a personal rapport, opting for one who gave him a good grade. Again, this does not speak well for David's personality, and his score of 2 on this letter reflects these glaring inadequacies.

INTERVIEW EVALUATION: DAVID HOROWITZ

During the course of our in-depth consultation, David described to me in as much detail as possible the content of his first interview with Johns Hopkins. In addition, David's high school college counselor received feedback from David's interviewer, warning her that David had interviewed terribly. Ms. Himmelfarb then communicated the contents of their conversation to David personally, urging him to prepare differently for his next interview. David relayed all of this bad news to me. The following evaluation is based on his recollections. Again, the maximum Ivywise Index ranking for each of the four Personal Support sections is 9 points.

David's Initial Interview:	1 point

• **Too quiet!**

David was painfully shy during his interview and did little to recommend himself to his interviewer. Normally some sort of social anxiety disorder can cause this behavior in others, but in David's case it was partially a product of his upbringing. The strict tenets of Jewish Orthodoxy preach modesty in all things. Unfortunately, modesty in the case of an interview can be perceived as both lack of passion and lack of conviction. The whole point of an interview is to share yourself with your prospective college in a way that no other application element allows. David would have been better off with no interview at all than this dismally quiet performance.

• No research!

In addition to his general shyness, David failed to research the offerings at any of his schools and was therefore unable to ask any well thought-out questions during his interviews. At Johns Hopkins, this contributed to the lackluster impression he gave of his candidacy. Even if Johns Hopkins was not originally his first choice college, David should have spent a good deal of time getting to know its offerings in order to give at least the impression that he applied there for a reason. As it was, David never tried to wow his interviewer with any in-depth knowledge of the school, nor did he try to sell himself with any gusto. As a result, Johns Hopkins was forced to conclude that David never had any intention of attending their school. If a college gets this feeling during the application process, they have no motivation to accept the student, especially if they are worried, as most selective colleges are, about their yield—i.e., the percentage of admitted students who accept their offers of admission. Johns Hopkins ended up waitlisting David only because his superior academic standing made him an attractive candidate despite these glaring red flags. In a sense, Johns Hopkins was saying to David: Show us you care, and maybe we can strike a deal.

• Monologue instead of dialogue

David failed to ask any questions during his interviews, erroneously believing that the interview was a one-way street, a chance for him to answer a few biographical questions and be done with it. In this, he was wrong. The interviews were his best chance to get to know the colleges he was considering. In a sense, David failed to realize that he was shopping for a school as much as the school was shopping for a student. By thinking of the interview as a dialogue, and not a monologue, David would have appeared more vivacious and interested.

He also would have given himself a chance to test whether the schools on his list were appropriate to his needs. Even though David hadn't seriously considered Johns Hopkins to begin with, it became clear during the admissions process that its blend of strong sciences, engineering, international studies, and humanities was well-suited to his interests—which he didn't realize until it was almost too late.

Considering David's scores from the four aspects of the Personal Support section:

David's Counselor Letter:	5 points
David's First Teacher Recommendation:	7 points
David's Second Teacher Recommendation:	2 points
David's Initial Interview:	1 point

We arrive at the following average, out of 9 possible points:

David's Initial Personal Support Score:	**3.75 points**

PERSONAL SUPPORT IMPROVEMENT STRATEGIES: DAVID HOROWITZ

Clearly, it was too late in the game for David to approach another group of teachers for new letters of recommendation. In addition, David's counselor's letter contained nothing truly negative, so there was no reason for him to visit her again, hoping to get to know her better, then asking her to write another letter on his behalf. Instead, David concentrated his energies on setting up and preparing for a second interview at Johns Hopkins, now his number one choice, using IvyWise strategies and tips to bolster his confidence and empower him with a wealth of knowledge about both himself and his target school. To begin with, David used the extensive research he had begun to do for his new and improved "Why Johns Hopkins?" essay (see Chapter 6) to formulate a number of questions he might ask his interviewer. Prepared in this way, David was able to express his knowledge of and overwhelming interest in the specific offerings at Johns Hopkins. I also gave David a thorough personal interest questionnaire that allowed him to craft responses to numerous possible interview questions, ranging from academic interests to world literature to international politics. Once he felt he was comfortable with the results of his research (both into himself and into Hopkins), David contacted his Hopkins regional interviewer for a second interview. Since David was so reticent in his previous interview, I also urged him to overcome his natural shyness by going through mock interviews and copious sample interview questions in real time with me under the same high-pressure conditions he would encounter in the actual interview.

David's Final Interview Score:	8 points

Bolstered by his extensive preparation, David was able to shine in his second interview. When he described to me how it went, I was thrilled. David's new research helped him demonstrate a heartfelt and detailed interest in Johns Hopkins. His newfound self-confidence allowed him to come out of his shell and share his unique perspective with his interviewer. As a result, he was able to increase his IvyWise ranking for this section considerably.

As a result of this increase in David's interview score, his overall average score for the "Personal Support" section of the IvyWise Index jumps:

David's Counselor Letter:	5 points
David's First Teacher Recommendation:	7 points
David's Second Teacher Recommendation:	2 points
David's Final Interview:	8 points

David's Final Personal Support Score:	5.5 points

PERSONAL SUPPORT PROFILE:
RONALD SIEGAL

For his letters of recommendation, I had Ronald approach teachers with whom he had an excellent rapport both inside and outside the classroom, teachers in whose classes, clubs, or organizations he had worked especially hard. Originally, Ronald was tempted to ask his freshman year Math teacher who had given him an easy A, but who did not know him well. I told Ronald that a recommendation from his Spanish teacher, who hadn't always given him an A, but who had taught him in several courses and knew him from various extracurricular experiences, would carry much more weight. This decision had three advantages: By knowing him well inside the classroom, his Spanish teacher was able to attest to Ronald's tenacity and extraordinary work ethic; by knowing him outside the classroom, she was able to comment on Ronald's personality and his contribution to his school and community; finally, by knowing him over a long period of time, she was able to comment on any progress he had made both as a student and as a young man. If a letter writer is unable to do this, the recommendation risks degenerating into a list of attributes or character traits devoid of life, adding nothing to an applicant's file. But a poignant series of anecdotes bringing the candidate to life as a person and a scholar can contribute invaluably to the personal profile of any application.

In addition to his counselor recommendation and his two teacher recommendations, I had Ronald request letters of support from two outside sources: his private art teacher with whom he had studied extensively for many years and the Executive Treasurer of the Cleveland Teen Center whose assistant Ronald had become during his junior year. Extra support letters such as these highlight a candidate's significant out-of-classroom experiences and skills. They also reveal characteristics such as responsibility and sociability by focusing on the candidate's success at tackling nonacademic projects and interacting with the community at large. Again, as with his academic letters, Ronald was careful to choose two outside writers with whom he had worked extensively and who could therefore attest to his full range of strengths and abilities.

Even prior to meeting with me, Ronald knew the importance of research. He understood the edge it would give him for both his "Why U. Penn?" essay and his interview. He also knew it would help him decide if the University of Pennsylvania was the right school for him on both an academic and a personal level. As a result of his detailed exploration of U. Penn's numerous scholastic and extracurricular offerings, Ronald was able to produce an excellent essay "picturing himself" in his first semester at U. Penn. There is no doubt that this helped to convince the admissions committee that Ronald knew what he was talking about when he applied early. In addition to this clear advantage on the essay, however, Ronald was able to use his extensive research to prepare for his on-campus interview with a representative of U. Penn's admissions office. This, coupled with his honest, probing assessment of his own strengths and weaknesses during an extensive interview preparation process, resulted in an exceptional interview, one in which he was able to express his interest in U. Penn and sell himself to his interviewer with utter conviction.

Over the next few pages, you will find Ronald Siegal's fantastic letters of support as they arrived with his Early Decision application to the University of Pennsylvania. I will not analyze each letter separately; rather, I urge you to take them all as models—not in the sense that you should ask directly for letters such as these from your recommending teachers, but in the sense that these letters represent the goal, the prize, if you will, of all the hard work you have already been doing to get to know your teachers outside the classroom and to demonstrate to them your many excellent skills and attributes. If you get daunted, just return to these letters and imagine everything that Ronald must have done in order to receive such a high level of praise. Imagine all the hard work he put into his classes, his art, and his volunteer work. Imagine the positive attitude he must have maintained throughout his grueling schedule. Try to picture the buoyant, effervescent personality it must have taken to light up the room the way his counselor and teachers claim Ronald did. That is what it takes to get letters like Ronald's, and that is what it takes to get into the selective college of your dreams. If you feel you are not already on the path toward receiving this kind of praise and support, fear not: *It is never too late to start* giving that extra effort and ensuring that your personal support profile is the absolute strongest it can be.

COUNSELOR RECOMMENDATION FOR RONALD SIEGAL

Ronald Siegal has been an exceptional member of our high school community for over three years. Not a day passes when I am not made aware, in some way, of his contribution to our lives. Whether it is the murals he painted on the walls of our central hallway as part of the National Art Honor Society, or an article on the latest exhibit at the Cleveland Art Museum for his column in our high school newspaper, the *Swan*, or the smile on the face of a freshman he helped counsel as part of my office's Peer Counselor program, I am constantly astounded by the depth and scope of Ronald's interests and activities. To think that he is also a hard-working student who has challenged himself academically with an extraordinary course load is truly astounding. He faces his busy schedule with the quiet self-assurance of a mature and professional young man who knows what he wants and how to get it. Kind, considerate, and never one to brag, it is all the more amazing that such an important role is played by such an unassuming young man.

I can remember vividly when Ronald first came into my office as a freshman. He wanted to get involved with the Student Activities Committee, the student organization responsible for such things as Homecoming, Junior and Senior Prom, and field trips to Chicago and New York. Even as a freshman he had a clear sense of his agenda: He wanted to organize an art-related activity, perhaps a trip to a museum or a gallery in downtown Cleveland. He attended the first meeting and, according to then President Clyde Barnsdale, it was as if Ronald had already been a member for four years. He argued his case eloquently in front of the seasoned committee and won not only their support for his idea, but a place on the committee itself. They provided him with a telephone and a list of contacts—and the rest is history. Four years later, countless students have benefited from the Swanee Gallery Crawl, two nights each semester devoted to exploring the gallery district in downtown Cleveland, taking in the sights, analyzing contemporary art, and eating at a banquet-style Chinese restaurant in the area—all organized by Ronald, completely funded by the committee. It is just this sort of gumption, this clarity of motive, and this fastidious follow-through that has made Ronald such a memorable part of so many in-school and extracurricular activities.

Active since tenth grade in the Cleveland Teen Center, Ronald is also dedicated to his community at large. The Teen Center offers a sports and recreation refuge to troubled inner city youths. Ronald first heard about the organization when he became a Peer Counselor here in my office in the tenth grade. He was actually helping another student explore the possibility of volunteering at the center when it struck him that he would be interested in it himself. As is Ronald's way, the next thing anyone knew, he had become their Hiring Interviewer, responsible for screening all applicants who wished to become Youth Group Leaders (the equivalent of a camp counselor) at the center. In addition to this regional work, Ronald has also been very active in the March of Dimes Birth Defects Foundation since the eleventh grade. He was the county's Youth Coordinator for their annual WalkAmerica fund-raising event, and he later served as the President of their Youth Leadership Council for the city of Cleveland. None of these achievements ever comes as a surprise to me, as Ronald engages passionately with whatever cause he chooses to adopt. He is hands-down the most dedicated student I have encountered in my seven years at Swanee, something his instructors attest to when they use words such as "driven," "hard-working," "dauntless," and "self-motivated" in their classroom evaluations. The same can be said for his college search. Ronald was literally the first person in his entire class (of over 300!) to visit me and establish a relationship with my office—all in the spring semester of his sophomore year!

This extraordinary work ethic, this adult sense of planning and preparation, and this dedication to his self-established goals both inside and outside the classroom—these are the attributes that will make Ronald Siegal an invaluable member of any college community.

I recommend him most enthusiastically and without reserve.

Sincerely,
Susan Cloverdale
College Guidance Counselor
Swanee High School

To Whom It May Concern,

I first met Ronald Siegal as his honors Spanish teacher in the ninth grade. The Ronald I met then I like to call "Reticent Ronald." He was reluctant to try out his superior Spanish skills in the classroom. When I asked him why a student with such an obvious ear for the language would hold himself back, he answered that he was afraid the other students would get discouraged. I explained to him that everyone has his or her strengths and weaknesses, and that it would be far better for him to lead by example. Ronald didn't require a second talking-to. From that moment forward, he was able to channel his considerable Spanish skills and his natural leadership skills into becoming the cornerstone of the many Spanish classes, outings, and experiences I have had the privilege of sharing with him. Because of his natural accent and facility with the grammar, I urged Ronald to join the Spanish Club, of which I am the faculty adviser. I will never forget the first time he sat down with us. He was clearly a bit intimidated by the other, more advanced students, and I could almost see the wheels turning as Ronald decided that he would someday master the Spanish language. Unsurprisingly, by the beginning of his sophomore year, Ronald had been elected Secretary of the Spanish Club.

It wasn't until later that Ronald's true talent began to emerge. Between tenth and eleventh grades, Ronald studied at an ASA-sponsored school in Madrid, Spain, where he did volunteer street cleanup work, studied the Spanish language and took courses in Art History. By coincidence, I was the faculty adviser on that trip and I witnessed first-hand Ronald's love of both knowledge and adventure. We took a field trip to the world-famous Guggenheim Museum in Bilbao, where Ronald was able to explain one of Dali's paintings *in Spanish* to a group of international students, placing the work in the context of surrealism and its contribution to the history of art. Not an hour later, this mature young man was scaling the medieval walls by the banks of the river like a youthful mountain climber, following the scent of a *bocadillo* shop, where I saw him eat with such gusto that I was reminded of his age, his vitality, and his love of life. By the time we got back to Cleveland, it was a different Ronald I had come to expect. This was Ronald the leader beginning to emerge, a Ronald I got to know well as his honors Spanish teacher in the eleventh grade. Again I was impressed by his diligent study habits, his honest, fearless approach to new grammatical material, and his willingness to help others find their way through the language. Not only did he remain with the Spanish Club, he became our vice president, organizing a trip to the La Raza Cultural Center in Cleveland, where Swanee students spoke Spanish the whole day while new citizens of Spanish nationality got a chance to practice their English.

By his senior year, Ronald was the logical choice for president of our organization. In the third week of the semester, Ronald held a special assembly at which he directed members of the Spanish Club in an uproarious stage-spoof of *Don Quixote*. As a result of this campaign to interest students in both the Spanish language and the Spanish Club, Ronald miraculously increased our membership by 50 percent. In addition to the considerable time he has devoted to the club—as well as to his numerous other extracurricular activities—Ronald has been the star pupil in my AP Spanish Language class this year. His finesse with the syntax, his subtle understanding of grammatical structure, and his natural ear for the tone, pitch, and rhythm of the language assure me Ronald will have no trouble acing his AP Spanish Language exam in the spring. Continually improving, continually challenging himself, Ronald is a joy to teach and a marvel to witness as he grows into a confident, considerate, and creative young man. I was not at all surprised to hear that, in addition to his duties as president of the Spanish Club and his relentless self-improvement in my course, Ronald has been giving private Spanish tutorials for the past two years, helping younger students discover the joys and pitfalls of the language while earning some extra spending money.

I recommend Ronald Siegal unequivocally as one the best all-around students I have ever taught.

Sincerely,
Sara Hernández
Honors Spanish Teacher
Faculty Adviser to the Spanish Club
Swanee High School

To: The Admissions Committee

From: Dr. Mark Fabian
            AP U.S. History Teacher
            Swanee High School

RE: Ronald Siegal

Dear Admissions Committee,

I instructed Ronald Siegal during what is reputed to be the most grueling course at Swanee High School, the dreaded Advanced Placement U.S. History double-course sequence that prepares students to take the AP U.S. History examination in the spring of their junior year. I mention this "reputation" not to lend credence to such an erroneous moniker. I mention it because Mr. Siegal, perhaps my favorite student in over fifteen years of instruction—and a young man of great spirit and intellect—took this reputation to heart. He walked into my classroom expecting an updated version of the Spanish Inquisition. "That would be European History, Mr. Siegal" I later informed him when his worrying over the topic of our midterm paper cost him days of valuable research time. You see, Ronald was under the impression that history was a discipline of crusty old men locked in dusty old libraries. I pointed out to him that although the study of history does require a considerable amount of painstaking research, it is also a discipline of conjecture, hypothesis, and interpretation. He seemed to lighten up. I knew from the way he approached his daily homework assignments that he would have no trouble with the painstaking research part of the course as long as he knew there was some "creative" light at the end of the tunnel. We were off to an auspicious start.

It was Ronald's suggestion that we meet every week outside of class for an extra hour on Thursdays. He initiated these sessions because of a poor grade he received on an early take-home examination. He had tried to bite off more than he could chew with this assignment, losing himself in a quagmire of secondary material in lieu of the simple and direct answers I was seeking. At first I could tell he was devastated by his lower grade, thinking perhaps that history was not his strength. Not one to let adversity stand in the way, however, Ronald eventually took matters into his own hands. During our weekly time together, I came to understand the origin of his reputation as a hard-working student with extraordinary self-discipline. As we settled on his first paper topic, "Slave Narratives as Alternative History," Ronald was shocked to learn that he could study what he considered to be works of literature *as history*. But once this breakthrough occurred, there was no looking back. Ronald combined his well-honed attention to detail with his proclivity for creative assertion into an intelligent, well organized, historically accurate, and thematically engaging work. In fact, Ronald's creative adaptation of the tenets of my often-conservative discipline caused me to reassess some of the methodological assumptions underlying my own work in the field. That is a compliment of the highest degree from a teacher of history.

Those hours spent discussing *The Emancipation Proclamation* and *The Gettysburg Address* as examples of "grand narrative history," in relation to the more mundane yet equally insightful depictions of everyday life contained in the slave narratives, were some of the most fascinating and probing conversations I have ever had with a student. Ronald is a mature, self-aware young man who has an enviable ability to relate historical events to his own life. His desire for clarity and understanding has made Ronald an expert researcher as well as an invaluable part of my classroom discussion. As Ronald learned to trust himself and his own unique approach to history, he contributed more frequently and with more poignant observations. By the middle of the second semester, Ronald was a leader in the class, invariably first to respond to difficult questions with both daring hypotheses and well-grounded analyses. I am sure that other instructors can attest to Ronald's uncanny ability to pick up information quickly and to synthesize it with his prior knowledge.

Ronald received an A for the two-course sequence, largely on the strength of his second paper, a brilliant exploration of "The Blacklisting of Hollywood Directors during the McCarthy Era." Again, Ronald chose a topic that interested him on the level of content, treating numerous Hollywood films as historical documents. And he chose it *early*, this time not letting himself worry over his theme or losing himself in what other people had already said on the topic. With time to spare, Ronald produced a well-structured, probing, and accurate analysis of his subject matter, again consulting with me often during our "Thursday Tea," as we came to call it. His eventual scores of 670 on the History SAT II Subject Test and 4 on the AP examination do not accurately reflect Ronald's ability nor his love of historical research—they have more to do with the pressure of the test-taking scenario. Given that, and given the wealth of memorable experiences I have shared with Ronald both inside and outside the classroom, I wholeheartedly recommend him to whatever excellent post-secondary institution is lucky enough to snatch him away from what I am sure will be multiple offers of admission.

Sincerely,
Dr. Mark Fabian

Maya Newman
Art Instructor
The Newman Art School
Cleveland, OH

Dear Admissions Officers,

For the past five years, Ronald Siegal has attended a biweekly, two-hour art class at my art school in downtown Cleveland. Together, we have explored a variety of media, including pencil, colored pencil, pen and ink, and oil pastels.

Ronald's artistic skill is matched only by his commitment to excellence. Never one to cut corners or find the simple solution to a complex formal or compositional problem, Ronald constantly impresses me with his uncanny renderings and fine attention to detail. Whether exploring his own unconscious in a free form, abstract work, or dedicating himself to the faithful reproduction of line and color in one of our many in-class exercises, Ronald consistently displays the highest level of concentration and imagination. In my many years of teaching art, I have rarely encountered such a natural gift coupled with such an exemplary work ethic. Fresh, innovative, and always highly evocative, Ronald's work never ceases to amaze me with its boldness, confidence, and accuracy, despite the handicap of color-blindness. It is truly a testament to his love of art and his thoroughly professional attitude that he has developed an elaborate way of compensating for this disadvantage, producing some of the most dazzling color drawings I have ever encountered.

Intelligent, trustworthy, and compassionate, Ronald is also a fine human being, a quality that certainly aids his artistic development. I remember one occasion in particular when a first-time nude model was having difficulty relaxing in front of our group. Of all the artists who were more experienced with nude renderings, it was Ronald, a relative newcomer at the time, who decided to tell a joke to put the model at ease. We all laughed at the familiar dream Ronald spoke of, in which he suddenly found himself without clothes at school—it could be worse, Ronald was saying to the model; at least she was there of her own free will and getting paid. Unfortunately, Ronald's sketches that day were less than ideal. When a fellow student critiqued what he called their "cartoonish" quality, Ronald did not gripe. He immediately agreed and diligently began to rework his sketches. That is Ronald in a nutshell—always willing to lend a hand and never daunted by the truth. He neither fears change nor seeks it but allows his creativity to mature at its own pace.

Ronald is truly a joy to teach and I will miss him sorely when he goes to college. I have no doubt he will make an excellent contribution to any college on both a personal and an artistic level. I recommend him most enthusiastically.

Sincerely,
Maya Newman

LETTER OF RECOMMENDATION FOR RONALD SIEGAL

Dear Admissions Committee,

I would like to draw your attention to an extraordinary young man among your many applicants. His name is Ronald Siegal, and he has been a crucial member of my organization for over two years. If only high school were longer and he could stay with us, I would feel much better about facing next year's budget meetings and fund-raisers. To say I have come to rely on Ronald would be an understatement. He has become an integral part of my office: filing, organizing, placing calls, keeping the books and, in general, making my life easier. Learning by doing, Ronald picked up these great clerical and computational skills almost instantaneously. Others in our office now rely on him to help them assess the viability of various projects from a budgetary standpoint and Ronald has successfully solicited and processed numerous new donor accounts, raising our overall endowment 15 percent during his tenure.

Above and beyond these great office skills, however, it is Ronald's personality that makes him such an important member of our team. The teens love him and the sponsors love him, a rare combination in a world where rough-and-tumble street kids don't often speak the same language as the corporate representatives responsible for overseeing our use of their generous funds. Ronald acts as a liaison, equally comfortable talking to the children about their latest art projects as he is sitting down with me to present our case for more funding to the directors. Open-minded, conscientious, and giving, Ronald is exactly what every nonprofit organization such as the Cleveland Teen Center needs: a volunteer whose heart reaches out to those he helps yet whose brain understands the business side of our operation. I am not alone here at the Teen Center when I say that Ronald's presence, charm, charisma, and caring will be sorely missed. Enviable is the school that is able to lure such an exceptional and generous young man away.

I give Ronald my highest recommendation.

Sincerely,

Hal Binkley

Executive Treasurer

Cleveland Teen Center

PERSONAL SUPPORT EVALUATION: RONALD SIEGAL

Ronald's Final Personal Support Score:	9 points

- **Great counselor and teacher recommendations.**

It doesn't get much better than Ronald's recommendation letters. All three required letters utilized personal anecdotes to illustrate the creative, caring, and persistent person that Ronald Siegal is. In terms of his application to the University of Pennsylvania, these excellent letters offered further proof that Ronald had an extraordinary work ethic and that he cared deeply about his community. The admissions committee understood right away that only a student with great diligence, persistence, and social skills could have obtained such glowing praise from his counselor and his teachers. By choosing teachers who knew him well and under a wide array of circumstances, Ronald ensured that his letters of support would shed light on the whole of his character, not just isolated aspects. Ultimately, his letters of support made him come alive as a person through the use of telling personal details. All in all, these are some of the strongest letters I have seen, and they overwhelmingly deserve the maximum number of IvyWise Index points.

- **Great and pertinent extra letters**

In addition, Ronald's outside letters of support attested to his ability to translate these excellent personal and academic skills into any situation, whether it be creating artwork or maintaining financial books. Outside letters can have a direct impact on a candidate's profile only when they come from people like Maya Newman and Hal Binkley: teachers and employers who have worked extensively with the candidate outside the classroom and whose letters shed light on characteristics of the applicant that we do not otherwise discover in the application. Although both his art classes at the Newman Art School and his volunteer work at the Cleveland Teen Center are mentioned elsewhere in Ronald's application, these letters give us a lively, story-driven view of Ronald at work in those fields as a vital, interactive member of his intellectual and artistic community.

- **An exceptional interview**

By doing elaborate research into the offerings at the University of Pennsylvania, meditating carefully on his own academic and personal interests and aspirations, and by going through a number of practice interviews with me in actual interview-type situations, Ronald was able to guarantee an exceptional interview with his U. Penn representative. Based on his highly favorable impression of Ronald, the interviewer was able to report back to the admissions committee that Ronald was an exceptional young man whose interests were a perfect fit for their school, despite what might be considered weaknesses in the academic sections of his overall application. This kind of unequivocal support from an interviewer can erase any residual doubt left by other, mediocre application elements and sway an admissions committee to vote in the applicant's favor.

PERSONAL SUPPORT PROFILE: STEPHANIE CHASE

As we have seen, major red flags began to appear in Stephanie's application during our discussion of her transcript and overall academic profile. The radical grade dip she experienced at the beginning of her junior year was left without explanation, and admissions readers at her top choice schools were forced to draw their own conclusions about the reasons behind it. Although she managed to pick up the academic pieces by the end of that same school year, the residual effect of her inexplicable decline at the beginning of what is arguably the most important time in high school more or less guaranteed that colleges like Yale and Wesleyan would waitlist her, essentially demanding that she make the extra effort to explain herself before they would reconsider her application. The negative effects of her choice to remain silent about the circumstances surrounding that period in her life were not isolated to her academic profile, however. By not explaining herself to her high school college counselor or to the two instructors she asked to write recommendation letters on her behalf, Stephanie also guaranteed herself a mediocre score on the Personal Support section of her college applications. If Mr. Hayden and her two teachers didn't know the first thing about Stephanie's problems at home, or about Barbara Murphy's death, or the reasons behind her drinking binge, then how could they possibly paint a complete picture of her in their letters of recommendation? How could they feel comfortable offering unequivocal praise for Stephanie when they knew she was actively deciding not to tell them about the most intimate yet important moment in her life? As a result, all three of Stephanie's letters expressed confusion and concern over that period in her life—as well as a certain reticence when it came to supporting Stephanie's character. The ghost of those few months cast its pallid shadow over what should have been glowing letters of praise.

As you read the following letters, along with my analysis of their relative strengths and weaknesses, try to note the residual effects of Stephanie's understandable yet devastating decision. Try to imagine what the letters would have said had they been written by people who truly understood the most important details of Stephanie's life. Then, based on the familiarity you now have with the IvyWise Index ranking system, try to determine each letter's score, even before my analysis begins. By continuing to test your analytical skills on David, Ronald, and Stephanie's applications, you will come one step closer to becoming an expert on the ins and outs of the selective college admissions process—an expertise that will surely come in handy as you sit down to write your own college applications.

RECOMMENDATION LETTER FOR STEPHANIE CHASE

Dear Admissions Committee,

From what I understand, Stephanie Chase is a gifted writer and performer. Although her participation in on-campus activities has never been as strong as I would like, she remains dedicated to the Drama club, which she helped to found, as well as to her editorial work for both the school newspaper and the school literary journal. In addition, she was the recipient of last year's coveted Saltonstall Award for Excellence in Historical Writing and of a National Gold Key for Creative Writing, both truly great accomplishments considering her lower grades in both subjects at the beginning of her upper year. Although some instructors have called her "distant," "standoffish," and "aloof," the majority of her course reports indicate a young woman of great intelligence, subtle understanding, and truly unique creativity. Clearly, Stephanie Chase would be a great addition to any college classroom, when seen from an academic perspective.

To really know Stephanie, however, you would have to step backstage, so to speak, to the other side of the facade she cultivates. You would have to find the shy, vulnerable, confused teenager who lurks behind the scenes while the more brash, public Stephanie performs her role of fierce thinker, alternative dresser, and independent spirit. Unfortunately, such insight is only rarely granted—and most of us are left with the feeling that we don't truly know Stephanie, even after sustained contact with her. From my perspective, I must admit that she has always seemed a bit removed, especially when it came to her own college admissions process. In general, Stephanie was not as on top of her deadlines and documents as I would have expected her to be, given her great academic achievement. In missing some important deadlines and refusing certain advice, I wondered if there weren't other factors involved, family pressures or personal difficulties that she did not feel comfortable discussing with me, but which influenced her decisions. Unfortunately, I will never know. No one will—unless she decides to tell us. Instead, we are left with the somewhat puzzling picture of a student who has the drive, determination, and creativity to produce, write, and direct her own play during her upper year as a fundraiser for breast cancer research (something she evidently had done during the summer as well) and yet who declines to make an acceptance speech for one of our school's top prizes, the Saltonstall Award; a student who wins the MVP award for the Girls Lacrosse team and yet who never mentions any desire to pursue lacrosse in college, not believing herself worthy. How could she be so vocal and so giving of herself on the one hand and yet so timid and aloof on the other?

I have known Stephanie's family for quite some time and the origin of her obvious difficulties remains a mystery. I know she has a tough act to follow in Dylan Chase, her well-known attorney of a father. Perhaps that explains her on-again-off-again relationship with a young man here at Egret whose imperfect influence on Stephanie's life has resulted in numerous missed classes, dropped activities—including the French club—and, on more than one occasion, a public screaming match that ended in tears. As far as Stephanie's interest in breast cancer goes, no one has ever had breast cancer in her family as far as I know, so its origin remains a mystery as well. Stephanie seems to have taken on this cause wholeheartedly, and yet all of her teachers are in the dark as to why. As I have said: This is typical—it's that 20 percent of Stephanie's personality that shocks, confuses, and seems destined to alienate her from those who would help her most.

From a personal perspective, then, Stephanie is a gamble. She can be gregarious, affectionate, even hilarious. At other times, she just wants to get the job done and get out. That's what makes her silence so frustrating. What is going on inside that turns her off so quickly? Whether she is naturally introverted or perhaps arrogant is hard to tell. She is clearly a gifted young woman whose intense private life is getting in the way. The school that accepts her will have to accept her on the faith that she will eventually work through these issues and blossom into the fantastic young person I know she can be. Believe me when I say, this is one student I wish I felt more comfortable supporting.

Please call me to discuss Stephanie's personal record further.

Sincerely,

Robert Hayden

College Guidance Counselor

Peter Egret Academy

COUNSELOR LETTER EVALUATION: STEPHANIE CHASE

Stephanie's Counselor Letter:	1 point

- **Not personal enough**

It is clear from the lack of personal detail in her counselor recommendation letter that Stephanie did not meet with Mr. Hayden very often, at least not above and beyond the necessary trips to ensure her application materials were in order. It is also clear that when she did meet with him, Stephanie was often unprepared for the encounter, noncommunicative, and generally dismissive of his advice. This is *not* something you want to have happen when you visit your high school college counselor. Since he or she will be writing a crucial letter on your behalf, you must treat this relationship with the respect it deserves. By being both courteous and generous in your personal dealings, you can help to ensure that a letter like this one never accompanies your college applications.

- **Unwilling to share**

The image we get of Stephanie from this letter is that of a naturally brilliant student who, for whatever reasons, refuses to share her brilliance. Her counselor comments that she seemed removed from the college admissions process and wasn't always on top of her documents. These are some of the worst things an admissions reader can hear from a college counselor. They suggest that Stephanie has no real interest in attending college or, worse, that she is a spoiled brat who is used to having Daddy and Mommy take care of nasty nuisances like applications. The last thing you want a college to think, especially if you come from a wealthy, high-profile family like the Chases, is that you are in any way spoiled or that you have taken your privileged position in society for granted and squandered your tremendous opportunities.

• Activities unmentioned elsewhere

Mr. Hayden mentioned Stephanie's breast-cancer fund-raising at home during the summers and as part of her writing, directing, and acting experience during upper year. These are great activities for a counselor letter to mention; the only problem was: Stephanie did not mention them herself anywhere on her original application. If you remember, her only mention of anything close to it appeared on her original brag sheet under the general rubric "charity fund-raising." This displays either an unwillingness to share on Stephanie's part or, worse, hints that Stephanie simply didn't care enough about these activities to do more than jot them down on the application. No matter what the reason, it looks sloppy and inconsistent to have certain activities mentioned in one part of the application but not in another. This is yet another reason to meet with your college counselor as often as possible and as soon as possible to establish firmly those activities that will be stressed throughout the application and that the counselor should highlight in his or her letter.

• Odd kid

Because of the inconsistencies and omissions mentioned above, we are left with an impression of Stephanie as one of those odd, quiet, genius, loner types who, while contributing fantastic things to whatever fields she excels in, is not exactly the most scintillating and gregarious member of her high school community. Stephanie's bizarre combination of acting ability and stage fright on the awards podium, of dedication to sports and community service and aloofness in the college admissions office, paints the picture of a young woman who has a lot of growing up to do before she is ready for college.

• The dreaded "call me"

Finally, and most poignantly, Stephanie's counselor's letter ended with the dreaded "call me." This is one of the worst red flags you can receive, as it indicates to an admissions reader that there are extenuating circumstances surrounding your college application, things that are too delicate or private to mention in a letter. Admissions officers from both Yale and Wesleyan ended up calling Mr. Hayden, from whom they heard, secondhand, about Stephanie's probation for drinking, as well as Dylan's masterful cover-up. Mr. Hayden relayed this type of information via telephone for fear of upsetting Dylan (potentially to the point of a lawsuit) if he had seen it printed in a letter to a prospective college. The "call me" was perhaps the most detrimental red flag on Stephanie's application, as it indicated that she had had severe emotional difficulties, the origins of which were unknown—as well as an overbearing family that had tried its best to cover up these difficulties.

TO: Admissions

FROM: Cyrus Bentham
        Instructor of English
        Peter Egret Academy

RE: The Inimitable Ms. Chase

Before I begin, I would like to state unequivocally that Stephanie Chase is one of the top three English students I have had the privilege to teach in my career of twenty-two years as an instructor. Always ready with an answer to even the most difficult question, always ready to challenge her fellow students, always eager to improve her own skill at writing, Stephanie is that rarest of creatures: a focused, dedicated student who is also an exceptionally creative young woman. Her true strength lies in her ability to analyze literature *from the inside*, from the perspective of a fellow writer and thinker.

I had the pleasure of meeting Stephanie for the first time during the spring semester of her lower year in my honors English course. My inclusive teaching style allows for a number of approaches to the classroom material. That year we focused our intellectual efforts on what I like to call the "Short Form." This includes everything from poetry and aphorisms to philosophical fragments and the more traditional short story. The one longer work of fiction we held up to the light of literary critique was Nabokov's *Pale Fire*, itself a quasi-academic critique of a poem, penned by the author himself, which overflows the normal boundaries of both form and content. Stephanie was the first to grasp the irony in this choice. Upon reading the title of the work on the syllabus, Stephanie commented that this novel was clearly appropriate, since it deconstructed the long form into a series of short form critiques and then reconstructed the short form into the long form it purported to deconstruct. She was grasping at larger concepts here—ones she would not have full command of for a while—but for a second year high school English student, this was a graduate school quality insight.

I was thrilled to learn that Stephanie had planned to take my year-long English course sequence in preparation for the Advanced Placement examinations in both English Language and English Literature. This is a grueling course, with intense work on grammatical principles as well as an exhaustive historical survey of English and American literature. In both fields, Stephanie performed at an exceptionally high level. She possesses the mind of a linguist and semiotician, able to parse out complex syntactical structures and determine their root rhetorical devices and grammatical principles. She also possesses the sensitivity and extraordinary reading skills of an advanced literary critic, able to place works of literature both in their historical and their formal context. What Stephanie did not know coming into the course, she learned quietly and quickly with very little urging from me. I got the sense throughout the course that she was listening intently to the vocabulary I used to discuss literature and was determined, whenever she encountered a new concept, to research and understand it by the beginning of the next class. If you have ever been in a junior English class, especially in this day and age when the combined effects of cinema and television have wreaked havoc on students' interest in language, you know just how exceptional these interests and abilities are.

I can remember one incident in particular, which succinctly illustrates my feelings about Stephanie. During the first semester of our year-long course together, I became concerned when Stephanie began to withdraw both emotionally and intellectually from class. Her insightful comments arrived with less and less frequency. Her weekly journal entries were spotty at best, more often melting into incoherent, notelike observations than penetrating their subject matter with the wit and pith I had come to expect. Coming into that year, I had been anticipating a rewarding interaction with Stephanie, who had been my most impressive student the year before. Although she still came to me during office hours, she chose never to reveal the origins of her obvious malaise. Perhaps it was hormones, boy trouble, or a general adolescent melancholia typical of many juniors when the reality of college and adult life sets in. Whatever the cause, I was sorry to lose her skillful participation, and I wracked my brain trying to come up with a way to draw her out of her shell. Right at this time, another student came to me and asked about Stephanie. The other students, of course, had also begun to notice Stephanie's withdrawal. This other student in particular felt the need to express her concern not as a friend but as a competitor—she believed Stephanie was a snob, the type of student who came into the first few weeks of a course guns blazing, establishing herself as the most gifted thinker and writer in the room, then sitting back and watching stone-faced as the others slogged their way through the material.

I was used to this competitive sort of comment at Egret. My alternative teaching methods—including creative writing assignments, student journal sharing, and gradeless papers—were largely a response to the overtly competitive atmosphere fostered on our campus. But this was something I had yet to encounter. I felt it was my duty to tell Stephanie she was having this effect on her fellow classmates. When I did, she smiled glumly and apologized for being so, as she called it, "out of it." I later saw her approach the student in question and apologize to her as well. That sincerity I found truly admirable. By the time the second trimester rolled around, Stephanie was back to her old self, made aware of her undesired effect on her friends and teachers. The reasons behind this "funk" remain a mystery to me, but I consider it very much in Stephanie's favor that she did the behind-the-scenes work necessary to turn herself around and save both her reputation and her grade.

Among the many accomplishments that set Stephanie apart from her classmates, her continuing dedication to her own creative writing stands out as the most formidable. In response to a paper assignment on the English Romantic poets, Stephanie chose to write a poem of her own, after the style of William Blake. This lengthy, soaring, melancholic, exasperated, yearning, ecstatic poem was the highlight of the year. It captured the essence of the Romantics' quest for ultimate self-knowledge through self-destruction; it played with the English language in a way that brought expression to the very brink of coherence yet returned home at the end of each carefully crafted stanza with the faithfulness of a carrier pigeon alighting from the great beyond. This poem, entitled *Prism and Scale of a Nightless Light*, was an obvious choice for submission to the Gold Key writing competition in the poetry category. Reluctant at first to share her work with the world, unsure whether it was the best among the many fine poetic *essais* contained in her brilliantly edited and illustrated journal of poetry, Stephanie finally overcame her timidity and submitted the poem. I was hardly surprised when the letter came announcing she had won. Taking it in stride, as she does all things, Stephanie signed and framed a copy of the poem for my office.

I hope Stephanie will continue to study with me in the spring of her senior year, when graduating Egret students are given the opportunity to choose an English elective in a specialization of their choice. As she excels at the poetic form, I would cherish the chance to explore the boundaries of language with her again. For now, let it be known that I recommend Stephanie Chase in the most superlative of terms. She will make an exceptional addition to any college campus.

Sincerely,
Cyrus Bentham

FIRST TEACHER RECOMMENDATION EVALUATION: STEPHANIE CHASE

Stephanie's First Recommendation Letter:	**8 points**

• Unexplained grade dip

Stephanie's English teacher, clearly one of her more ardent supporters, made reference to the difficulty Stephanie had experienced during the first trimester of her junior year. Difficulty per se is not a negative attribute. In fact, some of the best teacher recommendations focus on moments when the student struggled through adversity, overcame obstacles, and emerged a stronger, smarter, more resilient scholar and human being. The problem with this observation stemmed from its inexplicability. Although Stephanie visited Mr. Bentham often during office hours, the fact that he knew nothing about her personal troubles would indicate to an admissions reader that the majority of their time spent together was of a more academic nature. Of course, colleges don't necessarily expect you to become friends with your teachers, but a student who feels comfortable interacting with instructors on various levels in high school is a student who will continue to benefit from that kind of confidence throughout college. Had Stephanie felt comfortable telling her English teacher about the reasons behind her grade dip, she may have felt more comfortable talking about it with her college counselor and, in the end, she may have worked it into her application, thus saving her the stress of having to fight her way off the waitlist at Wesleyan. Because of this unwillingness to share her story, Stephanie's otherwise stellar letter of recommendation loses 1 IvyWise Index point.

• Important activities revealed

In addition to the above, Mr. Bentham's recommendation letter inadvertently reveals that Stephanie keeps a brilliant journal of poetry. If, as Mr. Bentham claims, it is of the highest quality, then an admissions reader might stop and wonder why Stephanie did not include it as a supplement to her application. They might also stop to wonder why Stephanie, at the very least, did not choose to include a copy of her award-winning poem, especially since she mentions the award on her initial brag sheet. It was up to Stephanie, the applicant, to make sure her admissions readers were aware of these accomplishments. Coming as they do in a vague brag sheet and a confused letter of recommendation, these omissions risk painting the picture of a painfully shy student unwilling to share her work. It also robs Stephanie of an opportunity to impress her readers with the brilliance of her poetry, something that is surely a rarity these days.

• Unequivocal praise

Despite these lesser red flags, this is one of the stronger recommendation letters I have encountered. It gives us direct insight into Stephanie's passion for poetry and the English language. It relays this passion through illuminating anecdotes that help Stephanie come alive as a person. In calling Stephanie "one of the top three English students" that he has ever taught, Mr. Bentham gives the highest form of praise a teacher can give. Phrases like this are what make an admissions reader take notice, especially when they know that the teacher in question is usually much more parsimonious with his praise.

Dear Admissions Committee,

It is both an honor and a pleasure to recommend Ms. Stephanie Chase as a candidate for college admission. Only rarely in my profession do I encounter such a captivating thinker and skilled historical researcher and writer. Throughout our year-long study of the history of the United States, Ms. Chase continued to improve upon her already substantial accomplishments, challenging herself to rise to ever greater academic heights. As you are most likely aware, Stephanie's final forty-five-page research paper looking at the little known African-American women contributors to the Suffragist Movement won our academy's coveted Saltonstall Award for Excellence in Historical Writing. As I myself had personally recommended Ms. Chase for this prestigious award, I felt quite proud of her deserved achievement. Combining her considerable prose-writing skills and documented strengths in historical research, Ms. Chase captivated the Saltonstall committee and assured herself a place in the annals of Egret history.

I must admit that our relationship did not start out as well as it ended. When our year-long course sequence began, Stephanie's presence in the classroom barely registered. Quiet, aloof, perhaps even condescending, Stephanie spoke only when directly addressed, and then with such penetrating intelligence that it was both confusing and frustrating to imagine why she only spoke when she did. I watched some of the other students roll their eyes whenever Stephanie deigned to finally open her mouth: perhaps worse than a braggart who takes up everyone else's time with mediocre commentary is the genius who refuses to share her insights. After a number of poor grades on both in-class quizzes and smaller paper assignments, Stephanie seemed to be settling into an underachiever role without much ado.

Then something happened. I cannot say exactly what it was, but Stephanie returned from our first trimester break with renewed vigor and an overhauled attitude. As her grades gradually improved and her classroom demeanor brightened, I came to the conclusion that whatever had been holding Stephanie back was circumstantial and not characteristic. By the end of our third trimester together, Ms. Chase had begun to act as a liaison and interpreter between some of the other less-gifted students and myself. Never worried about her own grades, willing to take time from her private research to explain historical concepts and principles to her fellow classmates, Stephanie emerged as a model student from the shambles of our first trimester together. Her presentation on the African-American Suffragettes generated one of the most lively and insightful class discussions I have witnessed in my seventeen years at Egret Academy.

A bit of a loner, but definitely willing to help; not always the most enthusiastic, but certainly the most insightful: that is how I would sum up Ms. Stephanie Chase.

Sincerely,
Joanne Schubart
Instructor of History
Dean of Faculty
Peter Egret Academy

SECOND TEACHER RECOMMENDATION EVALUATION: STEPHANIE CHASE

Stephanie's Second Recommendation Letter:	5 points

• Bad first impression

Unlike Mr. Bentham, Ms. Schubart had never taught Stephanie before their upper year encounter. Based on her first impression, Ms. Schubart was ready to write Stephanie off. Although Stephanie's performance improved radically over the course of the coming year, she had this one chance to make a first impression—and it was a bad one. The residual distaste of this initial encounter was pronounced enough to carry over into Ms. Schubart's letter, where admissions readers were alerted that Stephanie was both an inconsistent academic performer and a potentially standoffish person, neither of which are very desirable attributes from the point of view of college admissions. Let this be as a reminder that every encounter in your high school career can have far-reaching effects for your college admission profile. No single red flag is enough to deny you admission to the school of your choice, but an accumulation of smaller red flags, as in the case of Stephanie, can create an overall negative impression in the minds of an admissions reader.

• Little personal contact

In addition, Stephanie's second letter of recommendation is not very enlightening. Although Stephanie was clearly one of the best students in Ms. Schubart's class, and won the Saltonstall Award for that year, she did not take the time to get to know Ms. Schubart outside of class. The award is impressive, surely, but without a recommendation to back it up, its luster begins to tarnish. Had Stephanie entrusted Ms. Schubart with some of the more personal details of her life, Stephanie may have saved herself her low score on this section of the IvyWise Index. Had they met more often, Ms. Schubart, who had initially recommended Stephanie's paper on the suffragettes to the Saltonstall Committee, might also have urged Stephanie to submit the paper with her college applications as well as to the *Concord Review* for publication, both of which Stephanie neglected to do. Ms. Schubert had probably assumed that Stephanie would do this on her own, given both the high level of consciousness about the college admissions process at Egret and the fact that most students at Egret know about the *Concord Review* and have published there in the past. Opening up to a teacher outside of class often has this kind of positive effect: It can uncover aspects of a student's profile that the student has unwittingly left underexploited.

- **Documented improvement**

Despite the red flags discussed above, Stephanie demonstrated incredible improvement over the course of the school year, an upward grade trend that was sure to impress her college admissions readers. A conscientious classmate and gifted researcher emerged during her year with Ms. Schubart, indicating that great improvement might continue throughout the rest of high school—and beyond.

To Whom It May Concern,

As a close personal friend of Dylan Chase since our days at Yale, and his golf partner of more than twenty years, I am in a unique position to recommend his beautiful daughter Stephanie Chase for admission to college. Stephanie comes from a wonderful family whose influence and generosity would benefit any institution of higher learning. I have had the joy of watching Stephanie grow into a fine young woman. She has always been eager to learn, conscientious of others, and the best darn actress I've ever seen.

Sincerely,

C. Bart Sturgeon

U.S. Senator (R), South Carolina

OUTSIDE LETTER EVALUATION: STEPHANIE CHASE

Stephanie's Outside Letter:	o points

• **Generic form letter**

Although Senator Sturgeon has known the Chases for quite some time, letters like this tend to be generic because the writer has usually had little contact with the actual applicant. As this letter corroborates, influential supporters are usually friends of the parents who have been asked to use their positions of authority to sway an admissions committee. Again, unless the writer has illuminating anecdotes to tell, these types of letters do nothing to help with college admissions.

• **Against her will**

I later found out that Stephanie had no knowledge of this letter. Dylan simply thought it was a good idea and got Bart to write it. These strong-arm tactics served to estrange Stephanie further from both her family and the college admissions process.

• **The only outside letter**

The lack of other substantial outside letters implies that Stephanie did not spend the necessary time forging meaningful relationships with adults outside of high school. Why didn't she ask Jason Blume from her internship at Yale to write her an outside letter? If this is all she could get, in other words, it does not speak well of Stephanie's future efforts to cultivate relationships with professors and campus leaders in college.

YALE INTERVIEW EVALUATION: STEPHANIE CHASE

Stephanie's Yale Interview:	3 points

Stephanie's Yale interview was a disaster. Just about everything that could have gone wrong, did. First of all, it took place over the summer between her upper and senior years at a moment when Stephanie was much more concerned about her internship working for Jason Blume, a professor of English Literature at Yale University, than about brushing up on her Yale facts and figures. In this summer of reading, writing, and in-depth discussion, the impending college admissions gauntlet was the furthest thing from Stephanie's mind. Of course, if she had known about the interview with more than two days' notice, things might have been different. As it was, Dylan pulled another one of his fast ones—he called an old friend from Yale who had been active in alumni interviews and asked him to take an immediate meeting with his daughter. The friend, knowing Dylan's power and influence, said yes—and the next thing anyone knew, Dylan was ordering Elizabeth to take Stephanie to Manhattan for a complete makeover. After getting her hair straightened, her nails done, and her nose-piercings removed, Elizabeth even went so far as to force a very preppy Laura Ashley outfit on her poor, unsuspecting daughter, along with an equally "acceptable" Lilly Pulitzer bag. With no more than a day to prepare, feeling ripped away from her internship, and looking awkwardly like the grown-up her mother wished her to be, Stephanie had to drive herself up to an imposing Brownville mansion, the home of her alumni interviewer, and try to impress a complete stranger. Needless to say, these were less than ideal interviewing circumstances.

- **Didn't want to be there**

The interview reflected this inauspicious beginning. In general, Stephanie's answers were curt and uninformative, largely because she was uncomfortable and wanted the interview to be over as soon as possible, but also because, deep down inside, Stephanie did not want to go to Yale.

- **Early or not early? That was the question.**

When the interviewer asked Stephanie if she was going to apply early to Yale, Stephanie panicked, remembering her father's demand that she do so. Having utterly no intention of locking herself into a school she didn't want to attend but afraid that the interviewer would get back to her father with the news, Stephanie said yes (which gave Stephanie a few IvyWise Index points). When the interviewer asked her why, Stephanie didn't have an answer—she hadn't done the research necessary to answer the question with any authority. Not only did

Stephanie come off looking unstudied, but her fictional answer also came back to haunt her in another way: The interviewer reported back to Yale that Stephanie intended to apply early. As a result, the admissions office at Yale started an early application file on Stephanie, eagerly awaiting her materials by the end of October. When Stephanie failed to turn in an early application, this raised a pretty serious red flag at the admissions office: Here was a legacy with strong development ties to the school who had told her alumni interviewer that she wanted to apply early—and yet she had failed to do so. What was Yale supposed to think?

• No research

As we have seen, it also became apparent during Stephanie's alumni interview that she hadn't done any research into Yale and that she was only applying because of her family history. Stephanie was unaware of many of the specific course offerings at Yale, even those that might have interested her, given her scholastic talents and background. Besides her internship with Professor Blume, she had neglected to research or contact any other professors she might have been interested in studying with. This gave the overall impression of smugness, as if Stephanie had assumed she was a shoo-in and didn't need to bother with such mundane details as classes and professors. In addition, Stephanie went off on a long tirade during the interview about how the only school that truly interested her at Yale was the School of Drama. Not only did this sound, excuse the pun, *dramatic*, but it was further proof to her interviewer she had no idea what she was talking about: There is no undergraduate "school" of drama at Yale, only a major and a comprehensive program for graduate students. Let that stand as a reminder: Research and only research can save you from Stephanie's fate— as well as allow you to make an informed decision when it comes time to apply to college.

• Revealed too much of the wrong things

When the interviewer asked her to describe her family, Stephanie got a little ahead of herself and rattled off that her mother was an alcoholic and her father a philanderer. When she realized what had just come out of her mouth, she tried to cover it up with a nervous laugh. The damage, however, was done. Stephanie's poor judgment implied a disastrous home life that made the interviewer ill at ease. In addition, Stephanie should have written about these issues in an essay or mentioned them in some manner more appropriate than a flippant remark.

• Couldn't deliver the goods

Because Stephanie was an outstanding student of American history and had called it one of her favorite courses, the interviewer decided to quiz Stephanie on U.S. presidents. When asked to name all the presidents with the first name James, Stephanie drew upon her considerable historical knowledge and answered correctly. As Stephanie gloated that she had a great memory and logical mind, the interviewer then tried to stump her by asking a logic question: the infamous "Marble and Jar" question. "If it takes sixty seconds to fill a jar with marbles and each second the number of marbles going into the jar doubles, then after how many seconds is the jar half full?" Stephanie smiled and answered "thirty seconds." The correct answer is fifty-nine. Although quizzes such as this may not occur in every college interview situation, they are frequent enough—and important enough—not to be taken lightly. Stephanie should not have bragged—and she should have declined to answer the question if she was at all uncertain of her answer, opting instead to contact her interviewer later with an answer via e-mail.

• Didn't ask any questions

By the end, flustered and exhausted, Stephanie forgot to ask any questions herself. This seemed to corroborate her overall lack of research initiative and her lack of social skills, and was further indication that she had very little interest in attending Yale.

Averaging Stephanie's four scores from the Personal Support section of the IvyWise Index, we arrive at the following overall Personal Support score for Yale University:

Stephanie's Counselor Letter:	I point
Stephanie's First Recommendation Letter:	8 points
Stephanie's Second Recommendation Letter:	5 points
Stephanie's Yale Interview:	3 points

Stephanie's Final Personal Support Score for Yale:	**4.2 points**

WESLEYAN INTERVIEW EVALUATION: STEPHANIE CHASE

Stephanie's Wesleyan Interview:	**8 points**

Needless to say, Stephanie's interview experience at Wesleyan, a school much better suited to her needs and goals, was quite different. Stephanie wanted this one to work. She set it up herself, and she made sure she was prepared.

• Went as herself

Stephanie went as she was, wearing her nose ring and earrings, her hair back in its corn rows, her clothes returned to their normal combination of skate boarder chic and vintage casual. She looked and felt like herself, not the whitewashed Sunday school version of herself that showed up for the Yale interview.

• On their turf

Stephanie also went to the extra effort of setting up an on-campus interview, getting "out-of-towns" from Egret to visit Wesleyan for a day in the beginning of her senior year. This showed the Wesleyan admissions office that she truly cared about her application to their school and was willing to take time out of her busy schedule to further strengthen her relationship with its admissions office.

• Did the research

Most important, Stephanie came prepared. Because she was so genuinely intrigued by Wesleyan's liberal arts curriculum and its supermotivated and highly creative student body, she did exhaustive research into the school and knew as much as any student at Wesleyan did about its offerings, traditions, and educational philosophy. Comfortable with how she looked, armed with this deep knowledge about the school, and truly excited about the prospect of going there, Stephanie came to life at her Wesleyan interview, asking many questions, interested to find out more about the school. She was gregarious, insightful, and passionate about her collegiate future.

• That pesky early question

The only minor blemish during Stephanie's interview with Wesleyan occurred when the interviewer asked her, given her obvious enthusiasm for the school, if she was going to apply early. The once animated, totally at ease and personable Stephanie just sat there silent, unsure, wavering. This was a red flag in the making. In that split second, Stephanie jeopardized all of the hard work she had done to impress her Wesleyan interviewer. In reality, there was nothing to fear. If you are asked this question, and you are not 100 percent convinced you will be applying to the school in question early, do not lie. But do not hesitate or stammer either. Simply state that you are thinking about it but have not yet made up your mind. Stephanie's nervous "no" left a lingering doubt in the mind of the admissions reader, who later read a report of the interview. When the reader learned Stephanie's father had gone to Yale, he assumed her reticent answer came about because she was more interested in attending Yale as a legacy and would therefore be applying early there. Wesleyan had no knowledge of her disastrous interview at Yale, nor of the pressure she felt from her father to choose that school. Without that pressure, Stephanie would have chosen Wesleyan and she would have applied early. Hence the hesitation. Part of the strategy we later developed to get Stephanie off the waitlist was to convey this sentiment and make sure that the Wesleyan admissions office fully understood her strong desire to attend their school. As such, however, Stephanie's near perfect interview lost a single point on the IvyWise Index because of her ambivalent answer to the early application question, and her decision, ultimately, not to apply early to Wesleyan, her favorite school.

Averaging Stephanie's scores from the Personal Support section of the IvyWise Index, we arrive at the following overall Personal Support score for Wesleyan:

Stephanie's Counselor Letter:	1 point
Stephanie's First Recommendation Letter:	8 points
Stephanie's Second Recommendation Letter:	5 points
Stephanie's Wesleyan Interview:	8 points

Stephanie's Initial Personal Support Score for Wesleyan: 5.5 points

PERSONAL SUPPORT IMPROVEMENT STRATEGIES: STEPHANIE CHASE

Since it was too late to erase the deleterious effects of Stephanie's ambiguous recommendation letters, there was only one choice of action: Stephanie would have to come clean to her high school college counselor, telling Mr. Hayden everything that happened during that fateful first semester of her junior year, going back, if she had to, all the way to the root of the problem in her disastrous family life. At my urging, and after consultation with her psychological counselor, Dr. Diamond, with whom she had maintained an excellent rapport, Stephanie finally got up the courage to go into Mr. Hayden's office and tell her story. She started with her parents, their emotional distance, the pressure they had always put on her to succeed, and their own general unhappiness. From there, Stephanie traced her need to look outside her family for a figure of maternal love and support. She spoke with passion about Charlotte and Barbara Murphy, about the many ways they had practically saved her life with their open and generous acceptance of Stephanie into their home. Then she told Mr. Hayden about the hardest topic of all: Barbara's death from breast cancer and the subsequent bout of depression that led straight to Stephanie's grade dip, her drinking bust, and her disciplinary probation.

Better late than never, Stephanie's willingness to come clean to her counselor had the effect she was looking for. It made Mr. Hayden an ally, even if it was late in the game. Whereas before Mr. Hayden had felt shut out by Stephanie's silence and outraged by Dylan's insistence that Stephanie's drinking bust and probation be removed from her permanent record, now he felt like he understood his counselee, that he and Stephanie were suddenly on the same page, and, most important, that he would be willing to do whatever it took to help her get into Wesleyan. As he was trained to do whenever new information emerged concerning the status of an in-limbo applicant, Mr. Hayden put in a call to the admissions office at Wesleyan, with the goal of trying to undo the negative effects of his first phone conversation with them. Mr. Hayden told them everything that Stephanie had told him, adding that the Chases were a potentially huge development case, even for Wesleyan. The fact that Stephanie came clean about her past did not, of course, erase the events that led to her being waitlisted at Wesleyan in the first place, but now there was a personal side to it. Stephanie was able to tell her story in her own words—and it was her counselor's job to convey this story directly to Wesleyan. It no longer seemed to Wesleyan that Stephanie was trying to conceal her past. Instead, she came across as a courageous and self-aware young woman who had suffered a serious tragedy. Most important, Stephanie's grade dip was explained and Wesleyan could see that it was not the product of sloth or rebellion.

In addition to this meeting and the subsequent phone call from her counselor, Stephanie also wrote a personal letter explaining the situation directly to her area reader at Wesleyan (see Chapter 6). Together, they helped to influence the difficult decision the Wesleyan admissions office had to make: whether or not to accept the new Stephanie, as they now understood her, into their school. As a result of this explanatory phone call from her college counselor, Stephanie's overall "Counselor Letter" score for Wesleyan went up 6 points to a full 7 on the IvyWise Index.

Stephanie's Final Counselor Letter for Wesleyan:	7 points

Averaged into her former recommendation letter scores, this means that Stephanie's final Personal Support score for Wesleyan jumped from a 5.5 to a 7, an overall increase of 1.5 points on the IvyWise Index:

Stephanie's New Counselor Letter:	7 points
Stephanie's First Recommendation Letter:	8 points
Stephanie's Second Recommendation Letter:	5 points
Stephanie's Wesleyan Interview:	8 points

Stephanie's Final Personal Support Score for Wesleyan:	7 points

Although 1.5 points may not seem like a lot, every bit helps when it comes to applying to some of the nation's most selective colleges, especially if you are trying to get off the waitlist

and into the school of your dreams. The final effects of this increase in the Personal Support score for Stephanie's overall application to Wesleyan will be tabulated in the final chapter, when we look at each application as a whole and discuss certain extra-credit strategies that all three students were able to employ to further increase their chances of gaining admission to the colleges of their choice.

Chapter Six

 PERSONAL ESSAYS

In addition to the data contained in the more factual elements of the selective college application, admissions officers at the nation's most prestigious schools want to hear directly from their applicants, in their own voices, via the personal essays. Many selective college applications ask numerous short answer questions in addition to either one or two longer essay questions, all of which form the "Personal Essay" section of the IvyWise Index ranking system. Topics for these original pieces of writing range from open-ended questions, in which applicants are allowed to choose from a life's worth of people, events, ideas, or experiences that have influenced them profoundly, to more precise questions asking applicants to reflect on their specific reasons for choosing the college in question. Whatever the topic and format of the question or questions, a few things remain clear about the college essay:

(1) It must reflect your personality and your voice.

(2) It must shed light on significant aspects of your character and experience, providing insight into you both as a scholar and as a human being.

(3) It should be an intimate and lively portrait of yourself that none of the other application elements can provide.

(4) If the application in question asks you to comment on a work of literature or art, you must still relate the cultural object in question back to yourself and your personal experience.

(5) If you are asked why you are applying to a particular school, you should discuss how the school's offerings relate to your personal interests.

(6) No matter what the topic, all essays essentially ask the same question: ***What makes you tick?***

This question may seem straightforward, but it is extremely difficult to answer. The problem is: You have to choose. Of all the educational, emotional, transitional, happy, sad, funny, and silly experiences you have had in your life, you must focus on a single one that succinctly and artfully conveys a sense of who you are. You simply cannot write about everything, no matter how tempting each significant experience may be. Nor can you simply offer a factual account of your life's experience. You must choose a particular moment or aspect of your experience *in microcosm* that depicts the whole of your character *in macrocosm*. That is the trick. Again, no matter what the topic, question, or guideline, the personal essay is a chance for you to shine, to speak out in your own unique voice, and to show an admissions reader why you would be an invaluable member of the next incoming freshman class. For an exhaustive overview of the essay-writing process, as well as numerous exercises, strategies, and tips on how to choose an outstanding essay topic, pick up a copy of my book *The Truth About Getting In*. For now, I would like you to consider the following essay-writing criteria, the same general categories I use as the basis of my rankings for the Personal Essay section of the IvyWise Index. As you read through them, keep in mind that these are the same criteria that admissions readers at selective colleges and universities across the country use to assess the writing ability of their candidates during the college admissions process.

• Show, don't tell!

Your goal with the essay is to **show** your great qualities and characteristics, **not tell** them via some list of your accomplishments. Let the reader conclude that you are exceptional *without actually saying it*! In this respect, one of the best topics for your essay is an anecdote from your past, an utterly unique story only you can tell.

• Let the reader hear your own voice!

Use a language with which you are familiar. Your own voice will distinguish what you have to say more effectively than borrowed phrases. Trying to tailor fit your essay to the imagined "literary" expectations of an admissions committee is a recipe for disaster.

• Follow instructions and answer the question!

If an application allows for an extra sheet (rather than sheets) beyond the space given, make sure you attach only one page. In addition, *stick to the topic at hand.* For instance, you may be asked in your application to select a quotation, novel, or play that has had a profound effect on your thinking. Be sure to address the text in question and only that text, discussing what it has meant to you personally.

• Use the same essay for every single application unless they ask the same open-ended question. Be sure to change the name of the college in each!

• *Tell* about your character and personality through a mere list of attributes.

• Make up a story—college admissions readers are seasoned veterans when it comes to "voice," and they will be able to tell when you are being insincere.

• Be tempted to let another person offer too much editorial help.

• Use thesaurus words that you think sound sophisticated: Colleges want to get to know you, not *Roget*!

• Write about your SAT scores or your grades. The essay is a chance for you to express yourself as a human being, not a mere statistic.

• Write a long list of activities—those belong in the Brag Sheet.

• Write about a tragedy that happened to somebody else—colleges want you to be the star of your own story.

• Use gimmicks, like writing in a haiku style or entirely in Old English.

• Write about yourself in the third person—it sounds pretentious and arcane.

• Handwrite your essay—unless it's for Brown.

- **The great first sentence**

As a general strategy, it is always a good idea to have a catchy first sentence. If it grabs the reader's attention, the reader will be encouraged to read on.

As you look through David's, Ronald's, and Stephanie's personal essays, keep these points in mind. Ask yourself if the profiled essays have addressed these criteria adequately. If not, what are some of the weaknesses you notice in their writing? What are some of the strengths? How would you go about improving the overall power, persuasiveness, beauty, and insight of their writing? Of course, the better you are at pinpointing the strengths and weaknesses in their essays, the better you will become at spotting the strengths and weaknesses in your own personal essay(s).

PERSONAL ESSAYS PROFILE: DAVID HOROWITZ

In addition to the Common Application's longer, open-ended question and its shorter, "meaningful activity" question, Johns Hopkins University required David to answer a specific question about why and how he envisioned himself taking advantage of the many curricular and extracurricular opportunities on the Johns Hopkins campus. As you will see from his answers to all three

questions, David's essays suffered from a significant shortcoming: Not generally accurate or well-structured, they also left much to be desired on the level of personal detail. Chock full of generalizations and clichés, yet lacking in personal anecdotes or revealing details, David's essays failed to offer anything more than a polite rehashing of much of the same information already contained in his other application materials. David barely comes alive as the dynamic thinker, the dedicated reader, the impassioned piano-player, the budding scholar, and the dedicated member of his faith that he truly is. Without this type of insight, David's admission readers at Johns Hopkins were left in the cold, shut out from David's personal life, unsure whether he had anything to contribute to college life beyond his extraordinary academic skill. There is no doubt that this lackluster performance on his personal essays contributed in large part to David's eventual waitlisting at Johns Hopkins: They sensed there was a spark of life somewhere, a gifted thinker and an interesting person hiding behind an intellectual facade—but they were waiting for a chance to see him come out of his shell. Without further ado, then, here are David Horowitz's original essays as they were first sent to Johns Hopkins University.

Q: Johns Hopkins University is a dynamic environment where students balance their cere-

(5) An essay about the first time a father and son went shopping together; and a female applicant who wrote about taking architecture classes at Columbia and talking to a drag queen one night in uptown Manhattan. (J. T. Duck at Haverford College)

(6) An essay by a student from Israel who was selected to be in an international leadership conference and whose roommate and subsequent best friend there turned out to be Palestinian. The essay talked about their similarities and differences and the writer's emotional struggles when his Palestinian friend was tragically killed at a demonstration. (Adam Max at Emory University)

(7) Essays about family and family dynamics. (Lloyd Peterson, formerly of Yale and Vassar)

(8) Essays that best convey a sense of who the applicant is. Ideally, students should start writing them early—in the late summer before their senior year after most colleges have published their essay questions online. (Marianne M. Kosiewicz at the University of Virginia)

What are the WORST essay topics you have encountered and why?

(1) Tourist essays—they tend to be boring, obvious, and impersonal. (Leon McLean, formerly of Tufts University)

(2) Death: It is a difficult topic, so universal that it's tough to make personal and risks

sounding disingenuous if you play on your reader's pity. (An anonymous admissions officer at Brown University)

(3) Sexual involvement with teachers, or losing of one's virginity. (An anonymous admissions reader at NYU)

(4) Attempts at humor that fall flat, or gimmicky essays that fail in their attempts at being witty. (Dan Evans at the University of Pennsylvania)

(5) Summer camp essays—too generic, and usually quite trivial. (J. T. Duck at Haverford College)

(6) An essay with a lot of curse words, or a graphic essay about one's sexual exploits. (Adam Max at Emory University)

(7) Secret abortions, kleptomania, pyromania. (Lloyd Peterson, formerly of Yale and Vassar)

(8) A confessional, recounting all the reasons the writer is "bad," or any specific topic taken from another school's application—we know them all, so you should write specifically for the school you are applying to. (Richard Avitabile, formerly of NYU)

In your opinion, what are the worst essay mistakes a student can make?

(1) Bad grammar. Students often don't seem to be aware that admissions readers evaluate

bral need for academic discovery with a visceral need to unwind. Please include the following elements in an essay on an attached sheet. Include your name and Social Security number on this and any other attachments.

- Why you believe that you are a good match for Hopkins
- Areas of study you are interested in pursuing at Hopkins
- How you plan to unwind
- Courses you have enjoyed the most
- Extracurricular pursuits you have enjoyed the most

A: There are many colleges and universities in this country and throughout the world. These offer various programs, which suit the needs of different groups of students. However, Johns Hopkins University would be a particularly good match for me in several ways: I am looking for a school with sizable resources and a suburban flavor, yet with access to the liveliness of an urban landscape. As a person deeply interested in history, I am excited by the historic flair of the university. The university is close to my current home, yet far enough away for me to experience the diversity of a new environment. The size and breadth of the university's programs and courses would allow me to pursue my two life's ambitions: playing music and finding a fulfilling career, with possibilities ranging from law, to medicine to international affairs. The school's reputation for excellence in all areas of its wide spectrum of majors and programs leads me to choose Johns Hopkins over other colleges of equal size.

Although I do have an inkling as to my major and possible career choice, I am still open to new ideas and other modes of thought. Mainly, however I am interested in the following subjects: I am captivated by international politics and world affairs. I also have a profound interest in the sciences and medicine. Law, too, seems fascinating. In order to choose a possible area of study, I will need to investigate new options. To enhance this exploration, I will take a broad range of courses, and, in the process, hear fresh ideas and interact with new people. I envision my first year of college as a time for experimentation, both socially as well as intellectually. During the time I will use to unwind, I plan to broaden my horizons by making new friends from different areas of the country and the world, and to experience many of the different entertainments that the university and the city have to offer.

Throughout my four years in high school, I have enjoyed my English classes the most, especially 11th grade English. In this course, we read a variety of many interesting books, from *Frankenstein* and *Dracula* to Ayn Rand's *Atlas Shrugged* and other works. This class has had a

essays according to grammar and writing ability as much as topic and theme. Applicants should proofread and show their work to fellow classmates and teachers. (An anonymous admissions reader at NYU)

(2) *Students underselling themselves.* If you are shy or reticent, that is a reflection on your personality. The question an application asks, first and foremost, is *How well do you represent yourself?* (Dan Evans at the University of Pennsylvania)

(3) Not answering the question, and not understanding the balance between description and reflection. (Lloyd Peterson, formerly of Yale and Vassar)

(4) An essay that is so highly edited by others that it loses its own distinctive voice and authenticity. (Marianne M. Kosiewicz at the University of Virginia)

Off the Record:

(1) "A long bad essay is worse than a short bad essay." (Anonymous admissions officer at Brown University during an information session Q&A)

(2) "In the essay, you have to be on stage. You can share the stage with others, but the audience wants to see you." (Lloyd Peterson, formerly of Yale and Vassar, and now an independent college admissions counselor)

> (3) "If one views the grades and program of study as a skeleton, then the essays, the recommendations, and the activities put flesh and blood on the skeleton. That totality is what makes an applicant become a real person to the Committee on Admission." (Marianne M. Kosiewicz at the University of Virginia)
>
> (4) "Of all the essays I have read, roughly 70 percent do nothing for the student; 20 percent help the student because they do an outstanding job bringing the two-dimensional application to life; and 5 percent kill the applicant's chances due to poor writing or inappropriate topics." (Adam Max at Emory University)

profound effect on me, as I am now reading Rand's *The Fountainhead* and plan to read her other novels.

My favorite extracurricular activity has been playing the piano. I have been playing for nine years and hope to continue in college. The piano allows me to express my creativity, as I do not only play others' music but I compose as well. I am sure that Hopkins is the right place for me and will fit my character traits as expressed in my extracurricular and academic interests. The environment at Hopkins is certain to be relaxing yet invigorating with challenge. Hopkins can help me express one other of my character traits: my desire to be a hard-working individual open to suggestions and to making new friends. At Hopkins, I plan to make sure that I will do my best in all areas of my intellectual pursuit as well as in music and the study of the piano. In this way, I will be known on campus as a diligent student, with an amiable personality and an affinity for music. I hope that by attending Johns Hopkins University I will be given the opportunity to pursue my goals and aspirations, all the while contributing to the air of excellence in education at the university.

Q: In the space provided below, or on a separate sheet if necessary, please describe which activities (extracurricular and personal activities or work experience) have had the most meaning for you, and why.

A: My study of the piano has had the most profound effect on my life. It has enabled me to understand the importance of patience and diligence as well as reap the benefits of hard work.

PERSONAL STATEMENT

Q: This personal statement helps us become acquainted with you in ways different from courses, grades, test scores, and other objective data. It will demonstrate your ability to organize thoughts and express yourself. We are looking for an essay that will help us know you better as a person and as a student. Please write an essay on a topic of your choice or on one of the options listed below. You may attach your essay on separate sheets (same size, please). Also, please indicate your topic by using the appropriate number from below.

(1) Evaluate a significant experience, achievement, risk you have taken, or ethical dilemma you have faced and its impact on you.
(2) Discuss some issue of personal, local, national, or international concern and its importance to you.
(3) Indicate a person who has had a significant influence on you, and describe that influence.
(4) Describe a character in fiction, an historical figure, or a creative work (as in art, music, science, etc.) that has had an influence on you, and explain that influence.
(5) Topic of your choice.

A: (4) The arts, music, literature, painting, theater and other modes of expression convey certain messages to their audience. In literature, as in other forms, one reader may glean one message from the novel, while another may gather a completely different, sometimes conflicting message. In the course of my study, I have been exposed to many novels, movies, plays and art exhibits. Each of these leaves its impression. However, literature has had the most profound effect on me, specifically the works of two selected authors: Ayn Rand and George Orwell. Their novels have changed the way I view my world, and have opened doors to new lines of thought. They have helped me mature my thinking processes and develop new insight into the world around me.

George Orwell wrote about the fears associated with the rise of totalitarian, communist government. In his novels *Animal Farm* and *1984*, readers begin to understand the unspeakable nature of the effects of totalitarian government, especially through the lens of communist ideology. In his novels, the individual is championed in his struggle to find his identity and pursue the truth. However, the reasons for advocating individualism were not altogether clear to me. How could society function if everyone were to work for his/her own benefit and not for the benefit of others; certainly, man cannot stand alone and be completely self-sufficient without ever needing anyone else? I found the answer to this question in the novels of Ayn Rand. Rand had been a citizen of Russia. After emigrating, she passionately promoted individualism through her philosophy of objectivism. In her novels *Atlas Shrugged*, *The Fountainhead*, *Anthem*, and many other works, she clearly delineates the reasons for her philosophy and the philosophy of individualism through allegory and clear philosophy.

In *Atlas Shrugged*, which I believe to be one of her most profound works, the author portrays a society in which everyone does things for the good of others. In her story she describes many a situation where this spirit of brotherly love causes the workings of society to go awry. In one story, she tells of a company that begins to lose money. The society then expects this corporation to maintain its operation and continue to provide services to its public sector. This becomes very difficult: the company cannot afford to pay its workers and soon the workers, still working by government decree, begin to become sluggish in their duties and eventually desert the company. This, however, is not the great tragedy of the novel. In that society, the public good is elevated and revered and individual need is reviled. Anyone with any type of ambition and ability is repressed either actively or passively. Actively, through governmental edict forbidding invention in order that all will have the opportunity to obtain established goods; and passively, through failing to reward for innovation because everyone is on the same level; no recognition, honor, or reward, monetary or otherwise, is given to anyone over anyone else.

This novel assuaged my doubts as to the fundamentals of individualism. The message conveyed was that if everyone works for his own good, then society as a whole will be protected. However, taking this message to the extreme, never looking out for the good of others, is also equally tragic as doing the opposite, that is, only looking out for the good of society. These novels taught me to appreciate innovation and ideas, and competence, and excellence. I now have a greater understanding of how the world works and how better to achieve the utopia spoken of by communist thinkers. These novels also reflect me personally as they provide further incentive to do my best, knowing that I am not only being rewarded, but that I am serving society by advancing my education, and eventually my career.

PERSONAL ESSAYS EVALUATION: DAVID HOROWITZ

David's Personal Essays Score:	1 point

The weaknesses in David's college essays, as evaluated according to the stringent criteria of the IvyWise Index, stemmed from the following series of related factors:

• No personal insight!

In general, David's essays were too vague and confusing—they failed to paint a clear picture of who David is and what his unique interests and goals might be. More often than not, his writing indulged in vague, philosophical musings about the nature of art and the state of the world, without drawing any connections between these generalizations and his own personal experience.

• Did not answer the question!

In his personal statement, David did not answer the actual question. He wrote at length and in very general terms about many novels, rather than about a single work or fictional character that had influenced him profoundly. By not answering the question, David was not following instructions. If he could not follow simple instructions on a college application, then how can an admissions reader be sure David could handle his daily assignments at a highly competitive college?

• Not enough research!

For his "Why Hopkins?" essay, David did not adequately research the school's particular offerings nor did he paint a detailed picture of how he would contribute to campus life. Instead, David simply stated over and over that Hopkins would be a great fit, without explaining why. David offers no insight into his "character traits" and does not bring his application to life through personal anecdotes or lively prose.

- **Stylistic weakness**

The opening sentences to both David's "Why Hopkins?" essay and his personal statement are filled with vague generalities that are bound to have admissions readers rolling their eyes more than turning their heads. These lackluster openings did nothing to captivate his reader's attention, eschewing any poignant insight into his character in favor of bland oversimplifications. In addition, many of his sentences have a mechanical, belabored quality to them, as if it were a struggle to get them onto the page. Some aren't even sentences at all, merely a conglomeration of words: more a result of inattention than stylistic experimentation.

- **Not using the space provided!**

David's "meaningful activity" essay is far too short. He was given the option of attaching an extra page but chose to write only two sentences. He claims the form looked different online, where he initially filled it out. Nonetheless, the offer to use more space appears in the text of the question itself. What was David thinking? How could such a brief essay offer any personal insight into his piano playing? David later realized he had not taken advantage of all the space given him for this question. More important, David realized that he did not read the question's directions carefully. If the question specifically states that you can add more pages, you should always take advantage of this offer and paint a detailed and highly evocative picture of your passion for the activity in question. It would have been better for David not to mention piano playing at all rather than to provide only two tantalizing yet ultimately unfulfilling sentences about it!

As a result of these significant red flags, the potential impact of David's stellar academic profile was severely diminished by his reticence and awkwardness on the personal essays. As a result of his mechanical performance, David scored quite low for this section on the IvyWise Index.

PERSONAL ESSAYS IMPROVEMENT STRATEGIES: DAVID HOROWITZ'S "WHY HOPKINS?" ESSAY

To begin with, I had David radically rethink his answer to the essay required by Johns Hopkins in its Common Application Supplement. As we have seen, David's original answer was fickle and confusing. He essentially told the admissions committee that he had no idea what he wanted to study and that he would use his time at Johns Hopkins to figure it out. This is unacceptable, both from the standpoint of the IvyWise Index and from a college admissions perspective. Colleges want students with honed interests. This does not mean they want applicants who have planned all four years of college. It does mean, however, that they want applicants who know something concrete about what they will attempt to study. Once enrolled, students may change their minds in the middle of their sophomore year, but at the very least they should have a few particular passions that they will continue to pursue. The same can be said of an applicant's interest in the specific offerings of the target school. David, by remaining on the superficial level of wishy-washy generalizations, never once gave the impression he had researched the academic and extracurricular activities offered at Johns Hopkins. As I indicated earlier, he merely stated that Hopkins would be a good fit—and not even a great one!—thus evincing an utter lack of conviction in his own interests, abilities, and compatibility with the school in question.

In order to rectify this, I had David research everything he could about Johns Hopkins University, ranging from specific subjects and professors to clubs and community service organizations he would like to join while in Baltimore. This is the "imagining you're there" exercise from my book *The Truth About Getting In*. The philosophy behind it is simple: If you can picture yourself there, participating in classes, attending clubs and activities unique to the university's campus, and participating in the surrounding community, then an admissions reader will have no problem picturing you there, too. Once David had done this, he decided to structure his new "Why Hopkins?" essay around his major interests in Hebrew, International Studies, and Music. This focus made sense in light of his documented accomplishments in these areas in high school, and it helped offer support to the other elements of David's college application. Once he narrowed his scope to these three disciplines, we began to see the real David Horowitz come alive. With consistent focus on the Judaic Tradition, World Politics, and Music, David began to emerge as a unique human being, a true individual who could one day make a memorable and significant contribution to life at Johns Hopkins.

On the following pages, read through the results of David's hard work. I am sure you will agree that his new "Why Hopkins?" essay is much more compelling, revealing, detailed, and informative than his first. Notice, especially, the ways in which David was able to incorporate the results of his extensive research into the natural flow of his narrative. Also, study how David seamlessly interlinks his three major interests into a convincing and wholly imaginable "day at Hopkins." Finally, analyze how David paints a vivid portrait of his potential participation in Johns Hopkins daily life. If this essay had come across my desk originally, it would have convinced me that David was a dynamic student of passion, integrity, self-knowledge, and generosity of spirit—many of the very same attributes that his first applications needlessly eschewed.

JOHNS HOPKINS REQUIRED ESSAY

Q: Johns Hopkins University is a dynamic environment where students balance their cerebral need for academic discovery with a visceral need to unwind. Please include the following elements in an essay on an attached sheet. Include your name and Social Security number on this and any other attachments.

- Why you believe that you are a good match for Hopkins
- Areas of study you are interested in pursuing at Hopkins
- How you plan to unwind
- Courses you have enjoyed the most
- Extracurricular pursuits you have enjoyed the most

A: I am sitting in Professor Daniel Hansa's Hebrew IIC class at Johns Hopkins, discussing an Israeli newspaper's potentially biased report on a skirmish with Palestinian militants in the Gaza strip. We are speaking Modern Hebrew. The discussion heats up. The conflict seems irresolvable, the terror hopeless. That's when it hits me. The fact that we're speaking Hebrew is the key. Although written in ancient Hebrew, the greatest collection of Judaic texts, the Talmud, may offer some light at the end of the tunnel. Study of the Talmud, the ethical and practical compilation of Jewish law, renowned for its complexity, has always been an excellent source of legal issue resolution. Written over a thousand years ago, this collection of discourses from history's great rabbis is still an enduring juridical masterpiece. As I sit there at Johns Hopkins, I recall discussions from my Honors Talmud course at Singer Yeshiva High School. Although not taught exclusively for the promotion of the Hebrew language, nor directly about international politics, it was the most enjoyable of my high school courses taught in Hebrew. Only now, sitting in class at Johns Hopkins University, there's something different. I'm in college. The conclusions we reach could have a real effect on our geopolitical climate. I'm a stone's throw from the Johns Hopkins University School of Advanced International Studies and only a train-ride away from Capitol Hill. When I quote a passage from the Talmud concerning the need for people of different backgrounds to live in harmony, my fellow students listen. The ancient, historical text is alive and well, contributing to today's political situation.

These thoughts follow me out into the quad. Students lounge in the grass before class, preparing their thoughts on myriad subjects. I sit down with some friends from the campus Hillel who are discussing one of our weekly prayer meetings and special Shabbat meals. I take an article from my backpack in preparation for my next course, Professor Steven R. David's course on "Contemporary International Politics." The article was written by another Hopkins faculty member, Faoud Ajami, Professor of Middle Eastern Studies at the School for Advanced International Studies. I love this class and have been studying diligently, with the hope that Professor David will invite me into his selective seminar next semester entitled "The Middle East in International Politics." If all goes well, I will ask Professor David to write a letter of recommendation on my behalf for the International Studies Internship Program, based on my proposal for a trip to the Middle East to research religious and social relations among Israeli and Palestinian youth. When I return, I hope my international exposure will qualify me to take courses at the renowned Paul H. Nitze School for Advanced

International Studies in Washington, D.C. Doing so would make me a perfect candidate for the five year BA/MA program in International Studies, which would serve well as a stepping stone for a career in diplomacy or international law.

On the other side of the spectrum, I have always been fascinated by science. After taking AP Biology and AP Chemistry in high school, I have remained highly intrigued by advances in technology made over the past few years, especially in the realm of "wet technology," the incorporation of biological elements into the functioning of complex machines. No longer just the fodder of science fiction films, this fascinating sector of the bio-tech industry is growing rapidly and carries with it serious ethical implications. Are we going to grow human cells specifically for use in machines? How far will this go? What about technological implants into the human body to improve reflexes and senses? How much government regulation is necessary to curb the evil designs of Frankenstein-like doctors without hampering the legitimate development of helpful and necessary medicines and cures? This interest in history, ethics, and bio-technology will be joined by taking "Science in the Atomic Age," taught by Professor Stuart W. Leslie, an expert in the History of Technology and the History of Science-Based Industry.

No matter how far this interest in international affairs and emerging bio-technology takes me, I will never stray far from a piano. My primary means of "unwinding," it is also the most centering and invigorating exercise I know. Lessons provided by the Peabody Conservatory and Peabody Preparatory will allow me to improve my musical skills. I plan to take classes on the Homewood campus as well, courses such as Professor Susan F. Weiss's "Music in Performance." As an avid performer myself, I have always been fascinated by how a piece is arranged for performance and how each performance, in turn, changes the original composition. Maybe I'll be known at the local Hillel as the guy who can play both Debussy and Billy Joel?

Finding time for myself in this busy schedule, I relax in my room with the latest Tom Clancy novel. Jack Ryan is a true hero. Later, I have tickets to an Orioles game with some friends who are visiting from Georgetown. Maybe I'll take them by the Baltimore Aquarium on the way—it's a magically relaxing place in the middle of a tough, urban environment. Then it's off to Washington for the weekend—time to let my Georgetown friends play host.

We are scheduled to take a tour of the White House then go out for pizza and a movie (my favorite thing to do with friends!). On Sunday night, before studying, I have volunteered to visit a homeless shelter with some friends from the dorm. We organized a trip to a shelter near Camden Yards where a soup kitchen has been set up to feed Baltimore's considerable homeless population. It's only one meal, but I know it makes a difference in their difficult lives. On the way home, we discuss other ways that direct political action such as this can lead to social change. Maybe there is hope.

Monday morning comes, and I hit the quad again, ready to begin another exciting week of class. I stop in the middle of the hustle-bustle and I take a deep breath. I am at Johns Hopkins University, the college of my dreams, *and it feels good*.

PERSONAL ESSAYS IMPROVEMENT STRATEGIES: DAVID HOROWITZ'S "MEANINGFUL ACTIVITY" ESSAY

Next, David rewrote the answer to his "meaningful activity" essay, making sure to give a detailed and personal account of how and why the piano was important to his life. When you look over the following essay, notice the way David comes to life as an applicant, the way we are granted a privileged insight into his emotional state while playing the piano, and into the meaning that David's original compositions have for him. The thing to remember here is this: Many applicants play the piano. Many have probably played longer and with greater success than David. That is not what selective schools care about (unless you are a concert pianist with tour experience!). They want to know what makes David tick, why the piano has stuck with him for so long despite the long hours and frustration—they want to get to know David.

Q: In the space provided below, or on a separate sheet if necessary, please describe which activities (extracurricular and personal activities or work experience) have had the most meaning for you, and why.

A: My study of the piano has taught me the virtues of patience and diligence, as well as allowed me to explore my emotions in a different, more expressive language. My original musical compositions are a way for me to channel my creative energies into melodic form. Part mathematics, part sonorous exploration of an imaginative realm, they bring me both private pleasure and public acclaim from friends and family who gather to listen (patiently!) to my latest effusions. I imagine I am Debussy when I compose. His innovative style expanded the boundaries of Western music by incorporating Eastern musical theory into classical European scale structure. His style was such an emotional and daring departure from the established norm of his time that I draw faith for my own improvisations from his courage and wit. It is doubtful that auditors other than my unconditionally loving parents could hear the connection between my stabs in the dark and Debussy's radical innovation, but I press on. For it is in these moments that I feel most alive, most a part of some greater community, both profoundly at peace with myself and delightfully liberated from the confines of normal existence.

It is not easy to become an accomplished pianist. Believe me, my teachers over the years can attest to just how stubborn my fingers can be. But natural talent is not the key to musical achievement. I was not hailed as a child prodigy, the next Mozart. In fact, an early music teacher of mine politely returned the considerable sum my parents had paid her when she first heard me banging on the keys. Tickling the ivories, this was not. More like torturing them. But that was 8 years ago. Now in my ninth full year of playing, I—and my teachers!—have come to see that inborn proficiency has only partial bearing on the ultimate success of any human endeavor.

From trying to imitate the sounds I heard on my parents' favorite Billy Joel LP's, to impressing friends with my ability to reproduce pop-cultural tidbits like the theme song from "Friends," I have certainly come a long way. I got here by diligently practicing 1–2 hours per day, disciplining myself to achieve because I wanted to be a certain level of player and was committed to the effort it would take for this to happen. I recently put my enduring passion for piano into action by founding my high school's first School Band. The music we play ranges from classical to pop to Jewish/Israeli, in which my piano playing forms the backbone of our performance. We've gotten to be quite good in the short time we've been together, and each performance is a new adventure. Energy passes between the players and the audience in a magical, evanescent moment. When I play in front of an audience like this, I feel like I did when I first started creating my own melodies, as if I were in another world. The music I compose, and the music I most enjoy playing, contain both somber and triumphant moments, fluctuating between the hope and despair of the human condition. This is what I plan to continue in college, this emotional involvement in a world slightly better than our own, coupled with the sense of community between players and auditors created in the moment of performance.

PERSONAL ESSAYS IMPROVEMENT STRATEGIES: DAVID HOROWITZ'S PERSONAL STATEMENT

Finally, David decided to rewrite his personal statement, focusing on a topic that would shed more light on his experience and development. If you remember, David's original personal statement was all over the place, trying to analyze numerous novels at once and attempting to say something profound about two of the major authors of the twentieth century. Not only did he bite off more than he could chew—and not even answer the question!—but David should never have answered this particular question in the first place. The Johns Hopkins admissions committee had already understood from the rest of David's application that he was a gifted student with considerable academic abilities, especially in the humanities. It was therefore incumbent upon David to address *other* sides of his personality in his personal essay in order to give the committee a well-rounded and detailed picture of himself as a candidate. Instead, they saw the same intellectual student at work, the same analytic mind, and the same shy thinker who preferred to avoid difficult exercises in self-exploration. Something radical had to change.

But when David first came to me for an Application Review, he was at a loss in terms of what to choose as a more appropriate essay topic. Truth be told, he had been misconceiving the entire concept of a "topic." To David, a "topic" meant an academic subject area or philosophical point of view, not a life-changing event, experience, or character from his own personal history. David needed to make a major shift toward the personal, as awkward as it may have felt to be so revealing. In order to help David brainstorm some essay topic ideas, I took him through the essay-writing exercises in *The Truth About Getting In*. As a result of the probing and meticulous work David did on these brainstorming exercises, he was able to pinpoint a topic for his personal essay: He chose to write about his grandfather, a fascinating historical figure who had had a profound influence on David's emotional and intellectual development. In his new personal statement, as you will see, we come to understand David's personal involvement in the issues that interest him, the motivation for his love of international and Middle Eastern affairs, and, most important, we experience these things in the form of a story, an engaging anecdote that breathes life into David's formerly lifeless application.

PERSONAL STATEMENT

Q: This personal statement helps us become acquainted with you in ways different from courses, grades, test scores, and other objective data. It will demonstrate your ability to organize thoughts and express yourself. We are looking for an essay that will help us know you better as a person and as a student. Please write an essay on a topic of your choice or on one of the options listed below. You may attach your essay on separate sheets (same size, please). Also, please indicate your topic by using the appropriate number from below.

(1) Evaluate a significant experience, achievement, risk you have taken, or ethical dilemma you have faced and its impact on you.

(2) Discuss some issue of personal, local, national, or international concern and its importance to you.

(3) Indicate a person who has had a significant influence on you, and describe that influence.

(4) Describe a character in fiction, an historical figure, or a creative work (as in art, music, science, etc.) that has had an influence on you, and explain that influence.

(5) Topic of your choice.

A: (3) Many years ago, he made his way from Iraq to Israel. An ominous foreboding had hung in the air since the riots. He realized there was very little time left for the few remaining Jews in the ancient Iraqi/Babylonian Jewish community, a community that had existed for over a thousand years in this hostile land, the land that inspired the Babylonian Talmud, the ethical and legal centerpiece of Jewish thought. He had lived his childhood and teenage years in this beloved land and now he was forced to evacuate in order to pursue a second life in the relative safety of the newly established State of Israel. In the face of un-expected opposition due to prejudice—he was a non-European, Sephardic Jew in a predom-inantly Ashkenazic, European Jewish state—and his low economic standing, he had to pull himself up by the bootstraps with diligence and perseverance. He quickly rose through the ranks of the Israeli Foreign Ministry, serving in the United Nations in New York, as well as in other countries around the world. Later, after emigrating to the United States, he became a lawyer, and soon thereafter a professor, teaching Middle Eastern Affairs at The New School in New York.

This extraordinary man is my grandfather.

At the age of seven, at a family barbecue, I first heard his story. I asked him so many questions, he must have thought I was planning my own escape to some foreign land. Paying rapt attention to his answers about the state of the world and the conflict in the Middle East, my young mind struggled to understand such concepts as racism and prejudice, poverty and discrimination, failure and ultimate success. He was like a superhero to me, some relic of a great civilization that had passed, walking proof that courageous men fighting evil forces were not just idle fantasies cooked up by too many comic books and a love of G.I. Joe. Here was a living, breathing man who understood the meaning of perseverance, the triumph of spirit over oppression, the endurance of faith in the face of adversity. And there I was, a boy of seven, who had yet to experience much in life, and yet still there was some sort of connection between us. I understood him in more ways than I could ever have explained to him then. I saw myself in him as he must have seen himself in me. He was telling me, in his own anecdotal way, never to give up.

Three years ago, I encountered my own adversity, albeit on a much smaller scale. It was still only half-light outside on that damp September morning. I was groggy, but a nervous fire burned in the pit of my stomach, a vague sense of anxiety, even dread. I heard the screech of the brakes as the bus rounded the corner, the bus that would take me sixty miles from my home every morning and sixty miles back every evening for the next three years. A profound sense of loneliness washed over me as I stepped onto the bus, surrounded by tired, foreign faces. No one knew me. I knew no one. I would have to start all over again. After a childhood spent in the town of my birth and one year at the local high school, I had decided to transfer to a Yeshiva many townships away. I left the familiar faces and comfortable acquaintances of Pearl Bay, NY, for the distant outpost of Rumsfield, a lone sojourner on a mission to improve my academic life, to challenge myself at a school commensurate with my desire to study, explore and grow.

As I took my first steps through the pristine, modern structure that would be my intellectual home for the next three years, passing strange faces and unknown lives, my grandfather's words came back to me. "David," he said. "David, the world is the same wherever you go. There are good people and bad people, rich and poor, happy and sad. But they weren't always that way, David. Just as you will travel many roads and change along the way, so have they. Remember that when you meet new people, you could actually be meeting yourself." And I smiled. Of course everything was unknown, foreign and frightening—that is what I had wanted. It had to be that way if I was to achieve my goals of academic excellence. I had to be uncomfortable at first—everyone is in the face of a new experience. As my grandfather told me that day at the barbecue when I was only seven years old—risk is the catalyst for growth.

I had to leave myself behind in order to find myself anew.

PERSONAL ESSAYS IMPROVEMENT RESULTS: DAVID HOROWITZ

David's Final Personal Essays Score:	8 points

As a result of the hard work he did on his three essays, David's IvyWise Index score for the "Personal Essays" section of the selective college application jumped 7 points. In these new essays, David emerges as a much stronger writer, although not the strongest or most creative I have ever seen. We get a much clearer sense of who David is as a person, yet some of his prose remains flat, especially when compared to other applicants. In this way, David was unable to score a perfect 9 on the IvyWise Index for this section, but he was able to radically increase his chances of being taken off the waitlist and admitted into the freshman class of 2006 at Johns Hopkins University.

PERSONAL ESSAYS PROFILE: RONALD SIEGAL

When it came to the personal aspects of his selective college applications, Ronald Siegal was a model student. This was especially true for the Personal Essay section of the IvyWise Index. Two essays accompanied Ronald's Early Decision application to the University of Pennsylvania: the all-important "Why U. Penn?" essay and a more open-ended personal statement in which Ronald was asked to reflect on a significant, character-defining "first experience." For the first essay, Ronald charged out of the starting blocks, a man on an essay-writing mission. Even prior to meeting with me, Ronald knew the importance of research. He understood the edge it would give him for both his "Why U. Penn?" essay and his interview. He also knew it would help him decide if the University of Pennsylvania was the right school for him on both an academic and a personal level. As a result of his detailed exploration of U. Penn's numerous scholastic and extracurricular offerings, Ronald was able to produce an excellent essay "picturing himself" in his first semester at U. Penn. For those of you who have read my book *The Truth About Getting In*, you will remember this fantastic piece of work from the chapter "Writing an Outstanding Essay," where I highlighted it as model writing sample. Here, in *Rock Hard Apps*, you will have an opportunity to read it within the context of Ronald's entire application, gaining new insight into its overall strength and poise. There is no doubt that its excellence helped to convince the admissions committee at U. Penn that Ronald knew what he was talking about when he applied early.

At my suggestion, Ronald chose an experience for his personal statement that revealed a characteristic not otherwise present in the rest of his application. He chose to write about his color-blindness, both a unique characteristic and a condition that shed new light on his artistic achievement. His essay combined an anecdotal style with some serious reflection on the nature of color, perception, and creativity, all the while giving a clear emotional picture of how this ocular condition has affected him personally. You will notice that the essay is not flashy, or laden with jargon, nor is it asking for pity. Instead it paints a very realistic picture of how a young man with artistic talent has used his confidence and determination to deal with a condition that directly affects his ability to explore and utilize that talent. Our overall picture of Ronald as a candidate is that of a young man facing the challenges and joys of the world with circumspection, grace, and even humor.

Q: "What characteristics of U. Penn, and yourself, make the University a particularly good match for you? Briefly describe how you envision your first year in college. How will your presence be known on campus?"

A: Leaving Professor Poggi's course, *20th Century Art: 1900–1945*, on a cool fall morning, I envision an independent study next semester focusing on World War I and its influences on art. After speaking with Professor Poggi, we agree I should take Professor Bokovoy's course, *20th Century American Culture*, because it will help me with my research concerning cultural influences on art during the early 1900s. Both professors' courses will allow me to link two of my favorite subjects, art and history. I know I will have dialogues through e-mail with Professor Poggi and Professor Bokovoy discussing how World War I shaped art in the 1920s. Both professors told me they would assist me in determining the locations for primary sources and meeting other knowledgeable professors at Penn.

Later in the day, I visit the Institute of Contemporary Art and confirm my internship in the Education Department for next semester. I know the paintings there will provide the basis for part of my research. In addition, the university's urban setting allows me to go to many museums on a regular basis.

I have asked my professors about arranging more art-related community service activities on and off campus like I did in high school. Last week, I organized a Cubist Day and invited a guest speaker from a nearby museum to speak about Picasso's influences on art in the 21st century. This was similar to many of my high school activities with the National Art Honor

Society. I provide information about art, such as museum exhibitions or gallery openings to U. Penn students through an interactive web site that I personally designed. I know I will have to retain my excellent time management skills because in addition to my schoolwork, I am also a member of the Artist Guild and DART. I also joined the Skydiving Club much to my parents' chagrin. But hey, you're only young once.

After I return from the museum, I head straight to the library to do research on a paper analyzing Ionesco's *Rhinoceros* due in a few weeks. A few hours later, in the early evening, I recruit classmates for my new community wide art club. Having received permission from the University of Pennsylvania, the School District of Philadelphia, and the Philadelphia Federation of Teachers, we assist in the development of the new PreK-8 University-assisted public school in West Philadelphia. We enjoy painting murals in the school and at the playgrounds, and holding art classes after school for the students. I have asked local businesses to donate supplies, in addition to organizing our own fundraising events.

Finally to relax, I meet my friends at a nearby coffee shop to have dinner and discuss Saturday's amazing Penn-Princeton football game.

Q: First experiences can be defining. Cite a first experience that you have had and explain its impact on you.

"It adds a precious seeing to the eye . . ."

William Shakespeare
Love's Labour's Lost

A: Picture living in a world filled with red trees, brown apples, and purple skies— colors only you can see. I remember when I first found out I was color-blind: I began drawing and painting when I was two years old, but my trees had vermilion bark and my oceans were the color of grape juice. My mother took me to an eye doctor to see if I was in fact color- blind or just a very eccentric three-year-old. The doctor presented me with the "black book," filled with Pseudo-Isochromatic plates used to test for color-blindness. The pages were full of different colored dots; the test involved finding numbers and letters camouflaged within the dots. I could not find either. My mother and the doctor explained exactly what color-blindness was to me. A little serious for a three-year-old, I didn't laugh when they showed me a colorful clown to try to explain the difference between what I saw and what they saw. My mother told me to lighten up. Ever since, I have learned to embrace my difference as a gift.

My color-blindness has by no means hindered my passion in life: art. Ever since I can remember, I have had a Crayola marker in my hand. Many of my pieces are a reflection of my color-blindness. For instance, I used colored pencil for my recent work of a butterfly taken from a photograph. I drew the markings along the outer part of the wings using the colors I see. All of the brown spots looked green to my art teacher. I used light blue for certain sections of the bottom parts of the wings, but in reality they were lavender. Even when I was young, I drew strangely colored cars and helicopters—foreign to my peers, but inhabitants of my world.

Ironically, it's difficult to determine which colors I confuse. Do I always see brown when everyone else sees red? Imagine never being able to be certain about what you see. On the other hand, do those who are not color-blind all see the same colors? Is the color my art teacher calls red the same one my sister sees as red? How can one really know? Color is a subjective experience. When I look at Van Gogh's self-portrait at the Metropolitan Museum of Art in New York, I see a man that no other person sees. His facial colors are what truly draw me in. I see contrasting colors radiating from the center of his face, making him appear almost surreal. His beard appears red, but also brown. I have difficulty recognizing one of Van Gogh's characteristic painting techniques—directional brush strokes—because he uses colors that blend together in my eyes. Nonetheless, I am fascinated and continue to study his self-portraits.

Because I am color-blind, whenever I draw or paint I have to be more methodical than most artists. When I wish to, I use a series of steps, consisting of outlining and color choice, in order to ensure that I draw or paint the colors everyone else sees. This also helps me to remain within the guidelines of a specific assignment. In addition to my series of steps, I also seek feedback from my peers and teachers. They allow me to understand just how creative and different my art is—they also let me see my colors through their eyes. Sometimes, however, I draw and paint using the colors that make up my world. I turn my back on accepted notions of red, blue, and yellow and, in an act of benevolent revenge, encourage others to see the world through my eyes.

When I was little, my box of 64 crayons had only 30 colors. Chestnut, mahogany, burnt orange, burnt sienna, and ruby red all seemed to be the same color to me. Nevertheless, I still managed to win awards for my artwork at a very young age. I know I will want to continue both my study and my creation of art for the rest of my life. I like to think of my color-blindness as an edge for creativity, providing me with a personal way to express myself, my own unique palette.

PERSONAL ESSAYS EVALUATION: RONALD SIEGAL

Ronald's Final Personal Essays Score:	9 points

- **Research pays off!**

It is obvious from the quality of Ronald's "Why U. Penn?" essay that he did sustained and detailed research into all of the academic and cultural offerings pertaining to his particular interests at the University of Pennsylvania. U. Penn loved seeing this level of knowledge because it demonstrated that Ronald was committed to their school, having done the hard work necessary to prove to them he was a perfect fit by "imagining himself there." By employing this strategy Ronald's essay did so much more than merely list the reasons why he and U. Penn would make a great fit. Instead, it told a story, literally placing Ronald on the University of Pennsylvania campus and detailing a single day in his life as an imaginary student. Because his research was so thorough, it was immediately apparent to Ronald's admissions reader that he was a perfect match for their school, the kind of candidate who would take full advantage of all that their curriculum and community have to offer.

- **Insight into a unique characteristic**

The genius of Ronald's "Color-blind" essay is that it told the admissions committee at the University of Pennsylvania something truly unique about his life experience, something they would never have learned from his other application materials. Of course, Ronald's art teacher mentioned it in her outside letter of support, but Ronald's color-blindness really came alive in his own words as he drew connections between it, his extraordinary work ethic, and his unique perspective on life. In addition, the essay shed light on a characteristic that tied in directly with his passion for art, thus furthering support for the "artistic" elements of his application. More important, it was a thought-provoking and subtle exploration of the very notion of color-blindness, a notion that I found myself contemplating long after reading Ronald's essay. This combination of an anecdotal writing style, a revealing personal characteristic, and a depth of perception made for an outstanding read. The same would hopefully be true for the admissions committee at U. Penn. Either way, they knew that they had a unique student applying to their school—and they were right.

PERSONAL ESSAYS PROFILE: STEPHANIE CHASE

As with the other aspects of her personal profile, Stephanie's essays evinced an evasive quality that worked against her as a candidate for college admission. As you will remember, Stephanie had been unwilling to share the circumstances surrounding her dramatic upper year grade dip with anyone other than her psychological counselor, Dr. Diamond, who was bound by confidentiality laws not to reveal the contents of their sessions together. Although everyone was aware of Stephanie's depression at the time, neither the teachers writing her letters of recommendation nor her high school college counselor were aware of Barbara's death as the reason behind Stephanie's difficulties. They could only observe in baffled silence as Stephanie's grades fluctuated wildly at the beginning of her upper year, drastically impairing their ability to write fully supportive letters on her behalf.

The same phenomenon hampered Stephanie's otherwise stellar personal essays. Clearly, Barbara's death would have been an ideal topic for Stephanie's personal statement, as it would have shed light on her experiences at the time of her grade dip as well as revealed the reasons behind her passion for promoting breast cancer awareness. She could easily have submitted such an essay for both Yale and Wesleyan, in response to the Common Application's Personal Statement question. Trained, however, to keep her emotions to herself—and probably still reeling from the death of her closest adult friend and mentor—Stephanie chose to write about an incident with her boyfriend at the time, Henri, a black student of Haitian heritage. The essay, as you will see, contained some interesting political and sociological insights, exploring the trickier aspects of a cross-racial relationship, even in this day and age. In the long run, however, it was difficult to say who Stephanie was from this essay—Stephanie as a unique individual never fully emerged from it. Her reflections were poignant and her writing was truly inspired, but readers were left with the haunting suspicion that this harrowing experience could have happened to anyone.

The same could be said of the "meaningful activity" essay that Yale required as part of its Common Application Supplement, and which Stephanie chose to submit with her Wesleyan application as an expanded response to the same Common Application "activity" question that David had overlooked. Thankfully, Stephanie knew to take advantage of the Common Application's invitation to submit "a separate sheet if necessary" prior to sending in her applications. Steering clear of her painful ordeal with Barbara, however, Stephanie chose to write about her involvement in theater. This was a logical choice, as admissions readers at both Yale and Wesleyan were aware of Stephanie's interest in drama from her dismal brag sheet. Unfortunately, Stephanie's discussion of her "dramatic moment" in this second essay did very little to answer the pressing question on readers' minds after going through Stephanie's application: What happened at the beginning of upper year, and why wasn't Stephanie writing about it? Don't get me wrong—Stephanie's "meaningful activity" essay was brilliant, expertly depicting a harrowing moment that occurred during one of her productions and beautifully expounding on the reasons behind her profound love for the theater. My point is, this essay was more significant for what it did *not* address than for what it did: the fact that the play Stephanie wrote was a fund-raiser for breast cancer research written in direct response to Barbara Murphy's sickness and subsequent tragic death.

As you read through Stephanie's two essays, keep in mind the rest of Stephanie's application materials: Do these essays shed light on heretofore unknown aspects of Stephanie's character? Does a coherent character profile emerge from the essays? Do they provide depth and insight into Stephanie's past and present struggles and triumphs? Do the essays convey their information in an engaging, anecdotal form or do they rely on discursive paragraphs more appropriate to the term paper than the personal statement? As you answer these questions, I think the red flags that nipped at the heels of Stephanie's essays will become apparent. As you encounter them, try to come up with strategies for improving Stephanie's essays by placing yourself in the shoes of a selective college admissions reader. This perspective will certainly come in handy when you sit down to write your own college essays.

PERSONAL STATEMENT

Q: This personal statement helps us become acquainted with you in ways different from courses, grades, test scores, and other objective data. It will demonstrate your ability to organize thoughts and express yourself. We are looking for an essay that will help us know you better as a person and as a student. Please write an essay on a topic of your choice or on one of the options listed below. You may attach your essay on separate sheets (same size, please). Also, please indicate your topic by using the appropriate number from below.

(1) Evaluate a significant experience, achievement, risk you have taken, or ethical dilemma you have faced and its impact on you.

(2) Discuss some issue of personal, local, national, or international concern and its importance to you.

(3) Indicate a person who has had a significant influence on you, and describe that influence.

(4) Describe a character in fiction, an historical figure, or a creative work (as in art, music, science, etc.) that has had an influence on you, and explain that influence.

(5) Topic of your choice.

A: (1) Was that the first time we saw each other? On the tennis court? I think. Club tennis. For the undecided and undedicated athletes among us. I must have struck a ridiculous figure: everyone in their regulation whites, me in my Fugazi T-shirt and ³/₄ length, ripped khakis. I stood out even more than he—and I was white. Later, at the dance, he peered over at me through dreadlocked bangs. Which dance was it? The Bennington Bash? I think. The other lowers were bouncing up and down to the boisterous staccato of the latest boy band, while I was balled in the corner, curled into my headphones with the Cranberries. Could he hear my secret music all the way over there? I think. And then, for the last time that first day, outside Wheelwright. He was drumming with a friend, slapping a bench with urban abandon. I walked by and, with a sideways smile, began to move to his beat. My feet, his hands, communicating in tentative rhythm over space and time. How could we know that was, as they say, "the beginning of something?"

We were strangers, after all. Ignorant of each other. I didn't know he spoke French, for instance, or that he was from Port-au-Prince, a sprawling city of slums and sun-beaten colonial mansions—the sad, sweet capital of Haiti. I didn't know he was the son of a university professor who specialized in postcolonial literature. I didn't know his mother was a "believer," that she blamed her bad knee on a man in a broad-rimmed hat who had cursed her with a dead chicken at her doorstep because his wife's hair had turned green five days after a visit to Henri's mother's full-service hair salon. I didn't know these things then—and it didn't matter. We looked at each other that first day in a way that made eyes seem superfluous. We spoke to each other that first day in a way that made language seem redundant. We understood each other that first day in a way that made reason seem mad.

Was it to last? Who knows? We were young. Yet the suspicion that this idyllic life could not last had always been hovering around the edges of our consciousness. Even back then. It was high school after all. No one marries their high school sweetheart anymore. I was from the suburbs of Connecticut. I was meant to marry a stockbroker from Manhattan and bake Martha Stewart pies for my 2.3 children. What would my father say to a budding musician, surreal poet, and rip-kicking snow-boarder of Afro-French-Caribbean descent? Did I care? Could I afford not to? And his mother, what would she make of the white girl with the crazy hair and the ripped clothes, the ubiquitous headphones and the father who owned six homes? Would she put a curse on my mother because she liked to sip a gin and tonic every once in a while? Or would they yuk it up on the front porch, sharing a miniature cigar? Questions. So many questions when there are so many differences. Maybe questions were the problem. Who knows?

So it happened, one day, that Henri and I, two years into our controversial "relationship," and very much in love, were walking back to campus after a meal at the Loaf and Ladle, the local vegetarian spot in downtown Lakewood. We saw them coming a few blocks away. Three boys. Three "townies" as we called them—a horrific and degrading name for the local residents of the town that generously put up with the presence of a thousand students from places nothing like this one. They carried sticks, these boys. Not menacing sticks like the thugs in *A Clockwork Orange*, but sticks nonetheless—like they wanted to whack something. They stopped in their tracks when they saw us coming in the opposite direction. I recognized them from the bowling alley. I told myself they had seen Henri and me together before, that they were *accustomed*. They made a big deal about stepping out of our way, an exaggerated gesture of "after you," sticks and all. The ball was in play. They had hit a high, arcing lob and we either had to run or lose the point. We chose to walk, hand in hand, in total silence, dreading the possibilities.

That's when it happened. Some fellow students, male Egretians, as we are awkwardly called, appeared in the doorway of the Milk Bar, Lakewood's only real coffee shop. Had they seen us coming too? Sensed the impending doom? The inevitable confrontation? Or were they merely gallivanting, posturing like the "townies," ready to work the caffeine through their young limbs? Who knows? Either way, they had the tense aura of alert cats who sense their prey might be too large for their domesticated claws, yet who want to pounce nonetheless. The "townies" leaned on their sticks. The Egretians swaggered. Henri and I could do nothing but pass between them like a wedding couple parting the aisle between the Hatfields and the McCoys. That's when we heard it. The two words that would change our lives forever.

"Nigger-lover."

They crashed in on me like the shards of an exploding glass building. I looked to the townies and I knew. Fear. They wore fear on their faces like a mask. They stared in astonishment at the Egretians, shocked that this series of salacious sounds had been uttered. I could read it in the Egretians' faces too—one of them had said it, one of the "educated" boys, one of those who was supposed to "know better," who was supposed to be "one of us." Now suddenly everything had changed. The townies were on our side. The barrier was no longer one of class or privilege or upbringing. It was one of civility. And the Egretians were on the wrong side of the tracks. The townies palmed their sticks, looked like they might protest, then walked off, as if the words they had heard were a poison gas released into the air—and they had to run or else succumb to it.

The Egretians passed too. Tense, furtive, none of them willing to take credit for the cloud of noxious gas around us, taking refuge in their numbers, their faded crimson and white rugby shirts, their eyes of wealth and hatred. Henri squeezed my hand, sensing the rage boiling to my ears. He gave a gentle tug, as if to say: it's okay. Move on. Forget about it.

But I couldn't. To this day I am shocked and appalled that a vegetarian, straight-edge, suburban white girl and a Haitian-American poet, drummer, and tennis player cannot walk down the street among the sons and daughters of the American elite without being "put in their place." Martin Luther King had died so that comments like that would evaporate in the empty skulls of thoughtless racists before they even had a chance to foul up the air we are forced to share. Had they not learned? I wanted to retaliate, to hurt these rich boys, to incite Henri to rise up and teach them a lesson. But he had witnessed all this before. He had heard the words of hatred and weathered their symbolic blows. He knew retaliation, at least of a physical sort, was a waste of time. Of all our differences, this was perhaps the greatest, the hardest for us to overcome. What did it mean that I was so angry? Was it because, in an unexpected twist, the epithet was addressed to me? Was I calling on good, old-fashioned chivalry and expecting Henri to defend my honor? What did those abstract concepts mean anyway? Mean to me? Today?

Henri and I may not stay together much longer. Then again, maybe we are meant to travel this wicked world together, hand in hand, moving to the same bench-slap beat. Who knows? Relationships are tough enough as it is. But with the added weight of history and hatred bearing down on our backs, the miasma of ignorance and insolence tugging at our feet, and the glass wall of my own inability to answer these questions stopping us dead in our tracks—the difficulty of maintaining a "relationship" was the least of our worries. The trick was: the problem was in me. I was the one who couldn't forget. I was the one pressing for a fight.

It was as if I had both uttered those unconscionable words and been attacked by them. It was my own culture talking back to me, and I hated it.

Later that night, Henri called. He wanted to hang out. Not tonight, I said, and curled up into my music. Would we ever recover? Who knows?

ADDITIONAL ESSAY—REQUIRED

Q: Yale requires two essays: the Common Application's Personal Statement and one other of about 500 words.

Some users of the Common Application choose to write a full essay in response to the instruction at the bottom of page APP-3 to describe which extracurricular or personal activity or job experience has had the most meaning for the candidate and why. If you have done so and intend to use that essay to fulfill the Yale requirement for a second essay, then simply sign and date Form S3.

Otherwise, please write an essay of about 500 words on a separate sheet of paper describing an interest or activity that has been particularly meaningful to you.

A: I rocked back and forth on the balls of my feet. The floorboards creaked with anticipation. I followed the dialogue in my head as I had a thousand times before. But this time would be different. This time people were listening.

I stood backstage awaiting my cue like a cat crouches in wait for a bird that circles and circles its perch. The bird touched down. It was my cue. I sprang.

But instead of the warm glow of the footlights that I expected to find, I was enveloped in a wall of icy air. My mind faltered, sputtered and went dead, reduced to the same pinprick of light that overcame my grandmother's TV set whenever you turned it off.

I had forgotten my lines. What was worse: I had written them myself.

I mean, it's one thing if Shakespeare's iambic pentameter eludes you. That's some pretty heady stuff, right? And it's understandable if you forget a few of David Mamet's ubiquitous four letter words—do his characters really have to curse so much anyway? You might even get away with jumping in too early on one of Tom Stoppard's maddeningly illogical *bon mots*. But your own lines? What kind of fool forgets her own lines?

That night—it was only a dress rehearsal, thank god—I did.

I had stayed up late half the summer and the entire fall hammering out these words in my mind. Countless crumpled pieces of paper attested to my borderline obsessive perfectionism. Countless burned discs littered my desktop. Draft after draft of the play ripened on my computer screen, only to rot away in its trash bin. These were my words—and yet there I stood, frozen, sweat beads meeting-and-greeting on my upper lip and forehead.

At least I thought they were my words.

Besides learning to study my lines more diligently, even for a dress rehearsal, I learned a valuable lesson about language that night, something I'm sure Beckett and Ionesco knew at a far younger age than I—*language speaks us, we don't speak language.*

As I stood there on stage, with no one to ask for a cue because the prompt book sat at my abandoned seat in the back of the auditorium, I thought: so this is why they say never direct and act in the same piece. But as I strove in vain to recall the lines that I myself had written, it occurred to me that moments like this were precisely why I loved the theater. Whether I am writing, acting, directing or viewing theater, it's all about the words. Their inflection. Their intonation. Their context. Everything else is there for the words to sparkle— the actors, the lights, the stage, the audience. They are all there to maximize the effect of the words, to tease as much meaning from each word as possible—and with as little overt direction as you can manage.

I listened. Silence reigned in the auditorium. A few actors shuffled, realizing the Catch-22 I was in as writer, performer, and director of my own speechlessness. And I smiled. What a privileged space, I thought, this theater. Amid the awful drone of commuter traffic, the discouraging din of morning radio shock jocks, the callous cacophony of cable television, and the relentless sloganeering of our merciless, consumerist culture, the theater was a place of silence. Of quiet attention. Of careful consideration. Of words left to their own devices.

This is why theater has been such a meaningful activity for me—it moves me to listen more attentively, to write more carefully, to act more deliberately, and to strive for meaning in everything I do. Having written, performed, and directed an original one act play during my upper year at Peter Egret Academy, I know that I will return to this privileged space of dialogue and discussion, listening and lamenting, caring and communication, as often as I possibly can.

PERSONAL ESSAYS EVALUATION: STEPHANIE CHASE

Stephanie's Initial Essays Score:	7 points

Despite their overall excellence, Stephanie's essays contained a number of red flags that may have alarmed her admissions readers at both Yale and Wesleyan. Confronted with these two examples of her outstanding prose, they were sure they had a great writer on their hands. Although she had gone over the 500-word recommendation on her second essay, it was clear that both its form and its length were necessary reflections of its scope and its content. The problem was, admissions readers at both Yale and Wesleyan weren't sure exactly who Stephanie was. Was she a passionate theater performer, internationally traveled young socialite, or self-absorbed genius? Was she a renegade thinker, melancholic dreamer, self-reflective poet, or courageous young girl who had defied her upbringing? Stephanie's essays offered her readers no way to decide.

• "Significant experience" not personal enough!

Stephanie's essays were extremely well written, no doubt. Yet in terms of her "significant experience," admissions readers missed Stephanie's personal relationship to this difficult time in her life with Henri. Her stark, evocative introduction, although stunning, veered off too soon into extended description, after which it quickly digressed into an impersonal albeit interesting discussion of the difficulty of maintaining a cross-racial relationship in contemporary American culture. This is the danger of tackling a topic of such magnitude as racism:

It was difficult for Stephanie to point out the specific quality of the racism she experienced. Couldn't this event have occurred to any Caucasian who happened to have a black boyfriend or girlfriend? Of course, it is articulated through Stephanie's creative eyes and pen, but overall this topic is risky, especially since Stephanie is not herself of African descent. Events that occur because of other people make tricky topics, since the immediate connections to the writer are often hard to discern. In this case, although Stephanie was the victim of a racial slur, the overall lack of personal detail in Stephanie's "significant experience" is a symptom of many "relationship" essays. The topic can be deceiving—it seems as if you are being personal when really you are falling into the realm of relationship clichés. Caught between a rock and a hard place—wanting to say something universal about race and relationships, yet wary of clichés—Stephanie would have been much better off writing about another topic, something more personal that involved her own passions or problems, like Barbara's battle with terminal illness.

• "Meaningful activity" shows passion for theater

This stylistically direct account of a simple yet meaningful moment on the stage really gets at the heart of Stephanie's personal attachment to the theater. We understand what drove her to the stage in the first place, as well as what keeps her coming back for more, despite its obvious pitfalls. As is ideal in an essay such as this, Stephanie made her admissions readers aware of her theatrical and linguistic passions in the form of an anecdote with a lively and engrossing tone and structure.

• A tad melodramatic

I got the feeling from reading Stephanie's essays, however, that she may have attempted to compensate for her lack of revealing self-exploration with a slightly exaggerated, even moderately melodramatic tone. To my ears, this gave her essays a borderline insincere ring. Although they are beautiful, they came across as distant and overly concerned with sounding "literary"—more about form than content, or more like a tone exercise from a creative writing class than a heartfelt portrayal of Stephanie's fears and desires. In addition, Stephanie addressed only a single "dramatic" moment from her vast experience with the theater. She chose not to chart the development of her interest in the activity—a more customary approach to this type of essay question. Although we understand Stephanie's profound connection to the theater, we don't understand the extent of her involvement with it *over time*. The moment she chose to highlight is a great one, but it remains isolated. And although we know Stephanie is a great writer from her sonorous, trenchant prose, admissions readers at Yale and Wesleyan must have suspected that Stephanie was hiding behind the power of her own words, reluctant to speak plainly about her participation in theater over the years.

• Themes too universal

In the college essay, it is certainly desirable to draw universal conclusions from the specific events in your past, but if you try to raise your particular experience to the level of historical inevitability, you risk sounding overly self-involved and lacking in subtlety. Stephanie's writing treaded onto this dangerous ground more often than I would have wished. Especially in her "significant experience" essay, it's as if the entire history of race relations in the United States came to bear on this one moment of trial in her past. Philosophically, that may be the case, but admissions readers at the nation's most prestigious schools are far more interested in hearing their applicants' personal reflections on the difficult experiences in their lives than hearing sociohistorical maxims borrowed from an American history lecture.

• Wrong topics

Since Stephanie spent a lot more time reading and writing poetry than she did acting and directing in the theater—and since poetry was far more likely to be an area of concentration in college—Stephanie should probably have chosen poetry as the topic of her "meaningful activity" essay. This would have shed light on an aspect of her personality that did not emerge elsewhere in her applications. Don't get me wrong—Stephanie's theater essay was great, but the very fact that she never once mentioned the name of the piece she wrote, its topic, the reasons she wrote it, or its purpose (fund-raising) demonstrates that it was perhaps just an elaborate exercise in evasion. It's hard to imagine Stephanie having been so elusive with poetry, the activity closest to her heart. Unfortunately, precisely because it was so close to her heart, Stephanie opted to write about the far safer topic of the theater. In terms of her "significant experience" essay, although racism and racial politics appear to have played a role in her life—for instance, we know from Stephanie's award-winning history paper that these issues concerned her—Stephanie would have been better served writing about breast cancer, about the moment she first learned of Barbara's diagnosis, about an encounter in the cancer ward of the hospital, or about a particularly moving experience while fund-raising for breast cancer research. Such an essay would have forced her to confront some of the more painful aspects of her past. It also would have created the perfect opportunity for her to talk about Barbara's death. Finally, it would have given her a chance to mention her significant theatrical work—since her play was a fund-raiser for breast cancer awareness—without having to devote an entire essay to it. By writing about racism, in other words, her essay was actually redundant—and we never learned about her all-important and highly-skilled poetical explorations.

- **Great writing talent**

Despite these red flags, there was no denying that Stephanie is an outstanding writer as evinced by her educated word choice, provocative, lively style, and ability to see the larger cultural import of the events in her life. Again, this ability was hampered in these particular essays by Stephanie's lack of revealing self-exploration, an important aspect of writing that she will have to work on if she honestly wants to realize her dream of becoming a professional writer. Nonetheless, Stephanie's admissions readers at both Yale and Wesleyan could be sure of one thing: Given the right environment and the necessary time to mature, they had a potentially outstanding young writer on their hands. It is the quality of her prose that rescues her score for this section of the IvyWise Index.

PERSONAL ESSAYS IMPROVEMENT STRATEGIES: STEPHANIE CHASE

When Stephanie first came to me for an Application Review after her double waitlisting at Yale and Wesleyan, she expended a good deal of energy simply trying to muster the courage to choose Wesleyan over Yale. This, of course, was difficult, because it involved confronting

Stephanie's father, something she was loath to do. Finally, when all of this prickly family business was behind us, I felt it would be in Stephanie's best interest not to spend her remaining time worrying over a fleet of new essays for her resubmitted Wesleyan application. Her old essays were good enough: They displayed her considerable writing talent, they touched upon topics that were important to the development of her worldview, and they were a good enough match with the rest of her application not to warrant a total, time-consuming overhaul. Instead of rewriting her personal statement and "meaningful activity" essay, I encouraged Stephanie to focus her energy on explaining what happened to her when Barbara died. Wesleyan had to know the circumstances surrounding her grade dip and her drinking bust if Stephanie was to stand a chance of being admitted off the waitlist. In this same letter, Stephanie decided to explain why she had failed to apply to Wesleyan Early Decision, as well as to stress that it had always been her first choice, whether or not she had acted that way in the beginning. I believe it was largely on the strength of this letter that her resubmitted application to Wesleyan was considered with the attention it deserved. Stephanie made a difficult choice; admitting to the drinking bust was not easy. But in the end, whether or not she was admitted to Wesleyan, she had displayed a ton of courage, grit, and maturity.

Mr. Jay Burton
Area Reader
Office of Undergraduate Admissions
Wesleyan University

Dear Mr. Burton,

I thank you in advance for taking the time to read this letter. It was difficult for me to write. But since Wesleyan is the school I have always dreamed of attending, any difficulty paled in comparison to the hope of making my college dream come true.

There are two general topics I would like to cover in this letter. Each has significant bearing on my application:

(1) My grade dip during the first trimester of my upper year; the family tragedy that provoked it; and the disciplinary action taken against me for drinking in the dorms.

(2) The changes I have made to my application since I first applied to Wesleyan.

Let me start with the most difficult first. In order to understand what happened to me, you must understand that, ever since I was a waddling toddler, my parents expected me to go to Yale. That was, as my father liked to say, "my future." My parents have always done and thought what they imagined would be best for me, I understand that. But I spent a good part of my childhood living a lie, trying to please them, telling them I shared their dream. Deep down inside I knew I did not.

Please realize that I mention my parents not to blame them. I simply think it may help you understand my personality if you know that my family life has been troubled. For as long as I can remember, my mother has had a problem with alcohol. I think it has something to do with the fact that my father is gone most of the time, either at our apartment in New York City or on a trip visiting one of his high-profile clients. Even when they are together, things are glacial between them. As such, I never really had a role model, male or female, other than my nanny whom my parents fired when I turned nine. During grade school, then, I did what I think a lot of young people in my position would have done—I looked elsewhere for something resembling a family, *anything*.

What I found was so much more—the Murphys. Without the Murphys I never would have made it through to high school. Let me tell you about them, since they are the crux of the matter at hand. The Murphys are the quintessential family-next-door. Charlotte is my best friend. She is loyal, kind, and always up for an adventure. Her father is a professor of political science. He is very sweet and has ideas that are very different politically from my parents'. Then there is Barbara Murphy, my true mother. She was always there with a band-aid whenever I fell off my bike. She was always there with sound advice whenever I had a problem with a girl or boy at school. There were some weeks when I ate every meal at the Murphys' house, and Jess, their German Shepherd, is the closest thing I have ever had to my own pet.

You must understand the level of my attachment to Barbara Murphy in order to understand how devastated I was in the seventh grade when she was diagnosed with breast cancer. My whole world turned upside down. Of course, being the resilient and courageous person that she is, Barbara fought back. She went into remission and seemed to have conquered the disease. Still, it was tough to go away to Peter Egret Academy, so far from Barbara and Charlotte—it would have been hard even without cancer to complicate matters. Don't get me wrong—the academic life at Egret has been excellent, but I missed the Murphys terribly.

It was the beginning of upper year. I had spent the summer researching breast cancer at the local library and publishing a series of articles in the *Brownville Journal* about my experience with Barbara's illness. I got to see Barbara relatively often, even though my parents dragged me away on various vacations whenever they could. I was much more interested in volunteering at Barbara's hospital in my spare time, learning as much as I could about breast cancer, trying to spread awareness about this deadly disease with an organization of nurses dedicated to raising money for breast cancer research. After tearful good-byes, I was just settling into a grueling year of school at Peter Egret, when I got a call from an hysterical Charlotte who told me that her mother had unexpectedly died. I was speechless. Unable to attend the funeral because of Saturday classes and impending midterms—my parents were vehement that I stay at school—I retreated into a dark shell. I felt dead myself. In sympathy, perhaps. I tried speaking with Charlotte on the phone, but we just broke down into sobs every time. I felt so alone, so isolated, so helpless and unhelpful.

Basically, I stopped caring about school. I, who was so strict about attending classes, was suddenly being put on restrictions for missing so many. I stopped trying. English, History, French, Drama—none of them mattered anymore because none of them could make me feel any better, and none of them could bring Barbara back or help me overcome my guilt at not having done more to save her. I was lost. So lost, in fact, that when one of the notorious partiers on our floor invited me to her room one Saturday night—as she had done so many times before and always to no avail—I found myself saying yes before I was even aware that the words were leaving my mouth. For a few weeks thereafter, we drank together, almost every night, doing shots of gin and vodka, Bacardi 151, whatever we could get our hands on. The last of these nights, weaving my way through the hall, I inadvertently weaved my way right into my dorm head's door. The loud crash woke her up and she followed the trail of fetid alcohol to my door. A knock and a blurry, vertiginous four-step walk later and I was busted. Stephanie Chase, the good girl from the suburbs who always tried so hard not to ruffle anyone's feathers, was suddenly the biggest Monday morning story on campus—busted, drunk, in her room alone.

I still couldn't think straight, but there was one thing I realized as I got ready to face Peter Egret's complicated and spirit-crushing disciplinary procedure: I was starting down my mother's path and that I was depressed. Desperate, even. And I had unconsciously chosen a mode of flight that my mother had introduced me to. Alcohol was her preferred way of "checking out" and, crazy as it sounds, it was my ardent desire not to follow in my mother's footsteps that made me work harder than I ever have in my life to stay in school and to stay off alcohol.

Thanks to some great advice from my counselor, Dr. Diamond, and some encouraging words with Mr. Murphy, I managed to survive the disciplinary committee. I ended up receiving an eight-week probation for alcohol. Of course, my father, combative trial lawyer that he is, persuaded the administration to drop the charge from my official record so as not to jeopardize my chances of attending Yale. Again, I am not blaming my father for actions that I myself incited, but this gesture of shame, this cover-up, and this lie heavily influenced my decision not to tell either my college counselor, Mr. Hayden, or any of the teachers writing my recommendations about the incident. As a result, I couldn't explain my grade dip to them either, an unfortunate side effect of my decision to withhold the truth. That is why this is the first time you are hearing this story. That is why I am writing this letter to you today—to come clean, to tell you what I should have told you four months ago, and to plead for your understanding in reconsidering my application for undergraduate admission to your outstanding academic institution.

As you will see, I have redone my brag sheet. Initially, I neglected to include some pertinent information that I now realize may help shed light on significant aspects of my character and my experience. I have also enclosed a copy of my book of poetry that has been my prime extracurricular activity since early in grade school, along with copies of the articles that I published in the *Brownville Journal*. I was reluctant to include these with my initial application out of sheer ignorance that they might generate interest beyond my personal sphere. As many of the poems in the book were written in the darkest hours of the ordeal described above, I hope it will also function as a literary complement to this more sober assessment of those events. Also, at the urging of my history teacher, I have included a copy of my award-winning essay on African-American suffragettes. I believe this paper documents both my interests and my abilities as a writer of non-fiction. Finally, I spoke with the head of the drama department here at Egret, Mr. Lynch, and asked him if he might feel inclined to send a taped copy of the one-act play that I wrote during upper year about Barbara's struggle with cancer. As I mentioned in my brag sheet, I wrote, directed, and starred in this piece as a way to raise money for breast cancer research.

Most importantly, I decided to write this letter, both as a factual account of the events that led to my grade dip in the first trimester of my upper year and as a way of clearing my conscience. I was too scared and too sad to write about any of this on my initial application. I now realize that was a mistake. If I could do two things over again, I would spend more time with Barbara, and would write about what I went through after her death on my Wesleyan application. Actually, I just thought of a third thing I would do: I would apply Early Decision to Wesleyan because it is, and has been, my number one choice. It took me a while to convince my father of this fact. Once I explained to him some of the contents of this letter, he began to understand my experience with Barbara and my subsequent depression at Egret. He even apologized for never asking me the reasons behind my drinking. He had arrogantly assumed that I had done it to annoy him. Now, I am happy to say, my father is 100% behind me and my desire to attend your school.

I hope these new documents will help you see that, although I may not have convinced you the first time around, I am exactly the kind of student that an excellent, small, liberal arts college like Wesleyan is looking for: I am creative, analytical, and dedicated to my community. If I were to continue my studies at Wesleyan, I would take such classes as "Advanced Poetry Workshop" with Professor Elizabeth Willis or Professor Alfred Turco's "Introduction to Western Drama" in the English Department, along with "Acting I" and "Directing I" in the Theater Department. Continuing my creative writing, I would also love a chance to participate in your world-renowned "Wesleyan Writers Conference" during the summer. Other goals include a possible year abroad at Reed Hall through your "Vassar-Wesleyan Program in Paris" and even a spot on your Women's Varsity Lacrosse team. I would be a proud member of the Cardinals, sure to wear my Crimson Red and Black, head held high, ready to break into a verse of the "Wesleyan Battle Cry:"

So keep on fighting
'til victory crowns everyone;
and then it's fight, fight, fight,
fight for Wesleyan!

Thank you for your time and consideration.

Sincerely,
Stephanie Chase

PERSONAL ESSAYS IMPROVEMENT RESULTS:
STEPHANIE CHASE

Stephanie's New Personal Essays Score:	9 points

The very act of writing such a heartfelt letter was a breakthrough for Stephanie. Even if Wesleyan decided not to accept her off the waitlist, the experience of writing this essay brought Stephanie a step closer to putting a cap on the most depressing and difficult chapter in her life. Not that she would ever forget Barbara's death. Her one hope was to incorporate this terrible loss into her understanding of the world, to work through the pain, to reflect with fondness on the positive influence that Barbara had on her life, and to allow her memory of that extraordinary woman to motivate her toward a productive future in college and beyond. In writing this letter, Stephanie also happened to accomplish four very concrete goals in terms of the college admissions process. First, Stephanie effectively explained her grade dip from the first trimester of her upper year, offering a very concrete and sympathetic excuse for her momentary underachievement. Second, Stephanie helped her admissions readers overcome any doubts they may have had about the complexity of her character. Whereas her initial application may have presented a certain unwillingness to share—or even an unwelcome shallowness of character—Stephanie now emerged as a young woman capable of profound philosophical and self-analytical insight. It was, third, the missing piece in the puzzle of her application. Admissions readers at both Yale and Wesleyan had witnessed firsthand Stephanie's extraordinary writing ability, and they knew that a deep sensitivity to language of this sort didn't emerge from an emotional vacuum. Unfortunately, that is precisely what they had been faced with in her first application: a void, an emptiness at the center of Stephanie's self-presentation that left everyone asking for more. With this letter, she gave them what they were asking for. By writing at such length about her ordeal, and with such candor, Stephanie essentially replaced her interesting, though slightly impersonal, college essays with this probing reflection on a past experience of extreme emotional and developmental importance. As such, her letter filled exactly the same function that a new essay would have. And finally, the last paragraph shows that Stephanie has researched Wesleyan thoroughly. Stephanie engaged in lengthy and in-depth research into Wes. and extracurricular offerings. Essentially becoming a mini-expert in Stephanie was able to utilize her knowledge to write a penetrating fin. personal letter to Wesleyan in which she elaborated the specific classes would pursue if accepted. Stephanie came across as a highly interested can sion. By killing four birds with one stone, Stephanie would surely come ali of her admissions readers. As we mailed off Stephanie's revised application, w ∪ed our fingers in hopes that this eleventh-hour revelation would be enough to convince her admissions readers at Wesleyan that she was emotionally mature enough to spend four productive years on their campus. As a result of this hard work, Stephanie maximized her overall Personal Essay score on the IvyWise Index ranking system.

Chapter Seven

☞ EXTRA CREDIT AND
RESULTS

INITIAL APPLICATION RESULTS: DAVID HOROWITZ

As we enter this final chapter, let us add up the IvyWise Index points David received on the various sections of his first application, the one that landed him on the waitlist at Johns Hopkins University. Remember that 99 points is the highest composite ranking an application can receive on the IvyWise Index. Also keep in mind that the scores from the "academic profile" count twice as much as the scores from the "personal profile" because this is how the nation's most selective colleges judge their applicant pools. Finally, as you read through the results of each student's application evaluation, remember that only a score somewhere between 90 and 99 will ensure a student admission to a selective college, whereas anything lower requires mitigating or extra credit circumstances in order to be acceptable.

Academic Profile:

Courses:	8 points	×2	=	16 points
Grades:	9 points	×2	=	18 points
SAT I/ACT:	7 points	×2	=	14 points
SAT IIs:	9 points	×2	=	18 points

Personal Profile:

The Brag Sheet:		=	3 points
Personal Support:			
Counselor Letter	(5 points)		
Teacher Recommendation	(7 points)		

Teacher Recommendation	(2 points)	
Interview	(1 point)	
	Average: =	3.75 points
Essays:	=	1 point

David's Initial Application Score:	**73.75 points**

EXTRA CREDIT STRATEGIES: DAVID HOROWITZ

What extra credit strategies have you seen? When does extra support cross the line?

(1) Extra credit strategies cross the line when the information they provide is irrelevant to the candidate's overall profile. Friendship bracelets, political pins with the candidate's name and face on them, and diary or journal entries are cute, but they don't really help. Support strategies must resonate immediately with a reader—after all, readers only have a few minutes to look at supplementary material. (An anonymous admissions reader at NYU)

(2) Supplemental material can rarely hurt you, but a seventy-page paper on isotopes may not be of much interest to anyone. Admissions readers may pass it on to the appropriate professor, but unless it is an award-winning paper, it will not increase your chances of admission. (J. T. Duck at Haverford College)

David's initial application score of 73.75 on the IvyWise Index was clearly not enough to convince the admissions committee at Johns Hopkins University that he was serious about attending their school. Before he could even dream of receiving the letter of acceptance he so ardently desired, David would have to prove to Johns Hopkins that he had what it took to make it at one of the nation's most prestigious schools, that he was committed to the college application process in general and to their campus and curricular offerings in particular.

• Original compositions: + 3 points

The first thing David did as an extra credit strategy designed to flesh out his personality and character was to submit a CD of his original piano compositions to Johns Hopkins University. By letting them listen to his own pieces played on his piano at home, David granted the admissions readers at Johns Hopkins a privileged view of his personal life, as well as a hint of the fanciful, playful, and creative side of his personality that had so little chance to emerge in the rest of his application. These recordings were not meant to get David a music scholarship to the university; they simply weren't good enough. Had they been, David would have received 5 points on this section. Rather, the tapes were meant to make David come alive as an applicant in the minds of his readers at Johns Hopkins. In the end, the recording helped him to stand out from the crowd of other applicants—they would always remember that kid from New York who played like a cousin of Billy Joel!

- **Explanatory letter: + 1 point**

David also decided to write a letter *to the admissions reader* responsible for his waitlisted application at Johns Hopkins University. This letter accompanied his new and improved application and detailed the changes he made to it. It underscored the reasons for each change and stressed that David would have applied early to Johns Hopkins if had he done the proper research in the beginning of his college search and if he had been properly informed by his high school college counselor. By doing this extra work and writing this letter, David brought extra attention to his application, demonstrating to Johns Hopkins that he was a serious candidate and erasing any implication that the problems with his original application stemmed from lack of interest in Hopkins, rather than an excusable mistake on the part of a momentarily confused student.

Mr. William P. Emerson

Office of Undergraduate Admissions

140 Garland Hall

340 North Charles Street

Baltimore, MD 21218-2683

Dear Mr. Emerson,

In reviewing my application, it became apparent that a picture of me as a candidate for undergraduate admission may not have been completely developed. In order to give further insight into my personality and character, as well as to show how these correspond to the specific offerings and atmosphere of the University, I would like to resubmit 3 sections of my application for additional review. They are the following:

(1) A more detailed extracurricular, personal, and volunteer activity submission in order to give you a more complete understanding of these activities, more than the outline which appeared in my original submission.

(2) My answer to the shorter essay question: "In the space provided below, please describe which of these activities (extracurricular and personal activities or work experience) has had the most meaning to you and why?" The format of the on-line application seemed to limit a response to this question to only a few sentences. However, after further review of the application, I realize that much more space had been given and a more detailed answer both suggested and warranted.

(3a) My essay describing how Johns Hopkins University would be a good match for me. I now realize that to fully answer this question, I should have taken the opportunity to delineate in detail how I envisioned my course of study and how this course of study would complement my academic interests. I also wanted to indicate how I would contribute to the university, both inside and outside the classroom. In my previous response, I also seemed to indicate that I wished to pursue a career in many different areas. I now realize that I may have stated more than I could handle.

(3b) My Personal Statement. I would like to resubmit this essay, answering a different question. My previous statement did not give the reader a full portrait of my character.

By submitting an essay on a person who has had a significant influence on my life, I hope to give the reader a deeper insight into my personality.

In retrospect, I should have done more research into the unique offerings of your great institution. Had I been more aware, I would have discovered Johns Hopkins to be my first choice, and I would have applied Early Decision. Unfortunately, my high school's college guidance department failed to direct me appropriately, due to a lack of experience, as I am in Singer Yeshiva High School's first graduating class.

I thank you for your anticipated cooperation and appreciate your taking the time to reevaluate my application. I hope these clarifications will enable you to gain a better understanding of my qualifications for undergraduate admission.

Sincerely,
David Horowitz

FINAL APPLICATION RESULTS: DAVID HOROWITZ

David's Initial Application Score:	**73.75 points**
As a result of the work we did together:	
David's Essay score jumped from a 1 to an 8	= + 7 points
David's Brag Sheet score rose from a 3 to a 7	= + 4 points
David's Interview score went from a 1 to an 8 and his overall Personal Support score went from a 3.75 to a 5.5	= + 1.75 points
David earned 3 points for his original compositions	= + 3 points
David earned 1 point for his explanatory letter	= + 1 point

David's Final Application Score:	**90.5 points**

With this much-needed bump in his IvyWise Index ranking, David pushed his application into the "A" range. Upon further review of his resubmitted application, admissions readers at Johns Hopkins were able to see that they had a serious contender on their hands, an academic superstar who now displayed more of the personal qualities they were looking for in their applicants.

> **Most important, by bringing his application into tip-top shape, David received his long-awaited acceptance letter to Johns Hopkins University.**

INITIAL APPLICATION RESULTS: RONALD SIEGAL

For his initial, Early Decision application to the University of Pennsylvania, Ronald scored the following points according to the IvyWise Index ranking system:

Academic Profile:

Courses:	7 points	×2	=	14 points
Grades:	6 points	×2	=	12 points
SAT I/ACT:	5 points	×2	=	10 points
SAT IIs:	6 points	×2	=	12 points

Personal Profile:

The Brag Sheet:	=	9 points
Personal Support:		
Counselor Letter		
First Teacher Recommendation		
Second Teacher Recommendation		
Interview	=	9 points
Essays:	=	9 points

Ronald's Initial Application Score:	**75 points**

EXTRA CREDIT STRATEGIES: RONALD SIEGAL

In addition to bringing the personal elements of his application into the best possible shape, Ronald strived for a number of IvyWise Index extra credit points.

• An excellent portfolio: + 5 points

To begin with, Ronald turned in his art portfolio as an exhibit. Although this alone does not guarantee a candidate any extra IvyWise Index points, Ronald's portfolio was exceptional, evincing both a high level of competency and a high level of passion. More important, it corroborated his overwhelming interest in art as already detailed in his brag sheet and his personal statement. Together with the outside letter of recommendation from his private art teacher, this extra application element further stressed the theme of a student devoted to the practice and study of art on all levels, helping to account for the significant portion of Ronald's extracurricular time spent on art and art-related endeavors. Furthermore, it proved to the admissions committee at U. Penn that he was dedicated to his craft and not afraid to offer up his work for critique. Because of Ronald's color-blindness, it also provided stunning visual clues to this most intriguing of personal characteristics.

At a Glance:

Admissions at Tufts University for the class of 2006:

- Regular admissions rate: 26 percent.

- Early admissions rate: 43 percent.

- 40 percent of incoming class was admitted early.

Admissions at Brown University for the class of 2006:

- Regular admissions rate (2490/14,612) = 17 percent.

- Early admissions rate (526/2000) = 26 percent.

- 35 percent of incoming class (526/1485) was admitted early.

- Yield (1485/2490) = 60 percent.

Admissions at Yale University for the class of 2006:

- Regular admissions rate (2000/15,500) = 13 percent.

- Early admissions rate (500/2000) = 25 percent.

- 38 percent of incoming class (500/1300) was admitted early.

- Yield (1300/2000) = 65 percent.

> **Admissions at Columbia University for the class of 2006:**
>
> - Regular admissions rate = 12 percent.
>
> - 47 percent of incoming class was admitted early.
>
> **Admissions at New York University for the class of 2006:**
>
> - Regular admissions rate = 26 percent.
>
> - Early admissions rate = 52 percent.
>
> - 35 percent of incoming class was admitted early.
>
> - Yield = 39 percent.
>
> **Admissions at the University of Pennsylvania for the class of 2006:**
>
> - Regular admissions rate = 21 percent.
>
> - Early admissions rate = 33 percent.
>
> - 48 percent of incoming class was admitted early.

- **Staying in touch: + 5 points**

In addition, Ronald tried to get as many people on his side as possible. He kept in touch with his regional U. Penn representative from the middle of tenth grade on, communicating often and expressing his strong passion for the school at every turn. He kept in touch with his interviewer as well, e-mailing updates about his life and asking follow-up questions concerning classes at U. Penn. In this way, he kept his name in the front of everybody's mind and displayed impressive confidence in his own communication skills. Ronald's parents got involved in the process as well. Although I do not normally endorse interference from parents, especially if they think their three hundred letters to the target school's admissions office will make a difference in little Johnny's campaign for admission, in this case Ronald's parents were great. They provided moral support every step of the way and communicated often with Ronald's college guidance counselor in an attempt to maximize Ronald's chances of gaining admission to the University of Pennsylvania. When they wanted more direct, personalized help with the college admissions process, they listened to their son's suggestion and called me. If parents can maintain a balance between too little participation on the one hand and heavy-handed manipulation on the other, they can be a valuable asset in their child's bid for selective school admission.

- **Applying early: + 4 points**

Finally, and perhaps most important, Ronald applied Early Decision to the University of Pennsylvania. Despite his lower overall test scores and the steeper competition he faced from other early applicants, this bold act demonstrated in no uncertain terms that, if accepted, Ronald had every intention of enrolling at U. Penn. For students like Ronald who want to stress that a particular school is the perfect fit for their goals and aspirations, this is the best choice. Selective schools want to increase their overall yield and offering early acceptance options is a way for them to guarantee the enrollment of a number of top-notch applicants. This, coupled with the obvious passion Ronald displayed in his essays and his interview, made him a sure bet: U. Penn knew he would be an enthusiastic and involved member of the next freshman class if accepted. For Ronald, the advantages were just as clear. As we have learned, applying early to many of the nation's most selective colleges and universities is roughly the equivalent of raising your SAT I score by 100 points. Given that Ronald started with a 1340, this extra effort kicked his score up to a 1440, bringing his new SAT I average to 720. This raised his IvyWise Index ranking from a 5 to a 7. And since an applicant's academic profile counts twice as much as his personal profile, this gave Ronald a total of 4 IvyWise Index extra credit points.

FINAL APPLICATION RESULTS: RONALD SIEGAL

Ronald's Initial Application Score: **75 points**

As a result of the work we did together:

Ronald earned 5 points for his original art work   =   **+ 5 points**

Ronald gained 5 more points for his excellent

"communication" with U. Penn   =   **+ 5 points**

Ronald earned another 4 points for applying early   =   **+ 4 points**

Ronald's Final Application Score:	**89 points**

As a result of employing the strategies detailed above, Ronald was able to raise his overall IvyWise Index ranking from an unsatisfactory 75 to an excellent 89, putting him just within reach of consideration at the University of Pennsylvania. Although his score falls just short of the needed A-range, U. Penn took a chance on Ronald because of his excellent character. Since it is close to impossible to achieve a perfect personal score—the equivalent of scoring a perfect 800 on the SAT I Verbal section—U. Penn saw him as a 90 instead of an 89. By applying early, acing his interview, and writing a stellar "Why U. Penn?" essay, Ronald demonstrated his strong desire to attend U. Penn—and this clearly gave him an edge over other applicants who may have had better overall profiles but who didn't make the extra effort to stand out. The admissions committee at U. Penn knew they had a hard worker on their hands, someone who would take full advantage of everything they had to offer. They saw Ronald's potential.

In the long run, it was Ronald's passion for the specific offerings at the University of Pennsylvania—resulting in his bold decision to apply early—as well as his extraordinary work ethic that made our collaboration such a success. He is one of the best students I have ever worked with. He did everything on time and was extremely involved in his own advancement. All I did with Ronald was clarify the college admissions process, come up with strategies to maximize his chances of getting into the school of his dreams, then put the power into his own hands. Ronald's hands were ready. Now it was U. Penn's turn to recognize his extraordinary effort—and reward him for it.

> I am proud to say that, in the end, Ronald Siegal was accepted Early Decision to the University of Pennsylvania. He wrote me a letter saying it was the happiest day of his life. I keep it over my desk and look at it whenever I need a smile.

INITIAL RESULTS: STEPHANIE CHASE AND YALE

For her initial, regular admission application to Yale University, Stephanie scored the following points according to the IvyWise Index ranking system:

Academic Profile:

Courses:	6 points	×2	=	12 points
Grades:	7 points	×2	=	14 points
SAT I/ACT:	7 points	×2	=	14 points
SAT IIs:	8 points	×2	=	16 points

Personal Profile:

The Brag Sheet:		=	1 point
Personal Support:			
Counselor Letter	(1 point)		
Teacher Recommendation	(8 points)		
Teacher Recommendation	(5 points)		
Interview	(3 points)		
	Average:	=	4.25 points
Essays:		=	7 points
Initial Yale Total:			**68.25 points**

In addition to this point total for the application sections evaluated by the IvyWise Index, there were certain mitigating circumstances that helped to strengthen Stephanie's initial application to Yale University.

Admissions at Emory University for the class of 2006:

- Regular admissions rate (4142/9789) = 42 percent.

- 37 percent of incoming class was admitted early.

- 75 of 800 waitlisted students were admitted.

- Yield (1313/4142) = 31.7 percent.

Admissions at the University of Virginia for the class of 2006:

- Regular admissions rate (5500/15,040) = 36 percent.

- Early admissions rate (950/2300) = 42 percent.

- 28 percent of incoming class was admitted early.

- Yield (3040/5500) = 55.3 percent.

- Transfer admissions rate (826/2294) = 36 percent.

- **Legacy status: + 3 points**

Since Stephanie's father attended Yale University, Stephanie was considered a legacy applicant at that school. This is the case if one or both of your parents attended a college as an *undergraduate*. You are not a legacy applicant if any other family member attended the school or your parents only attended graduate or professional school there. Legacy applicants are given special consideration in the college admissions process because it is assumed they know more about the school than non-legacy applicants. Parents like Dylan presumably talk about their alma mater at home, attend or host reunions and fund-raisers, give alumni donations, and/or are involved with the school in some other fashion. Legacy students are therefore assumed to be making a more educated decision when they apply. They are also more likely to attend based on the strong family connection. Any student who is thinking of applying to a college as a legacy applicant should definitely apply early. Not applying early can appear like a snub to the school—which, in this case, was the risk that Stephanie ran by ignoring her father's wishes. As a legacy, Stephanie should have decided beforehand if she was truly interested in attending Yale instead of treating it like a safety school. Had Stephanie applied Early Decision to Yale, her IvyWise Index extra credit score for this section would have been a full 5 points. This is most likely the reason Yale waitlisted Stephanie in the first place—as a courtesy to her generous father, who would have been outraged if Stephanie had been rejected. Nonetheless, Stephanie still had an advantage as a legacy, even applying regular decision: While Yale accepts barely 13 percent of its general applicant pool, it accepts around 30 percent of its legacy applicants. For Princeton, the number is even higher, around 50 percent.

- **Development potential: + 5 points**

Because Dylan is such a wealthy and well-known public figure, and because he had given extensively to his alma mater in the past, the Yale University Development Office was able to assume with relative assurance that the Chases would continue to donate heavily to the school, especially if the latest member of the clan were admitted into the next freshman class. As I discussed in the introduction, money alone cannot buy a mediocre candidate a place in a selective college like Yale. However, if the family has extraordinary means (which the Chases do), a history of large donations to the school in question (which the Chases do), and the applicant is more or less qualified to attend (as Stephanie was), an admissions office at a highly selective college like Yale may receive a call from its Development Office alerting them to the great development potential of one of their applicants. For a student on the cusp between acceptance and rejection, this can make all the difference.

As a result of these mitigating circumstances, Stephanie's overall Yale application score, prior to coming to me for an Application Review, moved up 8 full points:

Stephanie's Initial Yale Application Score:	76.25 points

INITIAL RESULTS: STEPHANIE CHASE AND WESLEYAN

For her initial, regular admission application to Wesleyan University, Stephanie scored the following points according to the IvyWise Index ranking system:

Academic Profile:

Courses:	6 points	×2	=	12 points
Grades:	7 points	×2	=	14 points
SAT I/ACT:	7 points	×2	=	14 points
SAT IIs:	8 points	×2	=	16 points

Personal Profile:

The Brag Sheet:		=	1 point
Personal Support:			
Counselor Letter	(1 point)		
Teacher Recommendation	(8 points)		
Teacher Recommendation	(5 points)		
Interview	(8 points)		
	Average	=	5.5 points
Essays:		=	7 points

Initial Wesleyan Total: **69.5 points**

In addition to this point total for the application sections evaluated by the IvyWise Index, there were certain mitigating circumstances that helped to strengthen Stephanie's overall application to Wesleyan College.

• Development potential: + 3 points

As with Yale University, the wealth and status of the Chase family played a role in Stephanie's chances of gaining admission to Wesleyan. Since Stephanie was not a legacy at Wesleyan, however, its development office could not be sure of a donation sizable enough to make a difference in Stephanie's profile. Since she did not apply early, they knew there were other schools under consideration. Because of his public profile, they also knew that Dylan Chase had attended Yale, a rival of Wesleyan's, and that he had donated significant sums to that university. A sizable Wesleyan donation was therefore a long shot. Nonetheless, the very name of Chase was enough to interest any development officer. As a result, Stephanie received 3 extra IvyWise Index points for her family's development potential.

- **Extraordinary Communication: + 3 points**

Stephanie was so moved by her experience at Wesleyan that she effortlessly maintained near-constant contact with both her interviewer and her information session leader, updating them on any changes to her academic and personal status, as well as continually reminding them of her desire to attend Wesleyan. As a result, the admissions office at Wesleyan opened a file on her application very early in the admissions process, updating it accordingly after each communication. When Stephanie was waitlisted, the admissions office at Wesleyan already had a vast store of information about Stephanie's candidacy. As new materials started pouring in after Stephanie's consultation with me, admissions officers at Wesleyan could fit each new application piece into the Stephanie Chase puzzle. This helped flesh out a student whom they knew they were interested in, but about whom they still had significant doubts. In addition to these crucial members of the admissions office, Stephanie took it upon herself to start an e-mail correspondence with a professor in the English department who specialized in poetry. Had Stephanie not chosen to cover up her drinking bust on her first application, she would have received the maximum 5 points for this extraordinary maintenance of communication.

Stephanie's Initial Wesleyan Application Score:	75.5 points

EXTRA CREDIT STRATEGIES: STEPHANIE CHASE

IvyWise Index points of 76.25 for her Yale application and 75.5 IvyWise Index points for her Wesleyan application were clearly not enough to get Stephanie into either school the first time around. As we have seen, she was waitlisted at both schools, forced to scramble for a way to convince them that she was serious enough about attending to be accepted. That's when she came to me. By employing many of the strategies unique to the IvyWise system, Stephanie was ultimately able to increase her chances of gaining admission to the school of her choice. But choice was exactly the problem. After much soul-searching and a serious heart-to-heart with her father, Stephanie finally decided to devote her energies to one school:

Wesleyan. I knew from looking over Stephanie's academic and personal profiles that this was the better choice for her. The trick now was to come up with strategies that would make her a shoo-in at Wesleyan.

Of course, we had our work cut out for us—it is extremely difficult to get off the waitlist at a school like Wesleyan. With so many applicants for so few spots—as well as their pick of Early Admission applicants—selective colleges and universities across the country have very little trouble hand-selecting the students they want for each incoming class. A waitlisting occurs only with those students whose profiles are almost exactly what the colleges are looking for, minus something. Provided the student fixes that aspect of his or her application, and provided the college still has a spot left over after May 1, then only those students who display an overwhelming desire to attend the college in question will stand even the remotest chance of being accepted off the waitlist. Aware that we were fighting an uphill battle, most of the work that Stephanie did to get herself off the waitlist at Wesleyan revolved around developing extra credit strategies that would convince Wesleyan's admissions office that she was serious about attending their school, even suggesting that she should have applied to Wesleyan Early Decision as it was clearly her first choice. With this goal in mind, Stephanie strengthened her Wesleyan application in the following ways:

• **Excellent book of poetry: + 5 points**

At my urging, Stephanie decided to offer Wesleyan the fantastic book of poetry she had maintained since the fourth grade, including her National Gold Key award-winning poem. As a creative writing portfolio, this book was top-notch and it was sure to grab the attention of the creative writing professor with whom Stephanie was in contact. In fact, I recently learned that this professor had contacted the Wesleyan admissions office on Stephanie's behalf and that he has since spoken with Stephanie about getting her work published through his literary agent. In addition to being the potential start to a new career, Stephanie's book of poetry also functioned as a poignant, descriptive, and revealing document of her interior life as she was going through the nightmare of Barbara's death. Stephanie had written many of the poems in the anthology in direct response to Barbara's struggle with breast cancer. A number of them were even dedicated to Barbara on the day of her passing.

• Taped performance, published articles, and paper: + 3 points

With the help of the head of the drama department at Peter Egret Academy, a renowned theater director who prefers the bucolic life in Lakewood to the hustle and bustle of New York City, Stephanie was able to procure a taped copy of her performance in *Trigger*, the outstanding one-act play about breast cancer that she wrote, directed, and performed in during the winter of her upper year as part of her work with the Drama Club at Egret. This visual document attested to Stephanie's extraordinary ability in all aspects of theatrical production, offering firsthand proof of her dramatic writing ability, acting talent, and directorial skill. In a taped introduction to this heart-wrenching elegy for the woman who had meant so much to her, Stephanie revealed that she had raised over $4,300 for breast cancer research through ticket sales and audience donations. In addition to this tape, Stephanie forwarded a series of articles she had written for the *Brownville Journal* during the summer before her infamous upper year. The articles, written when Stephanie was still hopeful for Barbara's recovery, explored Stephanie's valiant efforts to cope emotionally with the cancer of a loved one. Combined with her taped theatrical performance, these submissions alerted both the English Department and the Theater Department at Wesleyan that Stephanie was an incredible potential major in either field. The submissions also helped to portray Stephanie's interior struggles with Barbara's sickness and death in two very different media: a public newspaper, on the one hand, and an avant-garde play on the other. At my urging, Stephanie rounded out her rapidly improving Wesleyan application with a copy of her Saltonstall Award–winning history paper on the African-American suffragettes. Both as an expository writing sample and as an excellent piece of college-level research, Stephanie's paper reminded her admissions reader at Wesleyan of the other side of her personality: the passionate and diligent writer of historical research papers and the dedicated explorer of issues of race and equality in America.

FINAL APPLICATION RESULTS: STEPHANIE CHASE

Stephanie's Initial Wesleyan Application Score:　　　　**75.5 points**

　　As a result of the work we did together:

　　Stephanie's Brag Sheet rose from a 1 to an 8:　　　　=　+ 7 points

　　Stephanie's Counselor Letter score went from a 1 to a 7,

　　　　and her overall Personal Support rose from a 5.5 to a 7.0:　=　+ 1.5 points

　　Stephanie's Essay score increased from a 7 to a 9:　　=　+ 2 points

　　Her poetry anthology earned her 5 more points:　　　=　+ 5 points

　　Her drama performance, published articles on breast cancer,

　　　　and history paper tallied another 3 points:　　　=　+ 3 points

Stephanie's Final Wesleyan Application Total:	**94 points**

By employing numerous IvyWise strategies for improving her selective college application, Stephanie was able to catapult her mediocre score of 75.5 into the college admissions stratosphere. In the end, all the hard work paid off.

> **Not only did Stephanie have a breakthrough with her father, allowing her to put her energies toward the school that was truly meant for her, she was also admitted off the waitlist and into the freshman class Wesleyan.**

CONCLUSION:
THE ROCK HARD APPLICATION
IN CONTEXT

Having followed David, Ronald, and Stephanie on their harrowing journey from college dreamers to fully matriculated college students, you have become an expert on the IvyWise Index and all that it requires. You have witnessed firsthand the thrills and spills of the high-pressure world of selective college admissions. Our three students started out in mediocre shape, but through hard work, determination, and a balanced regimen, they were able to turn their applications into lean, mean fighting machines. With their scores pushed near or into the 90's on the IvyWise Index, all three of our profiled college applicants eventually found their rightful, postsecondary homes—although not necessarily where they had wanted to go in the beginning. Johns Hopkins University, the University of Pennsylvania, and Wesleyan University are three excellent institutions where David, Ronald, and Stephanie are currently thriving. Last I heard, David had plans to travel during his junior year to Israel, where he hoped to put his emerging expertise in Middle Eastern history and politics to the test. Ronald had already begun to show his art at a local Philadelphia art gallery and was hoping to procure an NEA grant for the summer. Stephanie's first play will be produced as part of a young playwrights festival in Hartford, and she has already landed a poetry agent at a major literary agency. In addition, she has become very active in Wesleyan's chapter of SADD (Students Against Destructive Decisions), helping at-risk students steer clear of the emotional turmoil she experienced while drinking in high school.

Their continued growth and success are the best illustration of the way things work in the high-stakes world of selective college admissions—the road is bumpy, but if you put in the necessary effort and training, more often than not, you will end up at the school that's right for you, studying what you love.

If there is one thing I want you to take away from our exploration of David's, Ronald's, and Stephanie's college application experiences, it is this: Everything, including your most extraordinary achievements and your most grueling challenges, will be looked at *in context* by the selective colleges to which you are applying. Colleges want to see that you have taken full advantage of the opportunities afforded by your family, your high school, and your community. They are not looking at statistics; they are looking at how you function in relation to the world around you. That is why, if I had to choose one application from this book to highlight as *the* Rock Hard App, I would choose Ronald Siegal's, despite the fact that it received the lowest ranking on the IvyWise Index. The reasons for this lie in Ronald's zest and determination, his singular will to make the most of his given talents and surroundings. Ronald Siegal continuously went above and beyond his limited context, seeking out educational and community service opportunities where none existed before. This is precisely what colleges love to see: a profound appreciation for the gift of education along with the determination to make the most of one's circumstances. By comparison, Stephanie Chase, a child of wealth, privilege, and extraordinary education, underachieved in these areas. Her lack of substantial community service outside of a personal interest in breast cancer research, her great but not perfect SAT I composite score, the substantial bonus her application received simply because of her family's development potential, as well as the overall capriciousness of her choices both inside and outside the classroom: These are aspects of her personal and academic profile which, despite her higher point total, detract significantly from the overall attractiveness of her selective college application. Stephanie was supposed to do well, in other words. She had the time and money to explore a wider array of options and prepare herself more adequately for her exams, both in school and in life. Because of this context, admissions readers expected more from a student like Stephanie than they did from a student like Ronald. When they didn't see it, they responded with a waitlisting. David Horowitz, on the other hand, lay somewhere in between. He made definite sacrifices because of his orthodoxy and his commute. No admissions reader, given these facts, would have expected David to be on three varsity sports or to have engaged in extensive test preparation for the SAT. On the other hand, if Ronald couldn't afford these luxuries because of money, David couldn't afford them because of time. Admissions readers might still have expected a level of extracurricular involvement more commensurate with Stephanie's. David's admissions to Johns Hopkins University proves that they were willing to overlook certain weaknesses based on the context of his application. Ironically, David's overall score may have been stronger had he chosen to remain in the large public high school he attended for the ninth grade. In the long run, however, by transferring to Singer Yeshiva, David displayed much of the same determination as Ronald did, the determination to improve his lot in life through desire and hard work.

Keep this in mind as you begin your own college application odyssey. You've got a lot of work in front of you. If you try to take advantage of everything that your particular context has to offer, you should be well on your way. As a vicarious veteran of the college admissions wars, you have learned from David's, Ronald's, and Stephanie's failures as much as from their triumphs. Once you have written your applications and you think they are ready to go, read through the three applications in this book again and ask yourself:

Are my applications strong enough to be called Rock Hard Apps?

ACKNOWLEDGMENTS

Thanks to all of the students I have worked with on their college processes, especially those whose profiles appear in *Rock Hard Apps*. By sharing their information and experiences, and strengths and weaknesses, they have helped my readers and me to understand the complexity of the application evaluation process. Each student is not an average of numbers and letters, but a comprehensive case study.

I could not have written this book without the help of my close friend and editor Jeff Timon. Because of our work together on *The Truth About Getting In*, he is intimate with the IvyWise approach to selective college admissions. So, when I needed assistance compiling all of the data on the profiles of David Horowitz, Ronald Siegal, and Stephanie Chase, and organizing it into an easy-to-read manuscript, I called on Jeff. And he rose to the task. He gave me invaluable feedback as I bounced my thoughts and ideas off of him, especially as I was formalizing the IvyWise Index scale and determining how many points to assign to each application section. He visited several selective colleges, sitting in on their information sessions to get answers to the many questions I asked admissions professionals, which appear in the sidebars of this book. Jeff helped me to edit and revise the entire manuscript, making sure that it all made sense and that the narratives flowed. But most important, he encouraged me every step of the way. In fact, I could not have completed this book without his moral support and friendship.

I cannot forget the love of my family. Thank you especially to my mom Jane Barack, my grandmother Florence Lippman, my uncle Peter Barack, my aunt Elise Barack, my sister Emily Pine, my brother Chris Cohen, and my stepfather Ronald Siegel, who have been my biggest fans and supporters. My grandmother has supported me throughout my life. I speak to my grandmother weekly and to my mom daily. Having them there at the other end of the line—ever understanding and loving—has meant so much to me, especially when I stress over my heavy workload. My uncle Peter is not only a father figure to me, but also my company lawyer. He is one of the most intelligent people I know and I consult with him before I make any important decision. My aunt Elise is one of the most educated and well-read people I know. When it comes to books, including my own, I look to her for feedback and constructive criticism. My sister Emily and brother Chris are constant comic relief; they each have a unique and wacky sense of humor, which, while I was writing this book, enabled me to unwind and lighten up. Thanks to my cats, Icarus, Daedalus, and Littly Biddly, for the unconditional love and for always making home more interesting than the wild animal kingdom.

I have so many supportive friends who also kept me happy and sane though the writing process. Their love and encouragement enrich my life everyday. I want to thank the following people who always inspire me and who were especially present in my life while I wrote *Rock Hard Apps*. Thank you so much: Eric Costen, Desiree Langager, Samantha Gillison, Leah Forester, Tanaz Eshagian, Lulu de Kwiatkowski, Alfredo Gilardini, Danielle Queller, Mike Heimbold, Alison Rother, Jennifer Johnson, Doug Liman, Liz Granger, Alex Cohen, Tiffany Salerno Antoci, Dan Shiff, Amy Pesner, Carol Cheng, Brett Mayer, Brad Kaplan, Cate Crumpacker, Frank Roccogrande, Boykin Curry, Dwight Angelini, David Conrad, Jaime Davidorf, Melanie Staggs, Jilleen Stelding, Mehmet Kutman, Greg Kiez, David Chazen, Michael Davis, Jack Merrill, and Tara Peters.

A special thank you to Nina Bauer Shapiro, the Director of IvyWise Kids, and a great friend who puts up with me everyday, and to her husband Andrew Shapiro. A huge thank you to Dan Lipman and Lawrence Spielman, my accountants and business managers, who run my business and life on a daily basis. Thanks to Ed and Jon Schultheiss, my computer wizards. Thanks to Nikki Geula, the head of my tutors, and a kindred spirit. And Namaste to Kelly Morris, my yoga teacher, friend, and personal guru, who keeps my body and mind healthy, so I am able to focus and produce the work that I do.

Finally, I want to thank my agent Suzanne Gluck at William Morris and my editor

Mary Ellen O'Neill at Hyperion. Thanks to Suzanne, and her assistant Emily Nurkin. A special thank you to Suzanne, who helped communicate my ideas to Hyperion when I was conceptualizing my initial proposal. She single-handedly convinced them to go forward with the project and to trust me. Since then, both Suzanne and Emily have been a constant source of support through the writing process for *Rock Hard Apps*. Mary Ellen O'Neill was also my editor for *The Truth About Getting In*. She saw it every step of the way, giving me constant feedback. When I submitted an almost-final draft of *Rock Hard Apps* to Mary Ellen, I was relieved and re-energized to hear that she was thrilled with the manuscript. Her approval meant so much to me. While she gave me excellent notes, enabling me to cut down a book that was way too long, she remained a real cheerleader for this project. She also kept me to a strict schedule of deadlines, which allowed me to finish the book on time.

I wrote this book during a very busy year. While I researched and wrote *Rock Hard Apps*, I expanded my company, IvyWise, by opening an office in Los Angeles. I had to find the space, staff the office, and train the new employees. At the same time, I was counseling my full caseload of students applying to college. There were days when I thought I simply could not do everything. I understood exactly what it was like to be a high school senior today applying to college!